Arnulfo L. Oliveira Memorial Library

Native People of
Southern New England,
1650–1775

The Civilization of the American Indian Series

Native People of
Southern New England,
1650–1775

By Kathleen J. Bragdon

University of Oklahoma Press : Norman

Also by Kathleen J. Bragdon

Native People of Southern New England, 1500–1650
  (Norman, 1996)

(with Ives Goddard) *Native Writings in Massachusett*
  (Philadelphia, 1988)

The Columbia Guide to American Indians of the Northeast
  (New York City, 2001)

This book is published with the generous assistance of the Kerr
Foundation, Inc.

Library of Congress Cataloging-in-Publication Data

Bragdon, Kathleen Joan.
    Native people of southern New England, 1650–1775 / by Kathleen
J. Bragdon.
        p. cm. — (The civilization of the American Indian series ; v.
259)
    Includes bibliographical references and index.
    ISBN 978-0-8061-4004-9 (hardcover : alk. paper)   1. Indians of
North America—New England—History.   2. Indians of North
America—New England—Colonization.   3. Indians of North
America—New England—Social life and customs.   4. Indians of
North America—History—Colonial period, ca. 1600–1775.   5. United
States—History—Colonial period, ca. 1600–1775   I. Title.
    E78.N5B732 2009
    974.004'97—dc22

                                                        2008042297

Native People of Southern New England, 1650–1775 is Volume 259 in The
Civilization of the American Indian Series.

The paper in this book meets the guidelines for permanence and durability of the Committee on Production Guidelines for Book Longevity of
the Council on Library Resources, Inc. ∞

Copyright © 2009 by the University of Oklahoma Press, Norman, Publishing Division of the University. Manufactured in the U.S.A.

        1   2   3   4   5   6   7   8   9   10

To my parents,
George and Patricia Bragdon,
with love, gratitude, and respect

Contents

Illustrations

Illustrations

MAPS

TABLES

Preface

This book is a historical ethnography of the American Indian people of southern New England during the colonial period (ca. 1640–1775), with an emphasis on the linguistic and cultural premises that underlay Native life in the region, as enacted within community settings. I portray the indigenous people of the region in cultural and symbolic terms, much as other ethnographers have done when describing the living peoples with whom they have worked. The richly detailed interpretations produced by many of these scholars are the inspiration for my analysis. At the same time, this study is also sensitive to the critical reappraisals of older ethnographies, reappraisals that ask us to be aware of the ambiguities of colonial experience.

In the early seventeenth century, the six "nations" occupying what was to become southern New England were the Pequots, Massachusetts, Pokanokets, Nipmucks, Pawtuckets, and Narragansetts (Gookin 1806:147) (see map 1). The arrival of English newcomers, beginning in the 1620s, triggered massive population losses and led to many subtle and dramatic changes among

Preface

these peoples. In particular, the chiefly societies of the coast and islands underwent dramatic transformations that either lessened the power and influence of their sachem leaders, or consolidated that power. Some Native people of the region adopted Christianity, while others chose to adhere to their old beliefs. Nevertheless, Indian people remained culturally distinct throughout the colonial period. Every Native community had a different history, as did each member within it, and most groups responded in a manner that was consistent with their particular origins and traditional adaptations. However, Native people in different localities shared significant experiences as well, and their own statements indicate widespread similarities in perceptions and practices throughout the region during the later colonial period.

PREVIOUS STUDIES

This study is a continuation of my earlier book, *Native Peoples of Southern New England 1500–1650* (Bragdon 1996). In the years since its publication, a great deal of new research has become available, particularly in the field of archaeology (Kerber 2006). Several useful collections of studies concerning the Native people in the late seventeenth and eighteenth centuries are also available (Weinstein 1992; Calloway 1997; Calloway and Salisbury 2003). This second volume draws on this new research, as well as on the increasingly significant body of historical, archaeological, and linguistic research conducted by Native people of southern New England themselves (Herndon and Sekatau 2003; Lamb Richmond and Den Ouden 2003).

SOURCES

Although this volume relies on important scholarship on Indians and Indian-English relations in Colonial New England, it does not try to duplicate it. Instead, I focus here on that body of materials

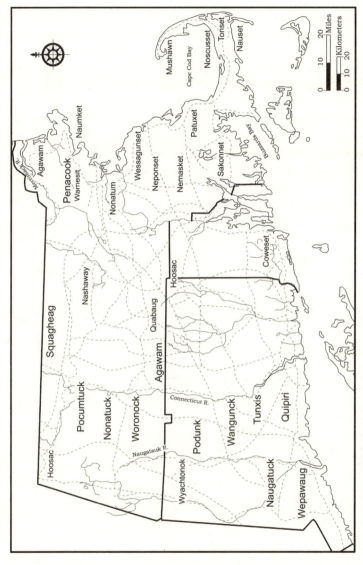

Map 1. Colonial Native places. By Heather Harvey.

written by Native people themselves, or in their languages, as well
as their reported speech and behavior, which provides many clues
to their cultural foci. From this perspective, their culture appears
to be both complex and distinct but, in common with other colonized peoples, has often been portrayed according to others' cultural categories. These materials are neither regionally consistent
nor universally representative. Most were written by converts to
Christianity, many reflect mundane or routine relations with
English overseers or other colonial authorities, and, with only a few
exceptions, they are confined to settled Native communities in
southeastern New England, including those on Cape Cod,
Martha's Vineyard, and Nantucket (Goddard and Bragdon 1988).
The Narragansetts, Pequots, Mohegans, and Niantics of the southern coastal and interior reaches of Connecticut and Rhode Island
were, for many reasons, less well represented by Native writers in
the colonial period, although contemporary materials in their languages are also available and have also been employed in this study.

While variable in quality, quantity, and representativeness, these
unique records allow a language-based approach to ethnographic
analysis, one that focuses on the symbolic world expressed in discourse and in the very structure of language itself (Sapir 1927).
The writings created by Native speakers of some of the New England languages and within the context of Indian communities also
provide insight into the symbolic categories toward which Native
language usage was oriented and the social context in which these
languages functioned. The perspective presented here is also
guided by the understanding that what distinguishes cultures from
one another in part is their distinctive ways of representing the
world through language (Chafe 1997:18).

ORGANIZATION

Although grounded in historical research, this book is not written chronologically. It considers various aspects of Native peo-

ples' colonial life experiences in southern New England, often bringing in data from a variety of locales within the region. The introduction describes the various American Indian groups known to inhabit the region during the colonial period and discusses the scholarly perspectives employed in the study. Chapters 1 and 2 introduce the concept of local language communities and demonstrate the relevance of language- and discourse-based analysis for understanding the symbolic and cultural underpinnings of Native life in the region during the period. These chapters provide the foundation for the discussion of family life in chapters 3 and 4. The material world in which Native life was embedded is discussed in chapter 5, while the cultural, social, and political implications of conversion and the adoption of Native language literacy among Christian converts are the subject of chapter 6. Chapter 7 links specific Native communities to one another as a demonstration of the significance of regional networks to the maintenance of Native lifeways of the time. Chapter 8 concludes this volume with a summary of the characteristics of Native life that remained distinctive and that formed the basis for the continued survival of Indian people in the region.

In short, this study makes the case for cultural distinctiveness among the Native people of southern New England during the colonial period, a condition that did not simply "happen" but was the result of active efforts, including resistance, accommodation, and reemphasis. It seeks to reveal the cultural logic at work among these colonized Native people, as expressed in their own words.

Acknowledgments

I am most grateful to the College of William and Mary, which supported the research leave that allowed me to complete the bulk of this work. The Massachusetts Historical Society and the National Endowment for the Humanities have also provided me with funds to see this book and related projects to conclusion. I thank the staffs at the American Antiquarian Society, the Massachusetts Historical Society, and the New England Historical and Genealogical Society for their assistance and support. In particular, I would like to thank Peter Drummey of the Massachusetts Historical Society and Dr. Harold Worthley of the Congregational Library for their continuing assistance. Archaeologists and friends Kevin McBride, Steven Mrozowski, and Brona Simon have generously discussed their research with me. Mike Nassaney, Patricia Galloway, Margaret Holmes Williamson, William Sturtevant, William Simmons, Ann McMullen, Neal Salisbury, Jean O'Brien, and Laurie Weinstein have also provided me with many useful insights. Dena Dincauze and her students at the University of Massachusetts, Amherst, have critiqued my work in great

Acknowledgments

detail, and I thank them all sincerely. Ives Goddard directed my study of the Massachusett language, and I remain grateful for his example and advice. I also owe a large debt to my Native colleagues, including the late Nanepashemet, Jessie Little Doe, Helen Manning, Russell Peters, Marcia Flowers, Bert Heath, and Ken White, who spoke to me at length about the history of their communities and who helped me understand how the present and past are linked. Several of my students have also helped enormously, including Shannon Dawdy, Neil Kennedy, Tim Ives, Erica Laanela, Nadejya Levine, Hank Lutton, Mark Kostro, and Carl Carlson-Drexler. An anonymous reader was helpful in clarifying my thinking, and Jane McKinney and Amy Den Ouden gave me many insightful suggestions on the final manuscript. Finally, I thank my husband, Marley Brown III, who provides, among many other things, a constant sounding board and audience.

Native People of
Southern New England,
1650–1775

Introduction

In 1703, some American Indian people living within the Township of Eastham on Cape Cod wrote to the commissioners of the missionary society known as the New England Company, complaining that

[h]aving . . . readily [received and embraced] all our methods and measures both as to religion and civil order from the English government here established under the crown of England; having thereupon abandoned all our former pagan idolatryes [*sic*] superstition and methods of government. . . . but those methods of civil order are now discontinued among us wherefore we the humble petitioners crave from yr excel. the revival of our former methods of civil order, observing to our grief by the discontinuing thereof immoralities grown audacious through the wane of civil discountenance, and we truly fear that immorality irreligion and ancient idolatry & customs wil [sic] return on us like a flood if not timely prevented and suppressed. (Massachusetts State Archives n.d.:30:91)

This comment, and others like it, suggests that "ancient idolatry and customs" survived among the Native people of southern

3

New England more than a century after the region was colonized by Europeans. For example, a story told to Captain Richard Mason by Mohegan Ben Uncas in the 1730s suggests that healing in the old manner had not died out among the Niantics, for when a young boy fell ill, "many of them suspected that the child was bewitched" (Barber 1733).

Such statements have been interpreted by historian Douglas Winiarski as expressions of a regional "popular religion" (2005). In the late seventeenth and early eighteenth centuries, Anglo-American clerics suspected that some among their flocks were secretly practicing witchcraft. Similarly, an "outbreak" of reports of divinely inspired visions among New England's white inhabitants occupied the attention of clerics and intellectuals in the eighteenth century, who reacted to this outpouring of emotion and spirituality with ambivalence (Winiarski 1998). Native converts to Christianity also reported similar experiences (Plane 2003). There were similarities between Native American spirituality and the ideas that came into prominence among non-Indians during the later colonial period (Simmons 1979); although superficially alike, these traditions had different origins. Native American religious practices in colonial New England were, in many cases, directly descended from indigenous belief systems or congruent with them.

In a similar way, also in keeping with the social anxieties of the time, Indians in the late seventeenth and early eighteenth centuries were often portrayed by their English contemporaries as wanderers. Many Englishmen linked the Indians' penchant for travel to the increasing presence of the "strolling poor" in the region (Jones 1975) and complained that they were unreliable in returning to habitual camping sites. For example, in the mid-eighteenth century, Josiah Cotton, minister at Plymouth, complained in his diary that the people who used to visit the area in the summer were now living elsewhere (1733–1748). Jean

O'Brien also writes of the many Natick Indians who exasperated their guardians by their mobility (1997a:168). But other evidence suggests that although Native people were indeed often driven by necessity to move from place to place, mobility was not random, that people who wandered were maintaining kin ties and taking advantage of seasonally available resources. Mobility was one of the strategies that made practicing a traditional way of life possible, and was one source for the continued strength of Native presence in the region to the present time.

Even in those areas of colonial settlement where Indians had been most closely supervised, Native peoples were persistently distinct. The above-mentioned Josiah Cotton believed that the Native people to whom he preached in the Plymouth, Massachusetts, area still resorted to powwaws (shamans and healers) and that his work "had had little effect" (Cotton diary 1756). At the end of the eighteenth century, in the papers of the Gay Head minister Zachariah Hossueit, are complaints of "fittling and dancing" at Gay Head, as well as "playing hundreds," and "yeards," and the "preacher knowing" (Howwoswe Papers 1782). Archaeologists working in many parts of the region now provide a picture of Native material life that shows many differences between them and their English-American neighbors (McBride 1996; McBride and Cherau 2003).

But what did the Indians' distinctiveness mean within the context of the colonial period in New England? The Native people of southern New England were deeply affected by the expansion of European, especially English, influence in the Americas. There are many examples of the transformation or reinterpretation of ritual practices and other aspects of southern New England Native life in the wake of colonization. However, few would argue that such changes were merely a response to the events and conditions of colonization, a footnote to the story of the expanding world system. Nor does this perspective help us to understand or illuminate Native historical experience in that region. For this, there is still merit in "writing for culture" (Brumann 1999). As Marshall Sahlins reminds us, although contemporary ethnographic literature pays greater attention to individual agency and invention than has been true at some periods in the past, the insights of earlier approaches, particularly those of the Boasian school, that understood communities and societies to be characterized by unique constellations of ideas still have resonance, even as ethnographic scholarship remains embedded in its poststructural moment (Sahlins 1999; Brightman 1995).

At the very least, the complaints and reports of powwawing, mobility, dancing, and gambling described above illustrate some of the ways the Native people of southern New England were set apart from their English neighbors and cause us to ask why this was so. It can only be that Indian practices, beliefs, and rituals were shaped by the colonial encounter, but also socially and culturally generated and sustained. These distinct practices are most effectively explained with reference to the sets of shared ideas that organized and explained Native life during the colonial period, especially within the context of their own communities, ideas derived from or consistent with those of the precolonial past.

NATIVE COMMUNITIES AND CULTURAL SURVIVAL

Members of Indian communities in southern New England referred to themselves in various ways. Although originally allied to particular nations, they often had other names as well. Some communities were called by the names of the places they lived, as was the case with Roger Williams's 1636 reference to the Wunnashowatuckoogs and the Wusquowhannanawkits, "who are the furthermost Neepnet (Nipmuck) men" (LaFantasie 1988:55–56). Occasionally Native people called themselves or were referred to according to their associations with particular sachems or rulers as when the author of *Mourt's Relation* wrote of "the Massasoits, our neighbors" (Heath 1963:52). In the eighteenth century, some Native people regularly called themselves "Indians," and this study sometimes employs that usage as well. For example, one petition written in the Native language to the commissioner of the New England Company from the Native people of Gay Head begins "maueog kuttummake Indianssog" (the poor Indians met together) (Goddard and Bragdon 1988:171).

Following the early-seventeenth-century arrival of Europeans in what would come to be called southern New England, Native populations were drastically reduced by the effects of introduced epidemic disease. Dean Snow and Kim M. Lanphear estimate that by the mid-seventeenth century, Native populations in some areas had declined by as much as 90 percent (1988:23). The aftermath of the 1636 Pequot War left many groups displaced, further strengthening English power in the region. Many Native communities were disbursed as their members scattered, and as their sachems sold off large tracts of land to English settlers. The final blow to Native sovereignty in the region took place with the defeat of Metacom or Philip and his forces in 1676. However, in spite of the curtailment of Native territories, severe population loss, and the decline in importance of the sachemships, many Native communities, some linked to one another politically and others autonomous, were to be found throughout southern New England in the late seventeenth century; and these were often noted on contemporary maps and described in English accounts (Rawson and Danforth 1698) (see map 2).

Communities were a feature of eighteenth-century Native life in New England as well. For example, the Native people who united to save their minister from imprisonment in 1753 defined themselves as "the whole [church] assembly and also the townspeople . . . as far as Nauset and here in Mashpee" (Goddard and Bragdon 1988:179). These people recognized themselves to be part of a group that came together in a socially agreed upon manner, for a

Map 2. Massachusett and Wampanoag communities ca. 1700. By Heather Harvey.

1. Magunkaquog	14. Acushnet	27. Nashuakemmiuk	40. Mannamit
2. Natick	15. Wawayontat	28. Talhanio	41. Weesquabs
3. Punkapog	16. Herring Ponds	29. Nunnepoag	42. Codtanmutt
4. Mattakesit	17. Mashpee	30. Sengekontakit	43. Saconeset Point
5. Duxbury	18. Pawpoesit	31. Christiantown	44. Wakoquet
6. Cotuhtikut	19. Ponanummakut	32. Chappaquidgick	45. Ashimuit
7. Assowamsoo	20. Punsnakanit	33. Seconchqut	46. Satuit
8. Quittacus	21. Meeshawn	34. Squatesit	47. Coatuit
9. Monimoint Point	22. Sokones	35. Oggawame	48. Weequakut
10. Cokesit	23. Elizabeth Islands	36. Wammasquid	49. Nobsquassit
11. Saconet	24. Elizabeth Islands	37. Comassakumkanit	50. Sawkuttukett
12. Nukkehkummees	25. Elizabeth Islands	38. Sandwich	51. Manamoyik
13. Assameskq	26. Gayhead	39. Pispogqutt	52. Nawsett

specific purpose, to the benefit of the community as a whole. This example illustrates that the community may not be a fixed place even though it is often referenced to one. Another example comes from Rhode Island, where Indians who worked among the English recognized their membership within the larger Narra-

gansett community centered on lands owned by the sachem Ninegret (Callander 1739:139). Some Indian communities were
associated with reserves, such as those established for the Mashan-
tuckets and Eastern Pequots in the mid-seventeenth century
(McBride 1996). Distant communities sometimes recognized a
common identity. A survey taken in 1767 reported that Indians
from Martha's Vineyard and "the continent" convened yearly at
Mashpee for a religious service "carried on by Indian ministers in
their own language" (Anonymous 1767:13).

These communities, which I define as groups of people who
recognize one another as members, interact according to a set of
shared ideas, and are engaged in culturally given ways of self-
replacement were the principal vehicles of cultural survival
among the Native people of colonial New England. Communities
were also the locales where the continuous expression and negotiation of ideas and expectations took place. Before embarking
on a discussion of the cultural premises of Native American life
during the colonial period in southern New England, as expressed in community experience, however, the following section
describes the sources that form the basis of commentary analysis
to follow and the theories that underpin it.

Among the most dramatic evidence for the presence and distinctiveness of Native communities during the colonial period in
southern New England are the documents created by and for
Native peoples in their own languages, particularly the language
known historically as Massachusett or Natick, dating to the period
between 1650 and 1770. These documents reflect all of the qualities of community described above. They are concerned with
land transactions, council decisions, and marriages, and embody
the social networks that made their production possible. This
book is structured around these unique manuscripts because
they are what James Deetz called "docufacts." For Deetz, these are
manuscripts whose creation (and preservation) is a testament to

the existence of real social groups, acting according to cultural principles, in the past (1996:33–34).

The endpage from the Massachusett bible shown in figure 1 is a poignant example of this type of document, and many hands contributed to it. It is a kind of conversation on paper among the several users of this Nantucket Indian-owned bible (Goddard and Bragdon 1988:380). The production of this document was a social act. Creating and maintaining writings in the Native language became common in some eastern Indian communities in the 1650s, and some have been found that date as late as the 1770s (Goddard and Bragdon 1988:56). In spite of the acculturative pressures these communities underwent, the persistence of vernacular literacy in the colonial period, and its historical significance later, suggests that there was a close association between this tradition and other aspects of Native culture.

But these documents are also testimony to profound threats to indigenous belief systems posed by missionary activity in the region. The adoption of literacy among colonized peoples is often thought to represent a loss of traditional perspectives (Bragdon 1997). But one of the many ironies of colonial encounters is the persistent way colonial authority is undermined and enforced practices subtly altered to convey other meanings (Comaroff and Comaroff 1991). As other scholars have discovered, in other colonial contexts, indigenous literacy often takes indigenous directions (Besnier 1995); in southern New England it had consequences no one could have anticipated. In the same way, the language usages glimpsed in these documents reflect the ambiguities of colonial experiences for all participants. A deep reading of these texts, and a thorough understanding of their role in social interaction, however, takes us beyond the surface appearance of mimicry (Bhaba 1994) to an appreciation of the complexities of enactment, reenactment, and multiple reference (Silverstein 1990). At the same time, while acknowledging the

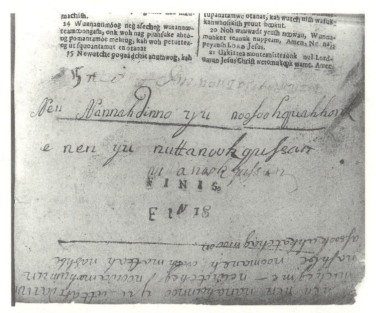

Figure 1. Bible end page (Courtesy of the Congregational Library, Boston, Massachusetts).

legitimacy of poststructuralist critiques concerning the "contested and unstable nature of cultural logic" (Sahlins 1993:15), this study pursues an ethnographic goal to investigate how the indigenous peoples of southern New England "changed their own authenticity" (Sahlins 1993:2).

THE ANTHROPOLOGY OF COLONIALISM

Claude Levi-Strauss has spoken for all who lament that the privilege of knowing something about societies different from those of the West comes at enormous cost to those societies (1974). Historians and anthropologists are now engaged in uncovering the many ways colonial regimes have penetrated and transformed indigenous societies around the world, have chosen the ways

11

these societies have been described and evaluated, and have controlled, to some extent, even the ways colonized peoples can express themselves. Thus, the historical records and artifacts that are all that is left to represent a particular place and people are already shaped by those with specific, and often self-serving, interests. Nevertheless, I believe that cultural analysis, such as has been central to much ethnographic writing, can provide fruitful perspectives on the past.

The many critics of traditional ethnographic research and writing suggest that culturalist approaches ignore time, agency, and hegemony. Although the goal of this study is not to address theories of culture directly, it is important to note that the concept of culture employed here does not imply coherence, homogeneity, or ahistoricism (Brightman 1995:540). Robert Brightman argues that "history, chaos, contestation, and strategy" have been givens in anthropological analysis for a generation (1995:540) and the insights derived from these perspectives constitute the repertoire of historical ethnography today.

Indian communities were unquestionably places of negotiation, sites for the many social and economic adjustments that had to be made during the colonial period. These interactions also took place within a material context was both setting and interlocutor in social relationships (Appadurai 1991). A focus on the language and discourse also permits us to examine the process of negotiation with reference to its physical setting.

One of the challenges of writing historical ethnography is the necessary reliance on biased contemporary reports written by non-Natives with a variety of motives and preconceived notions about the Native people they wrote about. A common theme of such writings in New England in the period following King Philip's War was the fall from power of once formidable Native foes. For example, the eighteenth-century historian John Callander wrote of the Narragansetts that "after [King Philip's] war they were soon reduced to

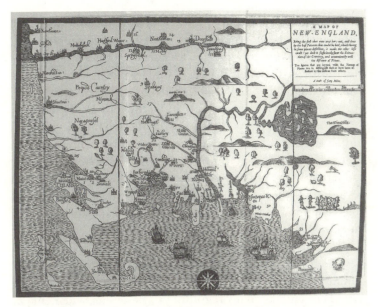

Figure 2. Foster's *Map of New England* (from Hubbard 1677) (Courtesy of The College of William and Mary, Special Collections).

the condition of the labouring (sic) poor, without property, hewers of wood and drawers of water" (1739:139).

Others wrote of the loss of Native cultural practices, such as powwawing (healing and divination through trance). In a well-known passage, Ezra Stiles, a minister from Newport, Rhode Island, and future president of Yale University, wrote that "the Vessel of sorcery [is] shipwreckt and only some shattered planks and pieces disjoyned floating and scattered on the Ocean of the human Activity and Bustle" (Dexter 1901:385–86). Still other reports attributed to Indian peoples the flaws that English-American settlers saw or feared to see in themselves.

Contemporary observers often failed to inquire more fully into the thoughts and experiences of the indigenous people they met and were unable to recognize the vital substance of their lives. Although they were "eyewitnesses," these colonial writers cannot, therefore, be the only sources we consult. Other information demonstrates that many people of indigenous descent in southern New England not only flourished during the colonial period, but also survived it as members of distinctive groups. This cannot be accidental, nor is it only the result of their exclusion from non-Indian society. It can only be due to the effectiveness of those "webs of significance" they created for themselves and those cooperative ways of living that served them during the colonial period. That those ways of thinking and living were expedient goes without saying, but, to paraphrase Marshall Sahlins, what is functional must also be cultural (1999).

Most histories of this period treat Indian peoples of southern New England as though their communities were increasingly diminished culturally from some hypothesized stable state in the past. They cite the many regretful or self-serving statements by non-Indian contemporaries about the disappearance of Indians from New England (Ghere 1997). Most of these histories also depend on census figures that not only deliberately under-counted Native people, but were collected to justify their further dispossession (Silverman 2005:230). Those few studies that postulate continuity in Indian communities in southern New England generally focus only on material culture and foodways. This study looks instead at Indian communities in the colonial period as participants in particular cultural modalities, as members of communities that were always recreating themselves through a process Marshall Sahlins describes as the "inventiveness of tradition" (1999:408). Colonial Native communities were remarkable entities, the products of many dynamics, and often "permutations of older forms and relationships, made appropriate to novel situations" (Sahlins 1999:409).

Introduction

HISTORIOGRAPHY AND THEORY

The interpretive models implicit in many studies of Indian people in New England and elsewhere are dependent on an idea of "primitive society" that is essentially evolutionary (Kuper 1988:190). That is, that people of a simple technology or organizational type are on a path toward a "modern" way of life that requires only an external trigger, such as the arrival of more "advanced" peoples in their region. Other studies suggest that cultural differences between the English and the Indians they sought to displace are less relevant in explaining Indian life and Indian response to Europeans than are the so-called universals of economic self-interest. In either case, the outcome of analysis based on these models is what M. Conkey and S. Williams describe as a "gathering up of the world's histories so as to reach a Euroamerican conclusion" (1991:113).

The idea that American Indian societies were timeless and primitive and, its seeming opposite, the notion that Indian societies were simply absorbed as minorities into regional and global economies are both in essence materialist perspectives. Without denying the centrality of economics, this study makes use instead of a culturalist approach. While recognizing the relevance of culturally consistent responses to contingency (Sahlins 1985), I also follow Franz Boas and his students in linking diverse ideational orientations to specific historical eras. In particular, I focus on the ways cultural values of spiritual power, advocacy, hierarchy, health, endurance, and collectivity motivated Native people, and how the emphasis on such ideas contributed to the histories of Indian communities during the colonial period. This perspective avoids some of the pitfalls of strictly economic analyses, which require us to make judgments about the relative acculturation of groups in contact and colonial situations based largely on their technologies,

15

subsistence practices, and so on, or on their involvement in the colonial economies that grew up around them.

Materialist approaches often emphasize individual agency at the expense of the role of community membership in people's lives. The values discussed above, which were emergent among Indian peoples in southern New England during the colonial period, were community values, and arose in the context of social life. In this view, the interplay of economic practice and ideational structure is a central feature of community identity.

How Indian people in southern New England defined themselves in terms of community practices and identities during the colonial period is a central part of this study. A community perspective does not deny the importance of individual agency or imply a static acquiescence to community mores and values. But, as Edward Sapir argues, it is only within the context of a cultural community that individual agency makes sense (1949). Even such individual experiences as grief are demonstrably subject to cultural shaping (Rosaldo 1998). Too many historical studies of Native people in Southern New England have singled out individuals only to characterize them as typical of presumed patterns of cultural change or loss. This study treats those rare individuals about whom we know more than the most basic facts as participants in communities, but not necessarily as representative of those communities or their values.

It is very common to describe communities as entities with physical boundaries. Modern community-based analysis avoids this trap by recognizing the fluidity of community membership at any given time and the likely possibility that individuals participated in more than one such community in their lifetimes. Indian people in colonial southern New England were not relegated to isolated enclaves, (although many lived on reserves), but rather participated in multiple groups throughout the period. Standard histories of Indian communities in New England during the colonial period are drawn largely from legislative archives or travelers or missionaries' descriptions of Native peoples, and may thus give a false concreteness to some groups that were in reality more diffuse and complex (see map 3). The legislative documents likewise omit references to many thriving Native communities who have thus, at least until recently, received little attention from historians.

Another factor links and divides these Native communities: what Anthony Giddens terms "historicity"—their recognition of their distinctive past. As colonial intrusion and racially motivated discrimination increased, Native people had little choice but to see themselves as "other" (1990). This historicity, one expression of ethnic awareness, was a central element in the folk stories of New England Indians, recorded beginning in the seventeenth century and still told among their descendants today (Simmons 1986; Crosby 1990). Historical awareness often figured as a rhetorical trope in disputes with non-Indians, as well as a feature of community reproduction during the colonial period.

Contemporary ethnographers use a variety of techniques to discover meaning, principally through participant observation and interviews. These methods are not available to ethnohistorians, who must rely on eyewitness accounts and on the information that can be drawn from other kinds of historic documents. An underused source in ethnohistorical writing is evidence derived from the study of Native languages. This is particularly true in southern New England where abundant sources for some languages are available, many produced or used by the Native people themselves. This study focuses on these materials and thus is concerned with the ways cultural ideas are expressed through language and speech.

The writings of Edward Sapir, cited above, remain authoritative sources for an understanding of the role of language in culture. Sapir argues that historical evidence about the habits and movements of people in the past is enshrined in language and that

17

language is the means by which people conceive of and articulate the world in which they live (1927). Added to Sapir's insights are the writings of sociolinguists who have documented the myriad ways that language and speech are employed to mark and rein-force culturally derived social categories, such as class, race, and gender. Sociolinguists also concern themselves with the ways speech events reflect the roles and interests of a variety of actors and the complexities of the outcomes of all speech encounters. Both these perspectives, the focus on language as a vehicle for cul-tural ideas and on speech as a site for negotiation, are employed in this book.

Language is not only about shared ideas. Marshall Sahlins (1985:ix) remarks that when cultural guides to appropriate action no longer fit changed social circumstances, and the forces that are shaping local events may be far beyond the village, people subject their cultural categories to empirical risks. Language as a social product is often the medium of symbolic risk taking. The Native communities I discuss were also what Michael Silverstein (1998:402) has labeled "local linguistic communities" where social relations were always being negotiated as the new colonial world came into being. The emphasis on Indian communities as lin-guistic communities does not ignore the violence they endured from English settlers and governments. On the contrary, a dis-course-centered approach to communities explains both their uniqueness and their reactions to the contingent events of their lives, which, during the colonial period, were both invidiously transformative and often destructive.

Native Societies on the Eve of Colonization: A Brief Overview

For the indigenous people of what would later be called New Eng-land, religious beliefs and economic practices, as far as can be reconstructed from partial and biased European accounts and

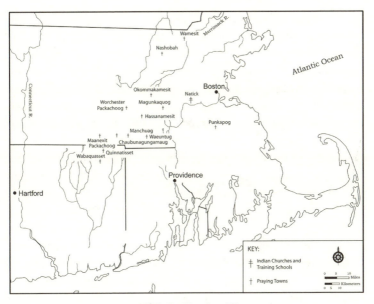

Map 3. Praying towns ca. 1675. By Heather Harvey.

from comparisons with similar societies elsewhere in North America, were in that state of balance described by Edward Sapir as one in which "indirect ends . . . were functionally . . . interwoven with . . . immediate ends" (1924:417). Indirect ends for Sapir were those of spiritual and emotional satisfaction and were achieved through the practice of centuries-old (if not millennia-old) rites of dream and trance exploration of the supernatural realm, aided by shamans and (in some places) by the use of tobacco and fasting to facilitate contact with supernatural beings who served as spiritual guides. For the people of the region, belief in the pervasiveness of supernatural power, called manitou, was one of the central premises of religious practice; its recognition was not limited to ritual expression, but was manifest in the immediate ends of daily life, in subsistence practices, social relations, and politics. For example,

19

hunters were guided by their spirit helpers to game, which was acknowledged through rituals performed before and after a kill was made. The symbolic role played by sachems, at least in the coastal societies in the region, resembled that of kings in other ancient societies around the world (Hocart 1927; Williamson 2003), and was both sacred and secular. A range of practices of deference described by early observers documents the special status accorded to leaders (Bragdon 1987, 1996). Men and women's spheres were separate but co-dependent, a relationship marked ritually as well as in everyday practice. Societal change, felt through influences from the west in the five centuries prior to the arrival of Europeans, and the effects of the introduction of new wealth items at the beginning period of European exploration are difficult to assess, but were probably leading toward the increased centralization of authority in many societies, a process interrupted by the effects of European-introduced diseases and subsequent, often violent, intrusion of Europeans themselves into Native territories.

The influence of Native theories of spiritual power, the effects of their gendered social and economic roles, and their views on the symbolic centrality of the sachemship can be seen in accounts of their interactions with the earliest English settlers in New England. For example, settlers were told that that their coming had been portended by strange sights and events, or foretold by sounds "heard in the aire" (Simmons 1986:65). The well-described encounter between the great sachem Massasoit and the Pilgrim leaders at Plymouth was preceded by overtures from lesser messengers, especially Squanto, in keeping with Massasoit's dignity. English settlers had little contact with ordinary Native women, who were most often occupied within the domestic sphere, removed from English settlements, but Native women of sachem lines played important diplomatic roles as well. Numerous historical and contemporary studies of North American Native spirituality, historical social organization, and ritual support this portrait, although each community and nation had its own particular practices. For example, dual kingship appears to have been a characteristic of the early seventeenth-century Pequot and Narragansett societies, but not of others, while ritual was reported by Native people to be more elaborated in these societies as well (these facts are likely to have been connected.)

What Peter Thomas has termed the "maelstrom of change" into which Native people were involuntarily plunged had drastic and altering effects on their societies, and some succumbed to what Sapir called "the cold air of fragmentary existence" (1924:414). Yet others did not, building new societies out of the chaos of the colonial encounter, societies creatively constructed from elements of their traditional past. The story of Indians of southern New England as victims of land grabs and disease, as pawns in colonial wars and regional conflicts, is an old one. This familiar story is derived from "official" sources and standard histories such as those reviewed above. But it is not the only story, and it does not explain Native life in the colonial period. For this we turn to early studies of Native languages and language use by English settlers in New England, as well as the writings of Native peoples in their own languages, to be described in the following chapters.

1.

Eidos and Ethos

The understanding of a simple poem, for instance, involves not merely an understanding of the single words in their average significance, but a full comprehension of the whole life of the community as it is mirrored in the words, or as it is suggested by their overtones.

—Edward Sapir 1921:145

THE NATIVE LANGUAGES
OF SOUTHERN NEW ENGLAND

Traditionally, linguists have identified five separate Native languages in southern New England, including Massachusett, Narragansett, Mohegan/Pequot/Montauk, Loup A, and Quiripi (also called Wapanoo) (Goddard 1978b:76). These languages are also distinguished by the variations they exhibit on the reconstructed Proto-Algonquian sounds *l and *θ. For example, the language known as Massachusett, Wampanoag, or Pokanoket substituted "n" for these sounds, while Narragansett used "y," Nipmuck "l," and the western Connecticut languages used "r" (see map 4).

There were other differences between these languages, for example, such features as locative (place) endings, and differences in vocabulary. Scholarly controversies over the boundaries of these languages, and the extent to which they were mutually intelligible continue, but it appears likely that multilingualism was common among Native elites in the region. These languages are part of the

Map 4. Languages of Southern New England by reflexes of Proto-Algonquian "l" and "θ." By Heather Harvey.

larger Algonquian language family that is widespread in North America. These are polysynthetic languages, organized around "roots" or "stems" to which various prefixes and suffixes denoting gender, number, and other grammatical features are added according to regular rules. Polysynthetic languages are extremely context sensitive; each word phrase can be precisely "tuned" to a

23

given situation, set of speakers, and nuance. It is this feature of the Native languages of southern New England that makes the following Whorfian analysis of symbolic meaning possible.

LANGUAGE AND MEANING

When the missionary John Eliot wrote the first published study of a southern New England language, *The Indian Grammar Begun*, in the mid-seventeenth century, he believed it was a contribution to scholarship because it described "these new wayes of Grammar, which no other Larned Language (so far as I know), useth" (1666:15). Among the new features of Algonquian languages that Eliot described was the first person plural exclusive/inclusive marker that allows a speaker to distinguish between a "we" including a hearer, and one that excludes the hearer, as well as the range of prefixes and suffixes that mark the relationships between subject and object, unfamiliar to Europeans but typical of languages of this type. Eliot also thought, as did many of his contemporaries, that linguistic expressions betrayed something about the character of a people. In keeping with his sense that the languages of America did not follow a classical model, however, Eliot found that there were exceptions to this rule. He wrote, for example, about what he called the "indefinite mode" of the classical languages, including "lofty" as well as "supine" expressions, but reported that "though the spirit of this People, viz. the vapouring pride of some, and the dull-hearted supinity of others, might dispose them to such words and expressions, yet I cannot find them out" (1666:20).

Roger Williams, the iconoclastic scholar, religious theorist, and diplomat banished to Rhode Island in 1636, also used the subject of language to point out the differences between his world view and that of the Indian people with whom he lived. His famous phrasebook, written in 1643 and known as *A Key into the Language of America*, uses a series of dialogues and stories to portray the Native people he knew best according to a series of oppositional qualities (Williams 1936). For him, they were childlike in their amazement over the phenomena of nature or at extraordinary human skills; they were shrewd to the point of fanaticism in search of a bargain. They were savage but displayed more Christian values than did Christians, were as weak as babies when in pain from toothache but were remarkably stoic when wounded or while giving birth (1936:126, 163, 144).

Another well-known description of the indigenous languages of southern New England appears in a letter written by Experience Mayhew, grandson of the first English missionary on the island of Martha's Vineyard and himself a fluent speaker of the Native language then called Massachusett or Natick (whose speakers are the ancestors of present day Wampanoags). Mayhew wrote in 1722 that it was "good and regular" as capable as any language of expressing a wide range of thoughts and emotions. He wrote, for example, that:

Indian words, especially, the names of persons and things are generally very significant, by far more so than those of the English, as the Hebrew also are: for with them, the way used was to call every place, person, and thing by a name taken from some thing remarkable in it or attending of it. Thus the place where I dwell is in Indian called Nempanicklickanuk, in English, "The place of Thunder-clefts," because there was one a tree there split in pieces (*sic*) by the Thunder. This is one reason of the length of Indian words, they are long that it may appear the better what they signifie. So Sin is called Matche-usseonk, an evil work or deed. (Mayhew 1722:15–16)

All of these writers made explicit their awareness that language was central to understanding the character of the Native people among whom they worked, a guide to their unique concepts and categories of thought.

Williams also noted that language played a role in defining self and otherhood in Native southern New England. For example, group membership was often couched in terms of language.

When discussing language variations in the region, he reported that his Narragansett and Niantic friends remarked on their own and others' linguistic identity thus: "nippenowantawem" (I am of another language) and "penowantowawhettûock" (they are of a divers language) (Williams 1936:9). In a dialogue illustrating a putative greeting are the phrases, "Mat nowawtau hetté mina" (We understand not each other), "eenàntowash" (speak Indian) (1936:8), and "npenowauntawâumen" (I cannot speak your language) (55).

Following in the footsteps of these colonial linguists, and in order to investigate cognitive dimensions of the colonial world that Natives of southern New England participated in, this chapter uses examples from the Native languages of the region to link what we know about Native thought to the practices and patterns described in the historic records. To discuss meaning, I use the concept "eidos" to refer to patterns of thought or cognition in the sense meant by Gregory Bateson, in addition to the concept of "ethos," the term he used to refer to "organization of emotions in cultural terms" (1958). Both of these concepts help to elucidate the perspectives of people in the past, the cultural ideas that made them unique.

A useful way of examining culturally defined patterns of thought and emotion among the Native people of southern New England is through what Wallace Chafe has called the "shadow" and "orienting" meanings of language (1998:14, 17). Shadow meanings are those implied by linkages and similarities between common terms. Orienting meanings are those that are suggested by the very structure of languages themselves. The Native languages of southern New England provide many examples of orienting meanings. One of the best known is the treatment of the grammatical category of gender. In English, for example, it is grammatically obligatory to mark the gender of subjects not referred to by proper names (and even these are often covertly marked), but male and female gender was not marked grammatically in Algonquian languages. For Algonquian speakers, a different dyad was required grammatically. This was the distinction between animate and inanimate. In a well known passage from *Indian Grammar Begun*, Eliot noted that he had previously, and mistakenly, assigned the term for "stars"— anogqsoh—to the inanimate category, as would have made most sense to English speakers (1666:5).

The orienting meanings of these languages thus were directed away from sexual gender, toward a focus on vitality and connection to the human condition. Algonquian-speaking people share a consciousness of pervasive sacred power in the natural world; many believe that all features of that world can be animated by this power, and that human beings can partake of this force as well. If sexual gender went unmarked in language, then perhaps other social categories, such as rank, were emphasized. Chapter 3 discusses Native women as people of rank, for example, rather than people of gender. Other orienting meanings in southern New England languages were associated with the domains of separation, division, and distance (see table 1).

In New England, directional terms were also linked to social and supernatural categories. Josiah Cotton records the term "qun-nunkque" (he is elevated), perhaps reflecting the habit of sachems to sit above those who attended them (Cotton 1830:27). The word that John Eliot employed in his translations for spirit or breath— nashauonk—also meant "between" (Trumbull 1903:325). This expression, implying separation, is found in a 1727 annotation in an Indian-owned bible, in the phrase kunnassannittumuog weto-muku got (your spirits are with God) (Goddard and Bragdon 1988:409). William Simmons has written persuasively that, in southern New England, major life transition rituals were marked by symbolic references to social distancing, often using color (1970, 1976). Similarly Margaret Holmes Williamson notes such marking among the seventeenth-century Powhatan, expressed

Native People of Southern New England, 1650–1775

Table 1. Selected Phrases and Orienting Meanings

Term	English Meaning	Shadow Meaning
Anunn8, anue	corrupt	beyond, further, more
Chepeck, chippeau	separation	division
Chepi	a spirit	separated, apart
Negonne,nukkone	first	old, leave behind
Manit, anue, anhit	God above, or "something that deals with us"	
Qunnunkque	high	politically exalted
M8naeu	deep	low, lean, hell

through the use of color, directionality, dress, and hairstyles (2003:219–20). Most of the significant descriptions of Native spirituality in southern New England were written by English observers in the seventeenth century, and little attention was paid to Native beliefs in the eighteenth century. However, the Native languages of southern New England, which continued to be widely spoken throughout the colonial period, oriented thought in ways that did not necessarily "emerge into consciousness" (Boas 1911:64). As Chafe points out, the subtle nature of these orienting meanings made them less susceptible to change due to the influence of other languages or cultural practices (1998:18).

SHADOW MEANINGS, SYMBOLS, AND RITUALS

Key linguistic terms in southern New England were also those referencing health and well being, happiness, hospitality, and wealth. Many of these concepts were reflected in the shadow meanings of words. For example, table 2 lists root or stem terms that formed the basis for a wide variety of words associated with concepts of health and well being.

The many terms in southern New England languages containing wunne- (good), include terms for handsome (wunnetue) and welcome (wunnegin). Many elements of eastern woodlands symbolism are consistent with these concepts and, like concepts of

Table 2. Key Symbols of Health and Well Being

Term	English Meaning	Shadow Meaning
Pahke	clear	transparent, reflective, hollow
Asq	new	raw or immature, not yet ripe
Wunniyeu	goodness	health, happiness, truth

social separation, are ritually expressed through color; paint, or the use of colored objects (Hamell 1987). Some color symbolism is reflected in many everyday terms from southern New England languages (see table 3).

George Hamell has written extensively about Native American color symbolism in the Northeast, and argues that colors were used in religious observance. Color symbolism was also significant in burial ritual, and grave furnishings were often marked by distinct color choices, particularly white and blue (Hamell 1987:75; Robinson et al. 1985). Native people also favored colorful clothing, as the description of Elizabeth Waban, a prominent Native resident at Natick in the 1680s, reveals:

Her Dress peculiar, she had sleeves of Moose Skin, very finely dress'd, and drawn with Lines of various Coulours, in Asiatick Work, and her Buskins were of the same sort; her Mantle was of fine blew cloath, but very short, and ty'd about her Shoulders, and at the Middle with a Zone, curiously wrought with White and Blew Beads into pretty Figures; her Bracelets and hr Necklace

Table 3. Color Symbolism

Term	English Meaning	Shadow Meaning
Wompi,	white	brightness, daylight
Musquanittuonk, musqui	red	anger, blood
Mooi	black	ordure, dung
Peshaui, 8noi	blue	deep water, sky
Aske, moskehtu	green	raw, new, grass, medicine

were of the same sort of Beads, and she had a little Tablet upon her Breast, very finely decke'd with Jewels and Precious Stones; here Hair was comb'd back and ty'd up with a Border, which was neatly work'd both with Gold and Silver. (Dunton 1867:217–18)

Another important element of all social gatherings and religious observances was tobacco smoking. The term "ushpeu" (ascend) also meant "to rise quickly aloft" and was linked to bird flight and smoke. The notions of soul flight, dream travel, and paths to the sky world are linked in the eastern woodlands with the smoking of tobacco, where the smoke quickly arose, like the flight of a bird.

In southern New England, people blacked their faces before going into battle, as well as at the death of a loved one, and early records suggest that newborns faces were blacked as well. During an epidemic on Martha's Vineyard, people also blacked their faces. William Simmons suggests that black was associated with liminal or transitional states (1970). White, on the other hand, was associated with purity and referenced in the widespread use of white shell in rituals and for personal adornment. The use of such color symbolism not only oriented thought, it organized emotion in cultural terms.

Some activities described by contemporary English observers appear to reflect native theories of healing, premised on symbolic oppositions. For example, when Narragansett men burned themselves (that is, were "cooked" or "dry") they let their own blood ("wet" or "red") with a knife (Williams 1936:188). Dryness was also associated with illness and aging. On the other hand, water and wetness were associated with fertility, rawness, and the underwater world. Daniel Gookin recorded a story about the origins of the Nipmucks that suggested women were impregnated by wading into the water (1806:146). Margaret Holmes Williamson (2003) found that early descriptions of the Powhatans suggest associations between raw and wet and sere and cooked with sacred directions, east being associated with cooked (or cultural

30

and female) and west with raw or wet (or noncultural and male). But all these oppositions are relative, so that what is "east" or cultural in one context is "west" and noncultural in another (Williamson 2003:228–29).

Some of the cosmological principles and structural oppositions found in expressions and descriptions of seventeenth-century beliefs and practices can be summarized as a set of oppositions and mediations enacted in various ways. Rituals and other cultural dramas such as healing events and dances spoke to these polarities, which were also reflected in social relations and the merging of opposite elements in the resolution of conflict or the restoration of order. They also permeated the calendrical rituals and were expressed in political ties and in trade, as well as in relationships between men and women. Some examples of these oppositions and mediations are summarized in the table below (table 4).

The earliest descriptions of Native cosmology in southern New England, drawn from observations and some Native testimony, describe a world in which the natural and the supernatural are conjoined. Their relations with the mysterious, unpredictable,

Table 4. Symbolic Oppositions and Mediations

Life	Not Alive
High	Low
Raw, new, green	Cooked, dry, fading
Pure	Corrupt
Sky	Underground/water
Superior	Inferior
Mediations	
Blood	Death/birth
Sacrifice or Loss	Renewal
Smoke	Burning, flying
Manitou	Life giving, Life taking

31

and powerful supernatural beings and forces known as manitou were as central a concern to the Native peoples of Southern New England as the achievement of direct enlightenment from God was to Puritan settlers of the region. The power of manitou ensured health and success in any enterprise. More importantly, the continuing cycle of life was in the manitou's control (Williams 1936:198–99).

The people believed that it was possible to gain the aid of manitou through prayer, fasting, and the sacrifice of goods. Dreams were analyzed to determine if they contained supernatural messages or lessons, and portents of many kinds were scrutinized for their meanings. Many Native people saw visions, especially in the sky (Simmons 1986:59).

Although the cosmos was divided into three worlds—the Upper or Sky world, Earth, and the Under (water) world—the boundaries between them were permeable, and it was possible to travel to supernatural realms in dreams, or during trance and soul travel. Manitou, of course, could and did appear in the human world, sometimes inhabiting animals, animating plants and minerals, and, on occasion, taking the form of human beings.

Manitou were especially likely to appear in certain settings, including caves and fissures, deserted stretches of forest, secluded swamps, high places, and in or near deep water. Groves of trees or arbors were often used for sacred rituals as well, while burials and burial grounds in historic southern New England were nearly always located near bodies of water. Important shamanic rituals were also conducted in protected and inaccessible swamps. The Pequot word, for example, for the swamp where they retreated to consult their supernatural protectors prior to the English attack on Mystic fort was "Cuppphock," meaning "enclosed place."

The first explorers, colonists, and missionaries who inquired into the cosmology of the Indians with whom they lived found that manitou was a word used to describe "Gods, Spirits, or Divine Powers, as they say of everything they cannot understand" (Williams 1936:103). This concept, closely connected to the ideas of the dual soul, soul travel, and of guardian spirits (Bragdon 1996b:184–87), is also common among other Algonquian-speaking peoples (Tooker 1979; Underhill 1965). As among these people, the Natives of southern New England sought the help of manitou, often thought of or encountered as animals or godlike figures such as Thunderbird and Serpent. These supernatural beings, "beings other than human" (Tooker 1979:76), might be persuaded through prayer, fasting, or sacrifice of food, tobacco, or wealth, to assist in hunting, war, or other enterprises, and to return health to ailing loved ones. Experts on these matters among the Natives of southern New England were shamans, known as powwaws, the taupaog, or "wise men," and, among the Pokanokets, the pniese (Bragdon 1996b:189–90).

The powwaws were particularly renowned for their close connections to the supernatural world, the strength of their spirit helpers or guardian spirits, and, hence, their abilities as healers and forecasters of the future. In pursuit of supernatural power, and as part of their ritual, shamans often performed "magical" acts, such as making objects appear and disappear, or creating smoke or fire without visible means. Some were said to be able to walk on water or to harm people at a distance. Powwaws frequently healed by "sucking" harmful objects out of their patients, thereby restoring them to health. Powwaws were often associated with snakes, which in Algonquian cosmology generally are the denizens of the underworld, associated with both birth and death. Their cosmic counterparts, the Thunderbird of the Sky world, and, in New England particularly, the Raven, were also linked with powwaws, especially since powwaws were believed able to fly to other times and places and to take the form of birds. Since tobacco has ancient shamanic associations in Native North America, its use is also associated with powwaws and, more generally, with the attempt to communicate with the supernatural world.

Descriptions by Europeans affirm that Native clothing, basketry, pottery and other objects, as well as human bodies, were decorated with "antick figures," drawings or tattoos depicting abstract designs and representations of animals, birds, and other images of significance lost to non-Indians (Williams 1936:165, 191; Wood 1977:103). These descriptions conform to petroglyphic and pictographic images carved on prominent outcroppings along navigable stretches of the Taunton River and in the Narragansett Bay region (Delabarre 1928:204). These signs and images show many similarities regionally and appear to represent or remark upon vision quests and other shamanic activities (Bragdon 1995). Images similar to these petroglyphs are also found on seventeenth-century documents as the "signs" or "marks" of sachems and others participating in land transactions or treaties. Roger Williams noted that when writing was introduced to the Narragansetts, they called it "painting, for that comes the nearest" (1936:42). While certainly not representations of the spoken word, these images constituted a visual code evidently widely understood.

The images appear to reflect shared ideas about dreams and visions, soul flight, ascent to the Sky or Upper world, and sexual potency (Snow 1976). In addition to petroglyphic representations, these widespread ideas were found on amulets, as decorations on pottery and baskets, and on clothing (Bragdon 1996b:187).

The pervasiveness of spiritual power in the world was also closely connected to Native theories of what Irving Hallowell (1955) called the "reality of a life beyond the grave" common to many people of the northeast and the association of dream journeys to the afterlife with serious illness or death.

In southern New England, English settlers were told of two souls, the cowwéwonck, who traveled in dreams and left the body during illness, the other called míchachunck—the "clear" soul—and located in the heart (Simmons 1970:54), representing the uniqueness of each individual (Williams 1936:130). Several seventeenth-century descriptions mention the attraction of mirrors and other shiny objects for Native people, which was not, as Roger Williams believed, for vanity only, but probably because they came to symbolize the "see through" or clear knowledge of an individual's essence. This belief evidently survived into the eighteenth century, as indicated by finds at the Fanning Road cemetery, on the Mashantucket Reservation in Ledyard, Connecticut, which included interments dating from 1666–1740 and included a burial described as follows: "a circular opening [was] dug in the earth, and the body placed in a sitting position. A stake had been forced into the ground perpendicularly in front of it: a nail was driven into the stake on which hung a looking glass opposite the face of the dead" (Hurd 1882:150).

Mirrors may have been a literal symbol of personhood—the reflection, or symbolic substitute for the essential soul that remained in the grave. It was also an aid to the traveling soul. Finally, its location may have been meant to direct the soul of the deceased on its journey. The spiritual beliefs concerning the dead held by Native people in southern New England seem to have shared in more widespread Algonquian belief systems, which were in some ways a reversal of those of English settlers. The earliest descriptions by ethnographers of Algonquian indigenous belief systems date to the early nineteenth century, but contain many references to ideas described by English settlers in New England two centuries earlier. For example, ideas of the Algonquian-speaking Berens River Saulteaux are described by anthropologist Irving Hallowell:

Despite the fact that in Native theory the soul (òtcatcákwin), detached from the body, makes the journey [to the spirit land (djibaiàking)] in any case, and that dream experiences are

35

classified as "real" experiences, categorically continuous with those of the waking life, a purely empirical distinction is made. The experiences described by persons observed to be dead, or fatally ill, are not said to have been "dreamed," while the "experiences" described by healthy persons are said to have been dreamed." (1955:29)

In southern New England, the dreamed was real, and the beings encountered in dreams were a living presence. They were part of the Native social world, and they were understood to work together with human beings. This personalization of the universe is characteristic of many Native American cosmologies (Brown and Brightman 1988:123). Native people in southern New England, as elsewhere, also sometimes explained specific events as "consequences of antagonism between beings representing opposed terrestrial and aquatic or subterranean spheres" (1988:135). For example, powwaws often diagnosed sickness as the result of the malign influence of the souls of the unburied dead, especially one lost at sea (Simmons 1970:53). William Simmons (1986) and Constance Crosby (1988) also remark on the pervasiveness of stories of "beings other than human" in folk stories from the region, collected since the seventeenth century.

In the later colonial period snakes represented traditional religious beliefs. Several surviving stories from southern New England involve Native ministers fighting off snakes, or shamans making use of snakes to attack others (Simmons 1986:284).

The role of shell ornaments (linked to the underwater world) in Native ritual during the colonial period is also a subject that deserves further study. Preliminary reports on the Long Pond Cemetery near the Mashantucket Pequot reservation, a cemetery dating to the late seventeenth and early eighteenth centuries, include references to animal shaped shell ornaments included as grave furniture, which were probably of local manufacture. The Pequots' control over significant shell resources in the early seventeenth century, and their reported ceremonialism appear

36

to have continued to distinguish these people in later decades as well (Kevin McBride personal communication 2006). High ranking women made belts of shell in the late seventeenth century (see chapter 4), although whether these were status markers or for use in diplomatic exchanges is not clear.

There are many places in southern New England with sacred significance to its Native people, some of which are documented as far back as the seventeenth century, where some of these conflicts are said to have taken place. Among the most important is Dighton Rock, a petroglyph site located on the Assonet River near Taunton, Massachusetts. Both John Danforth (1680) and Cotton Mather (1712) described this rock, and Danforth was told its characters depicted a battle between two groups, a theory also put forth by Chingwauk, an elder at Saulte St. Marie, to whom Henry Schoolcraft showed a copy in 1839 (Lepore 1998:230). Many tales from Cape Cod and Martha's Vineyard also tell of conflicts among culture heroes and giants, which resulted in dramatic changes in the landscape, still visible today.

Some of these stories were associated with shamanic practice, still common in Indian communities in the colonial period in southern New England. Dighton Rock and other pictographs referenced this activity and its results, these images linking peoples to one another through a regionally shared system of signs (Bragdon 1997).

The images found on petroglyphs, pottery, and amulets, also are used during the colonial period, as decorative images, as "signatures," and on historic period objects. Among the most interesting of these is the leather cover of a ledger book owned by Matthew Mayhew of Martha's Vineyard that depicts an anthropomorphized thunderbird image very like those found on petroglyph sites throughout the region (Richardson personal communication 2004). On occasion Native signatories to deeds used signs very similar to these images, especially the thunderbird.

Although powwaws were participants in calendrical rituals, these seasonal ceremonies were presided over by the taupaog, and were often sponsored by sachems or councilors, or by individuals who wished to bless their communities with a Nickommo or feast. These rituals and feasts often included dancing, gambling, and special foods, and usually lasted for several days. Some rituals, especially for mourning, were by contrast marked by fasting, prayer, and the blackening of faces. Both solemn and celebrative rituals were accompanied by the sacrifice of wealth, which was often burned, sometimes buried, or thrown into the sea, and the construction of sacred structures, such as "arbors" or "mourning houses" (Bragdon 1996b:217–30).

Many of the most thorough accounts of shamanic practice and Native cosmology in southern New England were preserved by missionaries writing of energetic missionary activity between 1645 and 1675. In these accounts, the shamans' practices were generally referred to as "sorcery" or "witchcraft," their beliefs "devil worship," and their spirit guardians as "familiars," or "imps." Karen Kupperman argues that some Indians presented themselves as sorcerers, using the names of Native manitou as Squanto and Hobbomok of Plymouth had done, to increase their own influence, and to play on the English settlers' fears of sorcery (2000:185–86). However, Kupperman also suggests that such Native intermediaries were in fact marking their liminality in the white world, as a shaman who entered supernatural realms also cut himself off from normal human experience.

The practice of allowing the supernaturally gifted to intercede for the community or for anyone in need was consistent with the special social role that shamans and other religious practitioners played and accounted for the fearful respect with which they were treated, which often was accompanied with, or replaced by, the certainty that such persons might use their powers to do them harm.

The pervasive spirituality of the natural world as a daily experience was periodically intensified by seasonal rituals and rites of renewal or by great feasts of mourning. While very few detailed descriptions of any of these ceremonies exist, many of them were accompanied by contests, gambling, and dancing. Others involved burning or destroying goods, or giving them away in large quantities. This aspect of Native worship, which also enhanced or marked the social prestige of the celebrants or sponsors, was consistently misunderstood by English observers, who viewed the destruction or giving away of property as senseless improvidence.

It has been widely assumed, based on seventeenth-century commentary and later historical theorizing, that the "seamless whole" that was Native cosmology did not long survive the arrival of Europeans on American shores. In particular, the terrible toll taken by disease has frequently been cited as the platform from which a full assault on Native ideas took place (Starna 1992).

Certainly the Massachusett, Wampanoag, and Nipmuck peoples experienced the most serious losses in the years immediately prior to the settlement of Plymouth and in the following decades. The success of missionary work among the Indians of this region is also evident (see chapter 6), although on Martha's Vineyard and Nantucket, where population losses were much less severe, Christianity prospered as well. A number of studies have suggested that ritual, in particular, intensified, or its significance altered, as a result of disease and the new realpolitik of the colonial world (Nassaney 1989).

William Simmons, whose important writings on this subject were among the first to address ideological change in the region (much of which he interpreted as a result of the devastation of epidemic disease), argues that "Native people came to see their culture had lost something which it once possessed, and which [the missionary Thomas] Mayhew translated as wisdom" (1979:207). But what

Simmons characterized as a "deep and rapid voluntary change to colonial ideology" among the Indians of Martha's Vineyard (Simmons 1979:215), was, in his view, the result of a "mutually understood expression of social dominance by the English and an active but not coercive effort by the missionary to offer the symbols of his culture." While not questioning the early and important impact that the combined effect of disease, invasion, and skillful persuasion had, I argue that this transformation was by no means unidirectional and that Native people continued to adhere to, or in some cases revive, a set of principles, practices, and beliefs that their ancestors had embraced.

There are also numerous pieces of evidence that hint at the preservation of certain elements of Native cosmology even in Christian communities. The regional networks that existed in Native New England, as well as their contacts with Native peoples to the west and north circulated ideas, perpetuated practices, and allowed a continued trade in sacred materials, including wampum.

For example, there are at least seven historic Native cemeteries in the region including Burr's Hill (Gibson 1980), RI 1000 (Rubertone 2001), and Crescent Beach and Long Pond on the Mashantucket Pequot reservation. Two others are associated with the praying communities at Natick and Canton. The earliest known historic period cemetery dates to the late sixteenth and early seventeenth centuries, and the latest contains burials dating to the mid-eighteenth century. All, including the Christian graves found at Natick and Canton contain grave goods of both Native and European manufacture. While debates continue about the significance of these burials (see Bragdon 1996b:236–41), it is clear that sacrifices to supernatural beings and preparations for an Indian afterlife were still significant concerns to Native people in the colonial period. These practices of Native origin were still alive in Indian communities in the later colonial period.

Practices with cosmological implications were often concerned with healing and mourning rituals even in the later colonial period. Some direct evidence for these practices comes from Martha's Vineyard, where the missionary John Cotton, Jr., recorded Native terms for a number of shamanic activities. Cotton paid special attention to Native "powwawing," which he called witchcraft. An example from a page of his wordlist illustrates the ways he explored this persistent aspect of Native life (see table 5).

Thomas Mayhew described similar face blacking among Martha's Vineyard Natives reacting to a "strange mortality" that raged through the Indian communities in 1643, a year after the establishment of the English colony. Native people began "to run up and down till they could run no longer," and "made their faces black as coale, snatched up any weapon, spake great words, but did no hurt" (Mayhew 1643).

Illness and possession were linked concepts, and powwawing endeavored to release the sufferer by thwarting the dream soul of the offending powwaw or removing the evil substance introduced into the body of the sick by sucking and spitting (Wood

Table 5. Powwawing Terms from Cotton's Word List

Neeskinneunkquac	Dirt
Mannonesk	Clay
Mooettequawonk	To black one's face
Suhkoowonk	To spit
Pawawon	A witch (related to "dream")
Qussampatuwonk	To bewitch (From queshau "he leaps," "a leaping man")
Nukquissemp	Kuk qupapoo, I, you, he (bewitches)
Qussepsh	Bewitch (Imperative)
Manetu	One is bewitched

Source: Cotton 1665–1678, *Journal and Vocabulary of the Indians.*

1977:101). Reports of powwawing continued during Cotton's time, and it was still unclear then whether or not "a powwow could kill a believer" (Mayhew 1643).

Words for healing, health, wealth, and well being were also important shadow meanings in Native usage. Among the many reasons Roger Williams found Narragansett and Niantic trading partners troublesome were their frequent excuses of illness. He recorded the phrase: "nowemacaûnash nitteaùquash I was faine to spend my money in my sicknesse" and commented "This is a common, and as (they think) most satisfying answer, that they have been sick; for in those times they give largely to the priests, who then sometimes heales them by conjurations; and also they keepe open house for all to come to helpe to pray with them, unto whom also they give money" (Williams 1936:169).

Not only did people give away goods during feasts and dances, but they also paid their mediators, the shamans. In exchange for the shaman's services, families and individuals paid large amounts of wampum, skins, jewelry, and other wealth, that the powwaw in turn burned, buried, or destroyed in sacrifice (Bragdon 1996b: 224–25). Thomas Morton reported, too, that "So great is the estimation and reverence that these people have of thes Ingling (*sic*) Powahs, who are usually sent for when any person is sick and ill at ease, to recover them; for which they receive rewards as do our Surgeons and Physicians. And they do make a trade of it, and boast of their skill where they come" (Morton in Dempsey 2000:30).

Rituals of curing are also described by later Native people. In fact, the gambling, the sacrifice of goods, the gifts of jewelry, clothing, and tools, the feasting, continued to be important acts of faith, part of the constant effort on the part of individuals and communities to ensure their own continuity and the renewal of the world.

A story attributed to the Native Thomas Cooper, a resident of Martha's Vineyard in the mid-eighteenth century, whose grandmother had been a "stout girl" when the English had arrived in the 1640s, describes in fascinating detail some of the elements of curing ritual and its associations with wealth and social status:

[T]hey could always lay [yellow fever] in the following manner. After it had raged and swept off a number, those who were well met to lay it. The rich, that is such as had a canoe, skins, axes, &c. brought them. They took their seat in a circle; and all the poor sat around without. The richest then proposed to begin to lay the sickness and having in his hand something in shape resembling his canoe, skin or whatever else his riches were, he threw it up in the air, and whoever of the poor without could take it, the property it was intended to resemble became forever transferred to him or her. After the rich had thus given away all their movable property to the poor, they looked out the handsomest and most sprightly young man in the assembly and put him into an entire new wigwam, built of everything new for that purpose. They then formed into two files at a small distance from each other, one standing in the space at each end, put fire to the bottom of the wigwam on all parts and fell to singing and dancing. Presently the youth would leap out of the flames and fall down to appearances dead. Him they committed to the care of five virgins, prepared for that purpose, to restore to life again. The time required for this would be uncertain, from six to forty eight hours, during which time the dance must be kept up. When he was restored he would tell that he had been carried in a large thing high up in the air where he came to a great company of white people, with whom he had interceded hard to have the distemper layed; and generally after much persuasion would obtain a promise or an answer of peace, which never failed of laying the distemper. (Bassett 1792:139–40)

This story includes many elements of Native theory: that the fire destroys and renews, that the sacrifice or giving away of wealth is necessary for health, that the community must be involved in cures, that singing and dancing were central to the cure, that someone must assume the role of advocate to the supernatural, and that the ceremony requires the use of a special structure.

43

In the late seventeenth and early eighteenth centuries, Englishmen who knew the Native people best continued to find that healing and divination practices of ancient heritage were still practiced among them. A few years after King Philip's War, John Cotton, Jr., wrote "[I am] writing a book refuting supernatural happenings (witches or devils) . . . a work very necessary to be done at this time, & I wish some able hand had undertaken it, for it is too common a practice in these parts to repair to a certain diviner among us to recover lost goods, & to any pretender English or Indian to know our fortunes one oute of order among us this year bottled and boiled his own urine to find out the witch that afflicted him" (Cotton 1665–1678).

Many people, Indian and white, consulted fortune tellers, used charms, and sought out Indian healers, in spite of the disapproval of their learned ministers. Edward Ward, who traveled in New England in the late seventeenth century noted, "Indians are Incomparable Physicians; Being well skill'd in the Nature of herbs and plants of the Country. But the English will not make use of them, because their ministers have infus'd this notion into 'em, that what they do, is by the power of the devil" (Ward 1699:16).

In 1716, Cotton Mather wrote two letters describing contemporary conjuring, reflecting just such fears: "you will pardon me syr, if I ask that it may not be judged altogether unphilosophical to suppose that these tricks were often performed by daemons who being after some sort invoked by the charmer stept in to answer his intention" (Mather 1716). He also described the use of snakes in curing rituals as well:

what has appeared a little strange to the spectators has been to see an Indian take a rattlesnake and handle the feared poisoners with as much freedom and as little damage as if he had (?) only an eel in his hands anon the Indian discovered that mystery he had anointed himself with the fatt of the bird aforesaid, and that gave him a greater security that what . . . for now the rattle snake would not so much as attempt the . . . bite upon him" (Mather 1716:422).

Although his father, Thomas Mayhew, reported in 1678 that witchcraft and sorcery were "out of use here," Matthew Mayhew stated that on Martha's Vineyard in the late seventeenth century, an Indian called George, who reported being "tormented," and "impotent," sought a local powwaw, who concluded that George was the victim of witchcraft. According to Mayhew, the powwaw then danced around a fire, with George and other Natives "lying by." However, other Natives broke up this curing ceremony, accusing the powwaw himself of bewitching the patients. When the powwaw was threatened with burning, the patients immediately recovered (Mayhew 1694).

This story suggests that Native people in Christian communities were divided about the use of such rituals, although the power of the curer was unquestioned. A similar healing ceremony, which reflects the same ambivalence, was reported in southeastern Connecticut in 1733, as Native people there attempted to cure a child with a strange condition:

[H]e continued 3 or 4 days in a very strange condition biting his tongue and striving . . . it was difficult to hold him. . . . many of them suspected the child was bewitched and there was a Nehantick Indian there which said it was. Upon which the grandmother of the child (being there) desired that he would make it apparent (?) and to do that he first pulled out of the belly [of the child] a leather string about three inches long, in which there was tied some hair. There was (*sic*) some Indians there which did not see him pull it out which said they did not believe he did. He said he wondered they did not believe it, and said that there was more in him yet, and to convince them of it he pulled another out of the small of his back, near as long as a man's finger, which also had some hair, and a wampampeag tied in the middle and there was several knots tied in the string, soon after these were pulled out the child died. The flesh where these strings were pulled out quivered much, and the strings after that were taken out moved about and the Indian which took them out with his teeth was immediately taken with great trembling, he and others thought he would immediately died. [But] some time after he was so well as to go home. The father of the child when he returned home from hunting the next week after the child died he enquired of the Indians about it who informed him about it as it has been represented. He immediately came to Capt. Mason with the grandmother of the child as was much surprised and concerned about it. He said that he thought there had been an end to such witchcraft (as he thought it to be) for he knew not an instance of it in his day before the old woman said she wondered the child should die in such a manner so soon after it was put to school. The sachem Mahom says that the Indian which pulled out the strings remains in a strange condition and can't obtain cure and they think he will not live long. This story is what I have chiefly from Capt. Mason which he has credibly informed of by the sachem Ben Uncas and several other of our Indians who said they were eye witnesses. (Barber 1733: n.p.)

Samson Occom, a Mohegan minister who served as a missionary on Long Island in 1761, reported that shamans were working there, and described their methods:

As for the Powaws, they say they get their art from . . . the devil, but then partly by dreams or night visions, and partly by the devil's immediate appearance to them by various shapes; sometimes in the shape of one creature, sometimes in another, sometimes by a voice . . . and their poisoning one another and taking out poison, they say is no imaginary thing, but real. I have heard some say, that have been poisoned, it puts them into great pain, and when a powaw takes out the poison they have found immediate relief . . . And I don't see for my part, why it is not as true, as the English or other nation's witchcraft, but is a great mystery of darkness. (Occom 1809:109)

Josiah Cotton, who worked among the Native people near Plymouth, Massachusetts, in the first half of the eighteenth century, claimed that Native people would use any occasion for an excuse to socialize. He wrote in his journal that "the year 1716 I left going to the Indians at Mattakees by reson of the distance, because it seemed as if the Indians made too much of a frolick of it etc." This comment by the discouraged missionary implies that dancing was only another example of the laxity of Christian Indians. Yet other information suggests that frolics and dances had important political purposes in the eighteenth century. The Mohegan reservation community provides a series of examples. In particular, the "black dance" held on the Mohegan reservation in support of Anne, daughter of Maahamet, to install her as leader of the community in 1736, was an overt statement of opposition to the colonial government. Den Ouden argues "the Mohegan resisters may have intended for the black dance to emphasize Mohegans' otherness, to articulate Mohegan identity in terms of a gendered opposition that defied both colonial understanding and governmental control" (2005:202).

This same incident was prefaced by internal skirmishing. Jonathan Barber wrote to Coleman in 1733 that

[The sachem of Mohegan] refusing to joyn with some of his people in a dance or frolick which they had, though he was importuned by his mother & . . . he said, what shall I now I am going to be a christian and now we have a minister joyn in a dance no I will not [his people] told him that his grand father & father used to doe so and that if he would not the Indians would slight him he said, he did not care for that and that he wronged nobody in refusing. . . . that week also some Indians formerly belonging to Mohegan which have been absent some years . . . had a great dance and the sachem again refused to joyn with them. (Barber 1733: n.p.)

In a similar way, the minister Isaac Simon of Mashpee complained in November of 1767 that he was

[S]taying at his mother mary simons house in mashpee and on Monday night a number of strange indians & squas to the number of near twenty come . . . at ten oclock . . . they come into the house and one of them offered them a bottle and he refused to drink and they went out of the house and went to dancing and frolicking and they came in again . . . and they sang and danced and frolicked round the house and continued the same frolick all tuesday and tuesday night he thretend them with a small penkive and stabbed one dead he made his escape and headed throu cheniquset river for fear he should be killed by [them] . . . and the [Indian] justice refused to medel in the affaire but came to barnstable court and "after the fellow was wounded he desired him to reed a book to him and he read an Indian book to him." (Simon 1767)

In 1784, the Gay Head minister Zachary Hossueit also complained in a memorandum written in the Native language, of fittling and dancing, hinting that two factions existed in the community. The persistence of Native language itself by the Christian minister at Gay Head illustrates the many ambiguities of belief in Native New England in the colonial period, as those structural and shadow meanings so embedded in the language lived uneasily alongside the strictures of Christianity and the by-then well-learned lesson that Indians were inferior both economically and spiritually to the English.

LAND, ENDURANCE, AND IDENTITY

The linguistic evidence from southern New England also speaks, literally, to the ways Native people themselves viewed and understood landscape and land as a productive entity, which also embodied and represented sociality and community (Goddard and Bragdon 1988:33, 373). The suggestion that use and possession are connected notions in Massachusett is reinforced by a pair of associated terms derived from the same stem auwoh (use), meaning also use up or wear out (Bragdon 1996b:167).

Tools and implements were among the most intimate possessions of Northeast Native peoples in prehistoric and early historic periods, often buried with their owners along with items of personal adornment and ceremonial objects (Simmons 1970; Gibson 1980).

Such tools were specifically mentioned in a Native language will written in 1749 on Gay Head (Goddard and Bragdon 1988:167), in which the Native woman Naomi Ommaush wrote: "Each one (of my kin) shall take, after I die, what I have not yet used (ne asque auwohteau)" (Goddard and Bragdon 1988:55). The will links the notion of use with the idea that these objects or items were to be used until worn out. Other Native texts imply that this was an idea associated with land use as well.

Words for "strong" are also common in Native documents. Menuhkequog (steel) is related to chohquog (hard knife) and often used to describe Englishmen, or "hard knife men" (Williams 1936:38). Menuhke (strong, firm) describes bravery and a stronghold (Trumbull 1903:55). In Native writings, menuhke also meant "long lasting" (Goddard and Bragdon 1988:175). To make something hard or strong was to "confirm" it (645). Menuhkinnum also means "he holds it fast" or "safe" (646). These notions would seem to be associated with endurance, especially with respect to land, an association also recognized in other societies (Róheim 1945:152). Their use in Native writings is also linked to the concepts of corporate ownership of land, the enduring nature of the kin group, and the moral requirements of loyalty to that group.

As noted above, the categories of animate and, its opposite, inanimate are pervasive in southern New England as in all Algonquian languages. These ideas might also be associated with hardness or durability, as it appears that stone and metal were sometimes classified as animate (Williams 1973:58). For example, pewter spoons, listed in the will of Naomi Ommaush in 1749, were marked with an animate ending (Goddard and Bragdon 1988:53, line 15) (see chapter 4).

The idea that land would only be abandoned if used up is attested to by Roger Williams when he wrote in 1643 of the Narragansetts that "This question they oft put to me: Why come the

Englishmen hither? and measuring others by themselves; they say, It is because you want firing: for they, having burnt up the wood in one place, . . . they are faine to follow the wood; and so to remove to a fresh new place for the wood's sake" (Williams 1973:59–60).

In a Native language document recording a land transfer, written in 1673, on Martha's Vineyard, the Native Sabiah Jootes wrote, "even though it is my children, they shall not meddle with it. For we have eaten it all, I and my children" (Goddard and Bragdon 1988:81). A will written in the Native language in 1735 by the preacher Peter Ohquanhit of Gay Head contains this passage: "When I die all this estate goes into the hand of my wife; she [will] own it the same way I owned any of it, and the same way I used it (auwohchamomp) she may use it. She may eat and wear anything from it as long as she lives" (Goddard and Bragdon 1988:169).

Both these texts use the expression "eat" (meechu) as a metaphor for land use. The stem for "eat" is also found in a related term in Massachusett likewise associated with land, meechummuonk (fruit, [such as apples]) (Cotton 1830:28), or "fruits, products" (Eliot 1663:Gen.3:3). This term appears several times in the Massachusetts' texts, often translated as "fruits" of the land (Goddard and Bragdon 1988:docs. no. 10, 11, 35, 44, 47).

Other metaphors link eating to an evaluation of relative humanness. Roger Williams described the Narragansett/Niantic description of the Mihtukmechakick or "Tree Eaters: a people so called living between three and four hundred miles West into the land from their eating only mihtuchquash, that is, Trees: They are men-eaters, they set no corne, but live on the bark of chestnut and walnut and other fine trees: they dry and eat this bark with the fat of beasts, and sometimes of men: this people are the terrour of the neighbour Natives "(quoted in Goddard and Bragdon 1988:doc. no. 13).

The Massachusetts' writings suggest that food and its lexical referents were an important domain in that language, and that, in one of its meaning extensions, eating was associated with land, its use, and its possession (Bragdon 1996b:135–36). Among the Massachusetts and Pokanokets, the idea of indefinite consumption was extended metaphorically in expressions regarding the use and ownership of land. One could eat from it and use it forever. The Mashpee document written in 1752 (quoted above) continues "we shall not give it away, nor shall it be sold, nor shall it be lent, but we shall always use it (nuttauohkonan) as long as we live, we together with all our children, and our children's children, and our descendants, and together with all their descendants. They shall always use it (wuttauohkonau) as long as Christian Indians live. We shall use it (nuttauohkonnan) forever and ever" (Goddard and Bragdon 1988:373).

In some respects, the Native language deeds resemble those of the English of the same region and period. English deeds from Martha's Vineyard, for example, generally follow a format similar to the deed cited below, in which the Englishman Ebenezer Rogers "sells" land to "Black Henry" Luce, the son of the Native daughter of Joseph Daggett, Alice, and the Englishman Henry Luce (Pierce 2007:12). "Ebenezer Rogers . . . hath bargained and sold, and doth by these presents sell, ratify, & confirm unto him the said Henry Luce, a certain tract of land . . . to have and to hold said land with the members, privileges and appurtenances to him the said Henry Luce his heirs and assigns forever, to him and their sole and proper use behoof and benefit forever" (Dukes County Deeds, November 19, 1699, Book 1:234) (see chapter 4).

Compare the following Native deed recorded in 1718 in Barnstable County: "I Jabes Wekkit let you have it, you Thom Pennas, all my land and all trees, grass, and all that grows there within the land. I Bashshonnis Wekkit am content. You own my land, and you use it (kauttohtauwun . . . kauttauwohkon), and you own it forever and ever" (Goddard and Bragdon 1988:49).

However, unlike the English deeds, this and other Native texts also convey the notion, common to all the land transfers recorded in Native writings, that one was not simply an individual randomly placed in time and space, but a member of a community that had deep roots in the past and equally strong connections to the future. When one had land in Massachusett, it was land that was to be used and eaten by oneself and one's posterity.

In a document dating 1679, the sachem Quateatashshit of Manomet in Plymouth colony wrote: "My bequest is not sold, this island forever, as long as the earth exists, but only they use it (wut-tauwohkanoo), these four children of mine, and in all their posterity forever and ever as long as they have descendants" (Goddard and Bragdon 1988:33).

The notion of use was closely tied to the idea of corporate identity, and the continuity of the land-using group through time. Several of the texts imply that land, if properly defended by its Native inhabitants will never be used up.

These ideas are also related to the Native perception of land as morally and socially significant, with each landscape feature serving as a mnemonic reminder of a sacred tale, a text to be read again and again by each new generation (Basso 1983; Feld and Basso 1996). To speak of land in this way is of course not to deny its commodification, but to question the applicability of western models of commodity to the New England case (Appadurai 1986).

And perhaps most significantly of all, the differences in perceptions of land documented between the English and Indians in these texts were differences that remained after 150 years of contact between the two peoples. These differences explain the continued resistance of the Indians of southern New England to the land hunger of Europeans, well after the time when the concepts of English "ownership" and "sale" were accepted and understood. More importantly, these expressions document the longstanding relationships between Native people and their surroundings, relationships tying generations together.

LANDSCAPE AND PERCEPTION

Place names, in addition to marking the extent of Native settlement, also testify to how Indian people referred to and made use of their lands, as resource locations, in their fixed sites along trade and travel routes, and with reference to their historical significance. In addition, much Eastern Pequot folklore concerns these and similar landmarks, which appear to have taken on additional significance through time. In these terms for use, place names "naturalize different worlds of sense" (Feld and Basso 1996:8). Native writings employ specific, localized terms for places instead of their English names continuing into the eighteenth century. For example, a set of documents associated with land at East Chop, on Martha's Vineyard, include a number of directional terms that must be local (Goddard and Bragdon 1988:61).

In similar ways, the brush and stone heaps of eastern Massachusetts and Cape Cod and in Narragansett country memorialize and mark Indian presence, as do the layering of experiences and stories that make these places and the paths that run through them part of a network of daily significance (Simmons 1986; Crosby 1988).

Other remarkable places were those with sacred springs and/or where shamanic visions took place. According to Ezra Stiles,

On the road from Sandwich to Plymouth there is a large stone or rock in a place free of stones; and that Indians immemorially have used whenever and as often as they passed this large stone to cast a stone or piece of wood upon it. . . . The Indians being asked the reason of their custom and practice say they know nothing about it only that their fathers and grandfathers and great grandfathers did so, and charged all their children to do so; and if they did not cast a stone or piece of wood upon it as they passed by it they would not prosper & particularly should not be lucky in hunting Deer. (Stiles 1916:162–63)

The folk stories, memorates, and sacred tales told by the Native people of southern New England populate the landscape with supernatural beings, historical figures, and culture heroes, and have done so since before the coming of Europeans (Simmons 1986). These stories, with histories dating back to the seventeenth century, along with landscape features such as pictograph sites, sacrifice rocks, and place names, gave a sense of pervasiveness to the Native presence in the colonial period that went beyond their physical presence (Crosby 1988). These sites were places where emotional links to the past were marked. It is important to recall that in the seventeenth century the Native people of southern New England regarded the land as theirs, by right and history, and even after Philip's disastrous war, traveled through it on paths their ancestors had cleared. Not only in settlement but also in movement the Native people of the region connected with one another, with their heritage, and with their living culture.

The kinds of orienting and shadow meanings described above were embedded in the Native languages of southern New England, influencing perception and action wherever those languages were spoken. These general orientations suggested by language, however, were also subject to reinterpretation in discourse. The dynamics of Native speech communities are discussed in the next chapter.

2.

Ethnographies of Speaking: Local Linguistic Communities

Kekuttokûunta (Let us speak together)
—Roger Williams 1936

We often imagine past communities as static and silent, when they were in reality full of sound, motion, scent, and color. Villages and settlements, camp sites, river crossings and trading posts, the scenes of daily activity in colonial Native New England had physical weight and familiarity. They were also the "locales" of social life, where people spoke to one another, holding conversations, rituals, and ceremonies, or where they disputed one another or worked together at tasks that required discussion and direction. To highlight these discursive aspects of social life, linguist Michael Silverstein uses the phrase "local linguistic community" to indicate that such communities are places of cultural reinforcement, negotiation, and change (1998). Language, in the Saussurian sense, and as described in chapter 1, is understood to be widespread, heterogeneous, superorganic, and operating at the level of the unconscious (Boas 1911). "Local languages" on the other hand, are those that people experience as "everyday" speech, for example, traditional formulas and greetings and familiar rules of verbal interaction, reflecting the contributions of peoples from various backgrounds and serving different functions depending on settings and participants. For sociolinguists, it is within the context of such dynamic local language communities that meanings are refined and shared, and it is through discursive practice that social relationships are explained and justified.

Language into Speech

But languages and the expressions they encapsulate are abstractions; their study reveals only part of what expresses, directs, and motivates human action. Human linguistic exchange is also a function of the social world, one in which people are born and die, make decisions, marry, worship, and work. When events occur and new people, objects, or practices are introduced into a social group, local languages reflect these changes. For example, anthropologists observe that when new rituals or other "event genres" (such as new religious practices), which often include new languages or dialects, are introduced into traditional settings, local linguistic repertoires and symbolic references are modified and adjusted (Hill and Hill 1986). Michael Silverstein argues that public events of this kind become sites not only for the incorporation of new ideas into old practices, but also "rituals of identity transformation in relation to an expanding field of intersecting cultural allegiances." Further, he points out, "shifting competence in these realms on the part of would be participants as a consequence of plurilingualism in speech communities [changes] the terms of performance and [adds] new sociopolitical contingencies to the outcomes of such events" (1998:411). At the same time, however, anthropologists who work in such plurilingual communities or regions also demonstrate how the local linguistic repertoire is still grounded by older expectations, perspectives, and concepts. Among the ways these patterns played out in southern New England is the use of newly introduced Christian religious rituals as part of the traditional negotiation of status and rank.

While the work of sociolinguists reminds us to pay attention to ritual and reenactment as a way of understanding the dynamics of cultural change, their findings should neither be interpreted to mean that culture is *only* about performance, nor imply that culture is merely opportunistic. People act according to cultural ideas learned through social interaction and experience, and many of these are ideas of longstanding. For example, in southern New England Native societies the idea of advocacy, where the person of higher status was expected to serve as an advocate for those who depended on them, was an idea that can be traced to the earliest historical records about religious practice, social life, and diplomacy throughout the colonial period. Similarly, the interpenetrability of the worlds of spirit and social life frequently alluded to in seventeenth-century accounts of Native life in southern New England, survives today in folklore and in the "kitchen table stories," that Indian people of the region still tell.

SPEECH STYLES AND REGISTERS

While the existence of seventeenth-century translations and grammars of the Native languages of southern New England allows us some understanding of language structure and rules in the region (Goddard and Bragdon 1988), its sociolinguistics can only be partially known, for English observers understood only some of what they saw and heard, and were present at only a few of the many types of events and rituals that took place in any Native community. From a variety of Native and English language sources, however, it is possible to reconstruct some of the genres of language use and to link them to social structure and cosmology.

FORMAL SPEECH

In the seventeenth and eighteenth centuries, language and status were clearly interrelated in southern New England. Sachems and

57

other elites were expected to speak eloquently and according to well-recognized rules of rhetoric. High status individuals placed emphasis on the sequence of speech exchanges (the higher-ranking individual speaking second) and on correct salutation, and observed certain speech taboos, particularly avoiding the names of the recently deceased. Ritualized insult was also highly developed (Bragdon 1987). This expectation was highlighted on Martha's Vineyard in the early years of the eighteenth century, when one Chappaquiddick sachem complained that the messenger from the English governor gave him orders, instead of making requests (Massachusetts State Archives, vol. 33:187, no. 20, 1767). It appears that such insulting speeches sometimes served as challenges to the authority of others, and that these challenges were also recognized and employed for political purposes in the later colonial period.

Some information from Native language documents on Martha's Vineyard indicates that certain archaic forms may have marked the speech of sachems as well (Goddard and Bragdon 1988:121). The role that multilingualism (the individual capacity to speak two or more languages) or multidialectalism (the knowledge and use of more than one dialect or speech register) played in this speech environment is also suggested by evidence from Roger Williams's *A Key into the Language of America*, written in 1643 (Williams 1973). This famous book, couched in the "emblematic" style so popular in the seventeenth century (Teunissen and Hinz 1973:61), is an account of the language and people of the western shore of Narragansett Bay, largely Narragansetts but including Niantics as well. For example, the terms for "ward" and "wife" listed in Williams's word list are not Narragansett words, suggesting that at least some people in the community were outsiders who spoke different languages or dialects (see also chapter 7).

The *Key* was composed at sea and organized according to a familiar seventeenth-century format. It has the immediacy of a traveler's account and, in some cases, records snippets of conversations, speeches, and commands, and the contexts in which they were enacted. After Williams' banishment from Boston in 1636, he established a trading post at Cummaquiddick, on the western shore of Narragansett Bay, where he and Canonicus, the elder of the two Narragansett sachems, entered into a mutually beneficial (at least in the short term) arrangement. Williams remained loyal to the English leaders of the region, especially the Winthrops and actively pursued the goals of the commissioners of the United Colonies, after their establishment in 1660. Williams portrays a number of lively conversational exchanges that give a sense of the local language in use in the area of his trading post near Providence, Rhode Island, in the mid-seventeenth century.

Williams, as a trader and an English emissary, first became familiar with the Narragansetts during the crucial years in which they, as allies to the English, helped to scatter and subdue the powerful Pequots, and as they attempted to consolidate their control of the coastal regions to the west of the Bay and on Long Island and to resist the equally expansive Mohegans, under Uncas. He wrote that "My souls desire was to do the Natives good, and to that end to have their language, which I afterwards printed" (cited in Williams 1936: introduction). He wrote eloquently of his hopes that the Native peoples of the Americas would "partake of the mercies of Europe" and cast his mind back to the "varieties of intercourses with them, Day and Night, Summer and Winter, by Land and Sea, [for] particular passages attending to this" (1).

Williams' *Key* is ideally suited to examine the Narragansetts' norms of language use, as it was framed, in his words, as an "implicite dialogue." For example, as described in the first chapter, to speak knowledgeably in Narragansett, one needed to know one's place. Roger Williams spoke of two "sorts" recognizable by their salutations, "some more Rude and Clownish, who are not so apt to Salute, but upon Salutation, resalute lovingly. Others, and the generall, are sober and grave . . . and as ready to begin a Salutation as to Resalute" (Williams 1936:1).

In his travels, Roger Williams learned to accept hospitality and to make small talk. He spent long nights in the forests of New England and conversed "as far as his language would take him" with numerous men. He noted both age and gender distinctions among them: "I once came into a house, and requested some water to drinke; the father bid his sonne of some 8 yeeres of age to fetch some water; the body refused and would not stir; I told the father, that I would correct my child, if he should so disobey me, etc. Upon this the father took up a sticke, the boy another, and flew at his father" (Williams 1936:30). A gendered division of labor, and women's monthly separation in special structures, also attracted his attention.

As a diplomat, Williams conversed on several occasions with sachems, including the elder "Prince" of the region, Canonicus, who served, with his nephew Miantonimi, as ruler of the Narragansetts in the mid-seventeenth century. Williams learned that trust and truth in speech were the basis of a sachem's relationship to his subjects: "Wunnaumwáyean if he say true: Canonicus, the old high sachem of the Nariganset By (a wise and peacable prince) once in a solemne oration to my self, in a solemne assembly, suing this word, said, I have never sufferd any wrong to be offered to the English since they landed; nor never will, he often saith wannaumwayean" (1936:58). And "Coánaumatous 'I believe you' this word they use just as the Greeke tongue doth that verbe πιςέυείυ; for believing or obeying as it [is] often used in the New Testament, and they say coannáumatous, I will obey you" (59). A lack of trust, however, marked their dealings with strangers. "Kuttassokakómme you have deceived me; obs. Who ever deale or trade with them had need of wisedome, patience and faithfulness in dealing for they frequently say cuppànnauem, you lye, cuttas-sokakómme you deceive me" (1936:162).

Williams also found the Narragansetts and others very astute trading partners. He wrote that "They are as full of businesse, and as impatient of hinderance (in their kind) as any Merchant in Europe" (William 1936:36).

Like Williams, other seventeenth-century observers of the Native people of southern New England found that skillful speech was highly valued. William Wood, who lived in an English fishing and trading center near what is now Salem, Massachusetts, recorded that, "In serious discourse our southern Indians use seldom any short colloquiums but speak their minds at large without any interjected interruptions from any, the rest giving diligent audience to his utterance" (Wood 1977:110).

The practice of diplomatic visits—common to both Native and English society—occasioned several encounters between leaders and their representatives in this period, during which both peoples acted according to cultural rules only partially understood by the other side. Wood's example above suggests that sachems were expected to address their followers and visitors or hosts in a dramatic, stylized form. These "harangues" as the English sometimes called them were occasionally very lengthy, accompanied by "great action" as well (Williams 1936:55). Ethnographic evidence from the nineteenth century tells us that other New England Algonquian speakers had the same lengthy style and that there were also songs sung only by chiefs (Goddard personal communication 1980). Two deeds from Martha's Vineyard dating to the late seventeenth century include quotes from the queen sachem Wunnatuckquanumow that appear to reflect an archaic speech style perhaps also limited to or typical of sachem's speech (Goddard and Bragdon 1988:79, 103). The addresses were attended to in respectful silence, regardless of length, the audience seated motionless in a circle sometimes "neer a thousand" around the speaker (Williams 1936:55). On occasion, followers would respond with cries in unison. The queen sachem of Martha's Vineyard used the newly introduced practice of writing to reinforce her own traditional claims to leadership in a ritual recorded verbatim, including a group of witnesses who spoke publicly in her support. Native people recognized a formal mocking speech as well, employing unflattering comparisons, threats, and gestures (Bragdon 1987:102).

The petition was another genre of pre-colonial Native speech: a "speech event" in which individuals or their representatives would approach the sachem with humble posture and gestures, and employ formal pleading terms in a request that the sachem speak for or defend them. The sense of community identification among Indian people is strongest in the surviving petitions written by representatives of various Native communities throughout the eighteenth century. For many Native people in southern New England, the petition became an acknowledged tool in the Native political repertoire, allowing Indian communities to circumvent or overturn local ordinances and violations of their lands and sovereignty. The function of Native leaders as advocates continued to be detectable in these petitions, as did many other aspects of Native social life.

The petitions in Native languages were unusual in a number of ways. Most of the signatures attached to these documents were transcribed by the writer of the document, often the minister of the congregation (Goddard and Bragdon 1988, vol. I: 22). Other petitions do not include attached signatures. Nevertheless, all claimed to speak for a significant portion of the community, as in the Gayhead petition of 1749 that represents all "proprietors" (see fig. 3).

Another feature of Native speech was the custom of using objects to make specific points in an argument. When Roger Williams debated English morality with the Narragansett sachem

Canonicus, Williams reported: "I replied that he had no cause (as I hoped) to question Englishmans [*sic*] faithfulnesse, he having had long experience of their friendlinesse and trustinesse. He tooke a stick and broke it into ten pieces, and related ten instances (laying downe a sticke to every instance) which gave him cause thus to feare and saye" (Williams 1936:58).

In an incident describing an encounter between John Eliot and Metacom (Philip), Cotton Mather reported, "he made a tender to the everlasting salvation to that king [but] the monster entertained it with contempt and anger, and after the Indian mode of joining signs with words, he took a button upon the coat of the reverend man, adding That he cared for his gospel, just as much as he cared for that button" (Mather 1852, 1:514).

William Wood lived on the early English frontier north of the Boston settlement and encountered Native people from a variety of communities, some of whom were usually far beyond the reach of English interference, and these people are rarely described in later sources. Roger Williams was living with the Narragansetts and Niantics while they were still a cohesive, self-governing group, and he was able to observe and participate in a limited way in the ways of life that reflected their own values and approaches. His correspondence describes many encounters with Native leaders and provides some glimpses into their seasonal observances. However, William's own philosophy of noninterference, and his fear of contamination from Native religious practices, made him an ineffective missionary, and the Narragansetts rejected the efforts of the English missionary organization known as the Society for the Propagation of the Gospel to provide them with teachers and ministers. Williams was not replaced by any significant English observer in the later years of the seventeenth century or the early eighteenth century, and thus we have less evidence of what went on in Narragansett communities after Williams's time. Some information does survive in court case records, however, that indicate that Narragansett leaders continued, well into the eighteenth century, to comport themselves in the manner of their forebears, to expect subservience, to extract tribute, to marry polygynously, and to pursue aggressive action against their own and their community's enemies (Plane 2000). Similarly, the Mohegans and Pequots were early victims of the reservation system, continually under siege from those who would encroach upon or acquire their lands, and appear largely in court cases in which they attempted to defend themselves (Den Ouden 2005).

The Native communities of the eastern side of the island of Martha's Vineyard were familiar with Europeans long before the island was settled by Englishmen in the early 1640s. At least two Native men from the island had been kidnapped by English explorers and taken to Europe in the first decade of the seventeenth century, and had returned with knowledge of English and of Englishmen. Indian people of the island owed fealty to Massasoit, a long-time ally of the English who settled at Plymouth in 1620. Thomas Mayhew, Jr., son of the principal English patentee of Martha's Vineyard, Thomas Mayhew, began proselytizing among the island's Indian population soon after he settled there in 1642. According to Mayhew his efforts to convert the Native people of the eastern end of the island met with early success. He wrote in 1647, "there were about twelve which came to the meeting as it were halting between two opinions" but, in 1648, "twelve young men publicly committed themselves to God's way" and by 1649 "twenty-two Indians were found to resolve to walk with God." Mayhew claimed one hundred converts by the mid-1650s. Mayhew wrote little about how he learned the language, but it is likely that he worked with bilingual speakers. Two Native men, Hiacoomes and Pannupuqua, a sachem's son from the eastern end of the island, were paid as interpreters in the mid-1650s by the Society for the Propagation of the Gospel. A number of other Native men were important in the missionary effort, and many served as Indian schoolmasters on the island between 1659 and 1663. These included the brothers James Sepinnu and John Tackanash (Wuttackaquannash), as well as the famous Japhet Hannit, whose mother dedicated him to the Christian God at birth. William Lay (alias Pannunnut), Momatchegin, Momenaqueam, and Nanoso, also served as Indian schoolmasters on the island between 1659 and 1663. Hannit, in particular, learned to read and write at the Indian school established in 1651.

According to Thomas Mayhew, Jr.'s grandson, Experience Mayhew, these men were fluent in English and Massachusett and were able to read and write in their own language. Mayhew, Jr., had made some progress in the language and began to lecture to a Native audience monthly and, later, biweekly, in their own language. The Native converts, who included women and children, prayed and sang, and learned the catechism. Hiacoomes also preached to the Natives, and he and Mayhew conferred over subject matter. Experience Mayhew also reported that Thomas had composed a catechism, which circulated among the Indians in manuscript form.

At the same time, with an island population of approximately two thousand Native people, and an English population of about one hundred, the majority of Native people there in the mid-seventeenth century knew of Christianity only through Native converts and had little contact with English settlers, and there is also good evidence that many remained aloof. Many never learned English to any extent. In 1698 Thomas Mayhew complained that only three or four people spoke English "and none to great purpose" (Gookin 1806:205). Both Samuel Sewell and Experience Mayhew regretted that so few Indian converts read or wrote in English as late as the 1720s. Experience Mayhew was often commissioned to translate documents in the Native language into English, so they could be entered into the county's records.

At least three Englishmen on the islands were also fluent in Massachusett. One was Peter Foulger, who later settled on Nantucket, but who acted as a schoolmaster on Martha's Vineyard after Thomas Mayhew's death in 1657, and John Daggett and his eldest son Thomas Daggett. John Daggett, along with Thomas Mayhew. Sr., was a co-founder of the island's English community and a master of political alliance. His eldest son Thomas married Thomas Mayhew, Sr.'s daughter (Thomas Mayhew, Jr.'s sister), and his youngest son, Joseph, married a close relative of sachem Sissetom, who was a close relative (possibly the brother) of Wampamog, the most important sachem of the eastern side of the island. While all these Englishmen were interested in establishing control over Martha's Vineyard and Nantucket, not all Englishmen who spoke Massachusett on the island invested in the missionary effort. John Daggett, a rival of Mayhew, was rather concerned to maintain the underpinnings of the Native system of land tenure and inheritance, from which his son and grandchildren directly benefited.

Another aspect of the complexity of social life on the island was the competing interests of several denominations in Indian communities. Congregationalists, Baptists, and Quakers sought to influence Indian people in southern New England coastal regions, and each had ceremonies that were understood to be distinctly theirs. This included adult baptism and the Quaker emphasis on voluntary expression.

Into this dynamic mix of Native rulers and their followers, Native converts, English missionaries of several denominations, settlers and entrepreneurs, stepped John Cotton, Jr. Cotton, son of the famous English-born Puritan divine John Cotton, arrived on Martha's Vineyard in 1666 and remained for three years, after which he was called to the ministry in Plymouth, Massachusetts, where he remained for most of his life. Although he had shown little interest in missionary work while at Harvard several years earlier, he was hired by the New England Company to assist the aging Thomas Mayhew, Sr., when Thomas Mayhew, Jr., was lost at sea. This task required that he learn the Indian language, a necessity for missionaries working in the region until at least the 1730s (Kellaway 1961:249). Typically, Cotton met with a group of ten to twenty people, and about ten Native people attended regularly.

At the time of Cotton's arrival, Native converts and ministers on the island probably had available to them several of John Eliot's translations, in addition to hand written copies of Mayhew's catechism. The translations included the *Indian Primer*, published in 1654, and another catechism based on Perkins's Foundations of the Christian Religion, known as *Indian Dialogues* (1671). Eliot also published the book of Genesis (1655), the book of Matthew (1655), a book of psalms, (1658), The *Christian Covenanting Confession*, the New Testament, and the 1663 edition of the Bible. Some or all of these may have been available to Cotton as well, for, as an employee of the Society for the Propagation of the Gospel, it is likely that he was sent to Martha's Vineyard armed with all possible assists. Cotton's job was to instruct Indian converts and to preach to them at several locations, primarily on the eastern side of the island. Cotton began a journal and completed a word list while on the island; his word list reflects the local dialect of the language then known as Massachusett or Natick, today more commonly referred to as Wampanoag. Comments from the Indians who attended Cotton's meetings also suggest that they read, or had read to them, translations of scripture, for they often asked specific questions about the texts. The picture that emerges from Cotton's journal is of a community, including a relatively small group of Native converts who were competent in their Native language, in Massachusett-influenced English, in missionary Massachusett, and in the liturgical texts provided for them through translation. Through time some among them became fluently literate in their own language as well. Other Indians had no direct relationships with bilingual or literate converts, but had family or economic ties with both the converts and the English settlers. Thus this small and isolated island was home to what Silverstein would call a complex "language economy" in which John Cotton briefly participated and that his word list only partially reflects.

English missionaries in collaboration with Native speakers were responsible for introducing or encouraging several new discourse genres to the Native society of the island, including sermons, scriptural exegesis, and formal question and answer sessions based on scriptural passages. A number of historians have suggested that these forms, highlighted in English publications of the period, imply a wholesale transformation of Indian society on the island. But the Christian Indians and their mentors were only one part of a much more complicated social scene. Here, both the missionary word lists and the Native-written documents provide perspective.

Native writings include "recorded oral land transfers" (Little 1980b), which appear to be verbatim records of the meetings or ceremonies in which Indian leaders transferred land to others. Since reported speech in many Algonquian languages is in the form of direct quotations, the documents give a flavor of contemporary speech. Such documents appear well into the eighteenth century, implying a continuity of this type of exchange, and of the sachem's authority to the extent that they controlled the transfer of land. While these texts may well represent a "predocumentary" category of speech event, their continuity into the colonial period and their transfer into written form also reflect a sense of historicity and a focus on legitimacy and authenticity that was certainly at issue in the contest between local rulers and English intruders. Further still, the ability to command the creation of such documents (they were never written by the principal participants) reflects an adaptation to the colonial context in which the Native writing system had become a tool of colonial control (Cohn 1985). Examples of the deliberate archaism can be found in the documents associated with the "queen sachem" Wunnatuckquanumow, of Nunpaog, who was known to the English as "Betty," and who lived near the principal English settlement at Edgartown. Her authority had been undercut by the breakdown of the tribute system of land allotment formerly linking Native rulers and their adherents.

Christian Indians and secular rulers such as Native teachers or ministers participated as witnesses in these formal land exchanges. For example in the recorded oral transfer from the sachem, the Native minister was present. However, analysis of all the names appearing in these records suggests that unless Christian Natives were entitled to the lands controlled by sachems, their presence at such ceremonies was less significant than those who appear to have played more traditional roles, such as councilor or "chief man." Documents in which sachems or their heirs were principal actors continued to be recorded in Native languages until the 1720s on Martha's Vineyard and Nantucket. After this time, although Native-language deeds were still produced, they usually ratified earlier arrangements.

The documents that appear to be associated with the Indian converts also appear to reflect prior Native models (Bragdon 1987). Oratory and exhortation, petitions for advocacy, the use of tobacco, and the emphasis on call and response formats in the eighteenth century had roots both in the Great Awakening, and Native formats (Simmons 1975; Simmons and Simmons 1982). In particular, the Native-language sermons of the Gay Head minister Zachariah Hossueit, recorded in the late eighteenth century, and undated exhortations in the margins of Native-language Bibles appear to reflect this style of oratory.

Petitions in Native language and in English were also written in the "old style." Several of these come from Gay Head, while others were composed at Mashpee; both were communities where Christian ministers were prominent local leaders as well. A translated example of such a petition from Gay Head reads, in part, "at Gay-head the poor Indians met together, we who are the proprietors. They made a humble petition, . . . Humbly we beseech you, we poor Indians . . . defend us much more regarding our land at Gayhead (Goddard and Bragdon 1988:173) (see fig. 3).

This passage uses phrases such as "we poor Indians" to mark relative status petitions and to demand that the sachem, commissioner, or other official advocate for them, as social superiors were expected to do (Bragdon 1987).

In dynamic social environments, where people of different backgrounds and languages live together, sociolinguists observe that people develop a number of strategies of communication. Among these are what sociolinguists call "code-switching" (the term used to refer to the practice of switching style, dialect, or language in different social contexts). Studies of Native American communities in the twentieth century show that Natives and non-Natives alike use a range of codes that signify attachments to particular social groups within the community, some more oriented toward the dominant culture and others more conservative or Native-centered. Oppositions such as preferences toward local/non-local, Christian/traditional, Native language/English language, and so on, are also detectable in conversations, rituals, and other speech events that sociolinguists observe. In the complex, multilingual context that must have existed on Martha's Vineyard in the mid-seventeenth century, such code-switching might have been common, although the specific oppositions may have differed.

Earlier, for example, on the mainland, the blustering Miles Standish was chagrined to learn that the pidginized Massachusett he was using was not the "real" Native language (Winslow 1624:281), and it seems likely that Indian people listened with only half an ear to the sermons of nonfluent missionaries. Thus, when John Cotton, Jr.'s missionary son, Josiah Cotton, famously records comments from the Indians of Plymouth that he was hard

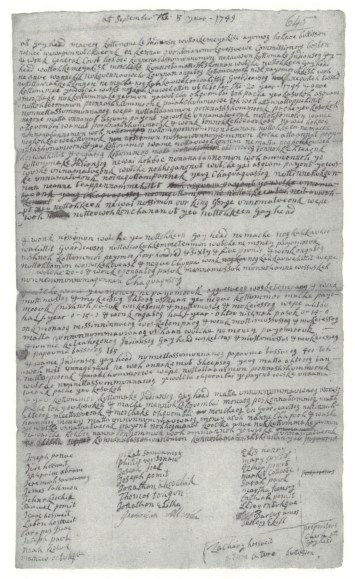

Figure 3. Gay Head petition, 1749, vol. 31:645, Massachusetts State Archives (Courtesy of the Commonwealth of Massachusetts).

71

to understand because he learned his Indian from his father who "learned at Nope," it is both a direct reference to the differences in dialect between the island and the mainland and an indirect reference to the middling skills of Massachusett-speaking Englishmen diplomatically couched in terms of differences in locality. In the 1750s the Native people of Mashpee asked to be relieved of an English minister, as so few understood him.

Competing dialects also played a part among Native speakers, as many of the first Native converts on Martha's Vineyard eventually made places for themselves on the mainland, working with and converting Native peoples scattered from Nauset to Bourne on Cape Cod, including those in Mashpee. Native writings suggest that some literate converts transferred or adapted their own education to other communities on the mainland. For example, one writing in Massachusett is a document from Monument Ponds making mention of Tom Tyler, son of the sachem Thomas Tyler, who married into the same Martha's Vineyard sachem family to which the Daggetts were allied (Goddard and Bragdon 1988:40). Dialect leveling (the decline in differences among dialects) in these communities has previously been attributed to the impact of Native-language Bible literacy, but no work has been done on the role these early Native preachers from Martha's Vineyard had in this same process. Another part of this study compares Josiah Cotton and John Cotton's word lists, as well as mainland Native writings, with this issue in mind.

As Silverstein points out, the three characteristics of local language communities, that is, language perceived as a seamless construction in which all participate equally, and in which all share the same knowledge; the social rules determining when and how language varieties are shifted (code-switching); and the "reflexive" ways that people engage in language and culture are actually the moments in the continuous process of the sociocultural life. Nor does this process occur in the same ways in all contexts.

Among the new Native communities on Martha's Vineyard, for example, what may have been a "power code," identified with astute and important local men and women, may have existed (Silverstein 1998:416). Examples of this type of speech are recorded in the wills left by local leaders, which combine knowledge of English legal conventions, Native inheritance principles, and assertions of personal authority. One document for example, is the will of the Gay Head Baptist minister Peter Ohquanhit, which states: "Know ye all people that this is how I set up for her my estate before I die. And it is witnessed by heavenly Jehovah, ruler of all the earth" and "This document was witnessed by Josiah Pomett, ruler, and Zachary Hossooit, Justice of the Peace" (Goddard and Bragdon 1988:169).

On the other hand, other people, including most women and traditional men used the more distinctive stylistic range of a less syncretized Massachusett, that is, showing less influence or interference from English, including the use of honorifics or titles as described above. These differences reflect the range of attitudes present within a single Native community about leadership and the position of Indians vis-à-vis the English.

On the whole, the influence of English on Massachusett was relatively minimal in the seventeenth and early eighteenth century, if the Native writings are any indication, so it appears likely that, as with the contemporary Tewa, the Massachusett speakers remained politically powerful on the island. Among the Tewa, who have successfully resisted borrowings from other languages for several centuries, the motivations are not a function of community-wide rejection, but rather due to the central importance of the ceremonial center of society, the kiva, the workings of which reproduce in cosmological terms the social structure of the community, centering around the elites who control community resources as well as esoteric knowledge (Kroskrity 1984:417). A similar situation appears to have been operant in the Massachusett-speaking community on Martha's Vineyard, in which the fluent use of the Native church community's sacred register became the grounds for legitimization in the secular community as well, both for members of sachem families and those from lower status backgrounds (MacCulloch 1966; Bragdon 1987).

As in other parts of the world where various forms of Christianity have been introduced, two processes were operant in the Native community of converts on Martha's Vineyard, one artifactual, associated with the mastery of scriptural literacy, the ownership of books, and the ability to produce writings, and the other nonartifactual, that is, participating in new forms of liturgy, devotional discourse, and public speaking. Native ministers were very active in the spread of literacy and took a leadership role in the acceptance of these new forms, which had the ultimate effect of creating an emergent local language community in which these new forms competed with older, yet related public speech event forms (Bragdon 1988). John Cotton, Jr., records that many of the meetings he attended were also regularly visited by Native ministers who were clearly central to the spread of new religious ideas. Of interest is whether this activity was part of a transformation of epistemology of language among Native speakers. So, for example, the earliest extant Native writings from Martha's Vineyard and Nantucket make use of community- or rank-based rhetorical devices such as iconic order (in which the more socially prominent person is named first) and direct quotations. The performative creation of social relationships, including the relationship of land-giving or -holding, often by employing hand imagery, was necessarily placed into competition with the "introduced concepts of personal intentionality underlying Christian belief and devotional language" (Silverstein 1998). One such writing from Gay Head, described below, refers to the individualized exchange of land as a commodity, reflecting personal intentionality, and is markedly devoid of community/ranked references.

In a letter written in the Native language to the Gay Head overseer Major John Allen sometime before 1763, members of the
Native community complained about the plan to appoint the
Native Elisha Amos as a judge. Amos had been accused of illegiti-
mately enclosing land and denying other community members
access to it, against local custom. As a clincher, they warned, "we will
be much more miserable because of this Elisha Amos, just as the
word of God says in Job 34:30 ("let not the hypocrite rule") (Goddard and Bragdon 1988:225). The community's outrage over
Amos's behavior suggests that, in spite of Amos's obvious familiarity with English legal forms and his contacts among the English
elite, the transformation of ideology had not yet taken place.

A set of Native writings associated with property controlled by
the Wicket/Sepet sachem family in Barnstable County on Cape
Cod has similar implications. These documents follow decision
making concerning this property for three generations, from
1712–59 (Goddard and Bragdon 1988:docs.4–6). In 1712, John
Sepet "let" Japes Wekket have a share of his land in exchange for a
gun. This document stipulated that no one would defraud Wekket,
including "the one who divides all my inheritance" (Goddard and
Bragdon 1988:45). In 1718, Wekket and his wife, Bashshonnis, let
Thomas Bennas have some of this land. A codicil to this same document records that Bennas returned the land to John Sepet in
1722 (49). Finally, "Old Sary Sepet" appointed "Old Jabe Wicked"
to oversee her land in 1759 (51). In this instance, the documents
themselves become part of the intergenerational "dialogue" concerning the use of shares of land. The documents, complete with
English dates, also roughly follow an English-style deed format.
Although couched in terms of an exchange, these bargains look
much more like continuing divisions by sachem families of land to
their relatives or to those loyal to them. The "local language community" thus must also be understood to include those knowl-
edgeable about English law, as well as Native custom, and those

who could write in the Native language on behalf of the principals. To argue, as some scholars have, that by the eighteenth century Native people in southern New England were simply "red" Englishmen, is to miss the significance of these writings that reflect distinctive Indian communities always coming into being.

Both of the Cotton word lists give some insight into this process; as Native communities came under increasing control by outsiders, new economic opportunities also developed that led necessarily to new kinds of social relationships. At some point during the collection of (largely) Christian-based word categories, John Cotton, Jr., also began to engage in a kind of ethnographic observation of the ways of life of his Native catechumens and other Indians on the eastern side of the island. The terms he collected reflect the lived physical, social, and ideological world of Native communities in early colonial period Martha's Vineyard.

John Cotton, Jr.'s word categories were linked to one another thematically. Emotions, including love and fear, as well as the concepts of work and family, were explored; but he was also teaching himself about the material life of the Indians of the island, in particular, their work for and with members of the English community. Like many Englishmen in New England, he showed little curiosity about kin relationships among the Native peoples, although he recognized the existence of multiple sibling terms and provided some important information about terms for aunts and uncles, husbands and wives. The frequent misuse of these terms in missionary translations may betray a lack of interest in and knowledge of Native concepts of kinship, which reflects the isolation of missionaries from the daily lives of their converts. On the other hand, it appears that some Englishmen on the island were avidly interested in the system, because of its connections to the allocation of land. At the same time, Cotton's word list shows a certain fascination with powwaws, the Native shamans and healers, whose work he linked to witchcraft.

As an example, feasting and dancing were heavily reported in Indian communities on the island (DCP 1:30; DCD 6:436). It is clear that the feasts described in these early sources had both social and cosmological significance, associated as they were with gift giving and games of chance. The social imperative to host feasts in order to establish or maintain social standing noted in very early ethnographic descriptions of the region are indirectly described in public records on Martha's Vineyard and alluded to in Cotton's list. The terms in table 6 provide an example.

As noted above, the Gay Head Native minister Zachary Hossueit complained a century later that dancing and "fittling" were still too important to Indian youths on Gay Head. This is not to say, however, that the role of such feasting remained entirely the same. Still, the continuity of certain festivals such as the green corn dance and other seasonal celebrations throughout southern New England throughout the eighteenth and nineteenth centuries suggests that these old cycles were still marked well into the nineteenth century (Willoughby 1935).

Communities on Cape Cod were similarly complex. Josiah Cotton, who served as a missionary to the Indians of the Plymouth

Table 6. Selections from Cotton's Word List: Dancing and Feasting

Pepekqh	Music, trumpet
Poopoonik	Drum
Mattokauwonk	To dance
Mattokesh, wauwiskory	Dance (imp), a good dancer (?)
Matishkary	A bad dancer
Nukkonyoud, nookheg	Meale
Waepi	Circle
Quunnuppuhsish	Encompass
Puhpoqunnitchohuwonk	To clap hands

Source: Cotton 1665–1678, *Journal and Vocabulary of the Indians.*

region until the mid-eighteenth century, wrote a word list based on his knowledge of their language. He admitted, however, that he was not a fluent speaker. We can imagine how English incompetence in the indigenous languages of the region was interpreted by Native people. These and other recordings also may reflect the day-to-day interactions of peoples from both language backgrounds, which were closest to the reality of discursive practices and their concomitant social relations in these always-emerging Native and English communities in these isolated corners of colonial expansion. Nevertheless, our understanding of this historical era has been heavily influenced by the way fluency in Massachusett was represented to other Englishmen. Josiah Cotton's word list is the best example, including as it does many minatory expressions in Massachusett deploring Indians tendency to drunkenness, theft, laziness, and fecklessness. One pictures the Native recipient of such admonitions politely failing to correct the grammatical mistakes of his Native-language "fluent" English interlocutor.

But Josiah Cotton's word list also recorded terms that harked back to ideas and practices observed by English explorers a century before. For example, Cotton's word list was organized into sections, one which he might have labeled "bad behavior" that included words for dancing, drinking, and avoidance of the kinds of manual work that were available to Indian men, none of which were congenial to them.

As the eighteenth century wore on, more and more Native peoples learned English, and some men and women of English background learned to understand Native dialects. In 1660, the sachem Nickanoose wrote, or had written, a letter that gives a flavor of Indian English on the islands: "I am Nekonnoossoo I give her my thaughter lant askomapoo half so: much I have lant I give her for nothing at nantukut askomapoo my thaughter I give her worryes she shall [not] have and all geterrations and she shall have and holt and she shall have right for ever no paty trouble her for this lant because I negonnoosoo my generation [spellings original]" (Little 1981:10).

Contrast this with a similar document in the Native language of the same period in Martha's Vineyard: "We thus convey it to him for him also to have it regarding all of it while he lives, Jacob Washamun and all his posterity, and for him to own it all by right. Trouble shall not come to him regarding this land. I am Nickanoose and I rightly own this land" (Goddard and Bragdon 1988:253).

Other Indian English examples from southern New England survive and suggest that it was characterized by simplified grammar, irregular distinctions of voicing (a feature not present in the Native language), and nonstandard word order. A story about Captain Thomas Waban, ruler of the Natick community in the early eighteenth century, and a similar one about Cadooda of Nantucket, record that when a case where two Native men were brought before them and they rendered judgment, their decisions were to "whip the defendant, and whip the plaintiff" (Badger 1835). Another Natick resident was also credited with the sole example of a Native aphorism recorded in southern New England, "tucks be tucks, no matter goose she raise them" (Dorson 1946).

Works by scholars in contemporary Indian communities suggest that Native American English retains other features of prosody, timing, pitch, and so on, that frequently color interactions between Indians and non-Indians, often undermining Native initiatives (Scollon and Scollon 1995). Ives Goddard argues that in the first century of more than 130 years of frequent contact and competition with English speakers, there were Native speakers of Massachusett of great literary skill in their own language, such as the Native preacher Solomon Briant of Mashpee, although his written skills in English were more limited (Goddard 1993). Ironically,

Indian English was thought to be more representative of Indian intellectual ability by surrounding non-Indians.

NANTUCKET IN THE MID-EIGHTEENTH CENTURY

A final example of the complexities of local language communities in colonial southern New England comes from Nantucket in the eighteenth century. English speakers and Native bilinguals sometimes lived side by side there, and often worked together. Zaccheus Macy, a member of a prominent English family, took an interest in the Native people who played such an important role in the local economy. A poorly transcribed but significant example of Native speech at midcentury is recorded in Macy's manuscript notes on Nantucket's Indians working at various trades. The manuscript dates to the late eighteenth century and recalls events he observed in his youth. Macy described a conversation between some Englishmen and the Native foreman at a building site: "once they were a framing a house and there was some white men looking on they brought one of there beames and the old master workman spake and said semoneeatch, autodque which in English is 'it is too short'" (Z. Macy n.d.).

On another occasion, Macy recorded that "once when one of our white men went into one of there [the Indians'] houses and spake thus taubeskeehow john tornoo damarus & john said mowtodpa for then the white spake and said auwitte poweshqua then john spake and said tom jespod muttumou, which in English tounge is how do you do John ware is Tom's wife" (Macy 1792:158).

Macy's description raises several interesting points; first, that some bilingualism survived on the island among English settlers and their descendants, and second, that bilingual Native men were fully integrated into the island economy. Had the Native population of the island not been so thoroughly devastated by the epidemic of 1763–64 (Little 1990b), the bilingual phase of language use might have survived for many more generations on Nantucket.

These vivid examples reflect the sociality of language use in colonial communities, and the linguistic context in which patterns of cultural continuity and change took place. The communities represented here were socially complex and multilingual, and probably reflect something of what was happening in similar communities elsewhere in colonial southern New England. With this composite portrait as background, the following chapter looks at the social institutions that can be identified through the use of language materials and how local language communities contributed to and reflected the new realities of the colonial world.

3.

Social Relationships
in a Colonial Context:
Families, Marriage, and Authority

Bringing Native communities in colonial New England to life depends not only on our appreciation of them as dynamic, discursive local linguistic communities, but also on our understanding of the underlying principles of their social relations. Often historic Indian communities in New England are described in terms of population figures, size of households, compositions of church membership, and so on. Beyond this, descriptions of the leaders of Native communities and their activities are frequently the focus of Native histories. Since many of these latter studies interpret Indian leadership only in terms of what Roger Keesing and Andrew Strathern have aptly labeled "the cold hand of economic and political advantage" (1998:345), they fail to provide a well-rounded portrait of Native life in the colonial period. This is because economic and political relations are consistent with cultural ideas about gender, authority, and power, but are rarely the sole origin of those ideas. Anthropologists who are concerned with cultural change note that the new economic realities and political constraints typical of colonial situations lead to new emphases, sometimes even to the overturning of older kinds of social relations among colonized peoples (Sahlins 1983), but that these changes too are part of cultural process, and they can only be understood in cultural terms. The Native writings and other linguistic data from southern New England allow us to read "between the lines" to discover the cultural ideas behind social action, the ways they were transformed or rearranged, and the true complexities of the Native colonial world.

HOUSEHOLDS

Indian societies in colonial New England were most often described by English writers of the period as being composed of family groups, which Europeans understood to be the equivalent of nuclear families, headed by a married couple. As is the case for many areas of Native North America, however, Native families and household groups in southern New England came in many forms. For example, clusters of houses uncovered by archaeologists at Gay Head, Mashpee, and on the Mashantucket reservation indicate that social groupings larger than the nuclear family often shared the same domestic space. Kevin McBride and Suzanne Cherau have found that two such clusters have been explicitly associated with two large and important extended families or lineages on Gay Head in the eighteenth century (1996). Further evidence for extended families comes from Ezra Stiles's descriptions of Niantic households he encountered in the mid-eighteenth century. Stiles found that, in one wigwam, nine people lived, including two adult men and three women, while, in another, were a man and three adult women (Stiles 1916). One of the wigwams Stiles described was larger than the other, to accommodate the larger number of occupants (see chapter 4).

The earliest descriptions of Native societies also note that polygyny (a man having two or more wives simultaneously) was practiced in the region. Mary Rowlandson, the Deerfield, Massachusetts, minister's wife whose narrative of captivity during King Philip's War is considered a literary classic, reported that the wives of polygynous men lived separately in the late seventeenth century, even while on the move (1913:150). If so, some communities included multiple households, each made up of a sachem's wife and her children. According to Ann Plane, the custom of polygyny lasted into the eighteenth century in some communities, especially among the elite. Ninigret I, the Narragansett sachem, for example, who died in the late seventeenth century, had at least two wives, and children resulting from both unions (Plane 1995:160). In addition, polygyny survived conversion to Christianity (167–73).

Monogamous relations were also common. In the mid-eighteenth century, Gay Head Native minister Zachariah Hossueit kept a list of marriages among Christian Indians that appear to follow the English model (Goddard and Bragdon 1988:69–72). Monogamous couples were, however, also common among the Native people of southern New England during the early contact period, and the coexistence of this form of marriage alongside both more informal living arrangements and the multiple marriages of sachem families is also consistent with earlier descriptions.

Under the scrutiny of the English, the practice of withdrawing from an unhappy marriage became more difficult for Indian women, as Ann Plane has convincingly shown (1995), but other evidence suggests that Native women were still able to avoid onerous marital connections. Natick resident Benjamin Tray wrote in his will, dated 1757, for example, "I give my wife Elizabeth Tray 10 shillings and no more she being eloped and not living with me to take care of me" (MDX Probate Record \#22768). Experience Mayhew included in the brief biographies of Christian Indians on Martha's Vineyard entitled *Indian Converts*, several abandon abusive or drunken husbands (1727).

As Plane also notes, Native marriage practices were partially redefined to accord with English definitions of marriage; polygynous unions thus became "serial" or successive marriages, and second and thirds wives became "concubines" (2000). However, English courts soon gave up the practice of overseeing Native domestic life and, except in cases where valuable property was in question, lost interest in their family arrangements, which evidently retained the flexibility of contact period marriage customs.

WIDER FAMILY TIES

Roger Williams wrote that he had known of many Narragansett married couples who lived together for years, and monogamous lifelong marriages were the ideal form in later Christian Indian communities. Yet there is good reason to believe that those ties that lay at the center of Native social life during the colonial period were not marriage ties, but the ties between siblings, parents, and others within the group anthropologist call consanguinial kin, that is, "blood ties," determined not by genetics but by cultural definitions of shared substance. In southern New England, for the purposes of reckoning the disposition of children or inheritance of property or leadership positions, people recognized descent from a single parent, a system known as unilineal, although ties with both parents' lineages were probably important. It is often the case that marriage ties in such systems are weaker, as spouses feel the tug of loyalty to (and have economic interests in) their own natal family group.

There is abundant documentation for Native recognition of lineal relations in the late seventeenth and eighteenth centuries in southern New England, but it remains difficult to sort out patterns. Perhaps this is because the kinds of transformations kinship systems undergo after massive population losses are not well understood. Patricia Galloway has suggested, for example, that the matrilineality (reckoning descent through the female line) reported for many southeastern peoples in the early contact period may have been an artifact of the disease holocaust period and "an ideal vehicle for post-catastrophe population recovery" (1995:51). But reconstructed terminological systems in the Native languages in southern New England resemble those of lineage systems elsewhere in North America, including other Algonquian language systems (Bragdon 1997), so that, to the extent that such terminological systems reflect social organization "on the ground," lineage organization appears to be of long standing in New England.

In spite of the tendency of colonial English observers in New England to describe Native families in terms of their own nuclear and patrifocal model, it is clear from Native writings that sibling ties and multigenerational connections remained important in Native communities. Kinship terms from Native language texts, for example (most of which date to the late seventeenth and the first half of the eighteenth century), include a full array of sibling terms, including those for siblings of the opposite sex, older brothers and younger siblings, and classificatory brothers (parallel cousins) (Bragdon 1997). Table 7 lists these interesting terms that show distinctions marking relative sex and relative age among siblings. The southern New England languages were further distinct in having more than one set of such terms. Ives Goddard concludes that these terms reflect the original Proto-Algonquian sibling system (1973:42).

In better documented lineage systems, anthropologists find that the relations between the children of siblings are marked in kin term sets as well. For example, in the system common among northern Iroquoian people, the children of brothers and the children of sisters called each other "sibling." The children of opposite sex siblings (cross-aunts and cross-uncles from the point of view of the next generation) on the other hand, called one

Table 7. Kinship Terms in Southern New England Languages from Early Sources

Term	Eliot (1685)	Speaker's Gender	Cotton (1664–1667)	Josiah Cotton (1830 [1707])	Williams 1936[1643]	Wood (1634)
Fa	n8sh		noosh	koosh	nòsh	noeshow
Mo	nokas		nitteah	wutchehwau	nitchwhaw nókace	nitka
So	nunnaumon			wunnaumonien	nummúckquáchucks	naumaunais
Da	nitaunes			nuttônnees	nittaûnis	taunais
Br	neemat	M	nemat	oowemattin	neémat	netchaw
Br	neetompas	F	nechi	wetompasin	wéticks	towwaw
OBr	nummohtonuqqus	F				
Si	netukkusq	F	nehtaht			
Si	netompas	M		wetomp		
Si	nummissesin	M				
Si	wetahtuoh	M		wetaht		
Ysb	wesummussoh	MF			weésummis	
U	8shesoh			ooshesin		
A	kokummes			nussukqus		
Grm	kukummussit(loc)			wutt8kumissin		
Grf				wutt8tchikkinneasin		
Wi	numittumwus			mittumwussis	mittummus weewo	web
Hu	nasuk			ouwasekkien	wasick	tommawshew

another "cross-cousins." This pattern is significant in that, in many societies, cross-relatives were considered eligible marriage partners, or as potential in-laws, while siblings and parallel aunts and uncles were not. Many lineal systems assign different ritual responsibilities and economic obligations to different classes of relatives, which are marked by these terms. This feature of lineal systems is harder to detect in southern New England.

For example, contemporary English translations of some Native documents gloss the Native term natonck, which, by analogy with other related languages such as Unami or Munsee, should mean "my cross-cousin," simply as "cousin." Since "cousin" in seventeenth-century English usage could mean any kin other than a sibling, and often was used for "wife," its meaning in the Native documents is unclear. In addition, of course, the English generally were unfamiliar with the Native kinship system and may not have been aware of the differences among the terms. The Native writings also include other terms containing the root awau (people), indicating some kind of kin relationship. Naomi Ommaush's 1749 will (see below), for example, contains the following expressions: nuttauwatueonk (referring to both a man and a woman); nuttawam (applied to a man or a woman); and nuttauwaeh (referring to a woman). Another Native language document uses auwaog for "wife." None of these relationships are clear.

To say that such terms indicate a strong emphasis on kin ties among Native people in southern New England during the colonial period does not necessarily distinguish them from the English of the same period, whose own writings recognize a wide range of such relationships. However, other records, and analogies with Native people who spoke similar languages and were also organized according to lineages, suggest that significant differences in social organization between the Indian and English communities in southern New England in the colonial period did exist.

The most striking distinction between the makeup of English colonial communities and those of the Native people of this region is the existence of larger, multigenerational kin groups in the Native communities. One Native language document employs the term wemotooonk (set of brothers), and another used wunnamaniinaonk, which should mean "set of male patri-lateral parallel cousins" (Goddard and Bragdon 1988:185). These terms may imply a lineage structure or other male-centered corporate kin group. Other groups are often referred to in Native writings as "descendants," "posterity," or "genera-tion." Most of these references appear in Native language docu-ments referring to some kind of corporate (property-holding) group. For example, a Mashpee document dating to 1752 con-tains the following passage:

This Indian land, this was conveyed to us by these former sachems of ours. We shall not give it away, nor shall it be sold, nor shall it be lent, but we shall always use it as long as we live, we together with all our children (nunechanunnoog) and our children's chil-dren, (nunnechanunnonog wunnechannooah) and our descen-dants (nuppometuonganunnoog), and together with all their descendants. (Goddard and Bragdon 1988:37)

The "descendants" referred to in this mid-eighteenth-century document of Mashpee were conceived of as a corporate body with rights and with communal ownership in land. Other phrases implied kin groups linked to specific sachems or families. The document in English attributed to the Nantucket Sachem Nick-anoose for example, contains the phrase "for I am Nickanoose, my generation" (Little 1980a). This suggests that Nickanoose was legitimate and the only representative of his generation, and therefore had the right to convey land to his daughter, Askamapoo, who was also a sachem. If these large family units were not lineages in the technical sense, they were corporate groups larger than the extended or nuclear family and were, moreover, conceived of as multigenerational. The term "house," found in a contemporary English translation of a Native writing for the word otherwise translated as "posterity," may indicate contemporary knowledge among the English of a kin unit larger than that of the extended family (Bragdon 1997). These social groupings played a central role in the allotment of land and the determination of leadership positions, and they probably also influenced patterns of post-marital residence, the education of children, and access to ritual knowledge, so were crucial to connections to the supernatural world as well. This larger kin unit, call it posterity, house, lineage, or even clan, was also a moral referent in Native societies, as members were expected to defend one another, in all contexts, be they economic, political, or spiritual.

The principal economic asset of corporate kin groups in Native New England was land, and people had access to this land through their sachems' allotments. Native language deeds speak of rules of land division. As discussed above, land was divided (chippohtonk) for people in exchange for the payment of tribute or allegiance, an agreement that had to be renewed periodically. Elizabeth Little argues persuasively that such agreements, said to be "forever" (micheme), in fact were valid only for the lifetime of the sachem (1996), who was the symbolic and functional head of a generation ([nip]pummetuonk). It was customary, however, for the sachem's heirs to reaffirm these agreements as well. Native people's contracts with their leaders, reaffirmed in every generation, were recognition of mutual obligation and a symbolic link between the generations embodied by each subsequent sachem, a concrete example of social reproduction.

Kin Groups and Communities

In the stratified social systems of traditional southern New England Native societies, members of some lineages come to represent communities and to advocate for them. It may be possible that the tempo of change in Native communities in the wake of colonization led to a newly emphasized identification between a community and a particular leader or family. Alternatively, Indian people were often forced to consolidate their holdings as English settlers expanded into their territories, intensifying personal and social contacts among the affected Native people. One way to look at this process is through changes in Native burial practices in the colonial period. In particular, the concentration of dozens or even hundreds of interments in bounded cemeteries became more pronounced through time, and many major Native communities were represented by them. Archaeologists working in the region have long pointed out that the late Woodland-period burials were more diffusely located, possibly organized by family clusters (Leveillee, Waller, and Ingham 2006:9). By the 1620s, however, large numbers of burials were clustered together, and differences among individuals were marked by the kinds of grave goods found with them. The pattern continued until the mid-eighteenth century (McBride personal communication 2006). This change in burial patterns might reflect the new importance of high-ranking corporate family groups to Native communities as a whole, as well as a newer conceptualization of community as bounded and embattled.

It is obvious that social reproduction in Native southern New England was a process that involved the active participation of both men and women, and thus land (female) and political authority (male) were two sides of the same coin. Alternatively, it can be argued more broadly that theories based on alliance and those based on descent are artificially opposed. On Martha's Vineyard, as elsewhere, the successful reproduction of community structure required alliances that reaffirmed authority over land, such that each generation was presented anew with the need to create such unions. The successful combination of authority and control of property allowed, in turn, the redistribution of such property in the traditional way. Since women were intimately connected to land, and their tenancy was thought to "use up" land, their role in social reproduction was central. I believe this conception survived in Indian communities on Martha's Vineyard for several generations after the arrival of English settlers, that Native rulers and their subjects reached a new equilibrium through alliance, and that this is reflected in documented land transactions among Native peoples on Martha's Vineyard, Nantucket, and Chappaquiddick in the seventeenth and early eighteenth centuries.

Another way this principle was maintained may have been the use of seasonal or cyclical residence. Little suggests that for marriages among sachem-related families, spouses spent time in each other's territories. For example, Wunnatuckquanumow, who married Washaman, "lived seasonally on both islands" (Goddard and Bragdon 1988:743).

As Little (1980b) recognized, there are a number of Native land transactions recorded for Nantucket, Martha's Vineyard, and the Elizabeth Islands in the early colonial period. Of these she recognized three types: (1) agreements involving tribute, (2) outright sales, and (3) confirmations of previous divisions (as described above). As argued elsewhere, these documents themselves are testimony to the changed conditions in Native communities during the early colonial period: the introduction of literacy, the increasing importance of land as a commodity mediating English and Indian relations, and the interference of the English in Native sovereignty. There are two sets of documents from Martha's Vineyard and Nantucket that imply that Sachems bequeathed land to their heirs, but there is reason to suspect that such documents were written ex post facto, when the Indian community's control over such land was in question among the English. For example, two documents dated 1663, but existing only as copies, record the sachem Towanquatuck's gifts of land to his son Saggeatanumou in 1644 and to his grandchildren Joel and Wunnatuckquanumow in 1663 (Goddard and Bragdon 1988:238–45). I interpret these as deeds written to "explain" Native principles of land tenure and authority in English terms. It seems more likely that premises of alliance and descent that underlay the sachem's authority to divide land were well understood within the Native community and, in any case, were previously confirmed not with written documents, but through oral transmission. The details of the documents that survive in Native writings also reflect a third scenario: efforts by Native agents representing rival Baptist sects were also accumulating land bases in an attempt to compete both with the island's Congregationalist Christians and the Native strongholds. In particular, the purchases of Isaac Takemme (Decamy) from Towanquatuck and his granddaughter the queen sachem Wunnatuckquanumow at Nashamoies (the Indian community south of Edgartown) appear to be connected to his prominent role in the infant Baptist Native community on the island (Backus 1871:2:507).

In systems such as those operating in Native southern New England, where labor was organized by lineage ties, what looks like a leader's ability to allot land is really what Jack Goody (1990) termed "homogeneous inheritance," where it is understood that all allotments are part of a societal fund. Such funds are closely tied with lineal forms of descent and inheritance that can be matrilineal or patrilineal (Strathern 1985:198). Often, a principal characteristic of a lineage-based economy is a system of social organization based on rank or status, which serves to naturalize the inequities of access to land and other valuable resources by legitimizing the leader's right to distribute them.

That the coastal societies of southern New England in the early colonial period were ranked societies is well known. English observers were themselves well attuned to status differences, and rightly noted that social differences existed among the Native societies they described (Kupperman 2000:92). Status differences were often marked in dress, deportment, the existence of a retinue of advisors and councilors, and other privileges (Bragdon 1996b:147). The highest-ranking individuals were the leaders, who generally were members of privileged sachem families.

Documents in Native languages and in English, written by or for Indian people, clearly show that status differences between common people and the elites and their descendants survived until the eighteenth century. In Natick, high ranking families were descendants of old proprietors, those who were among the first to settle in Natick and who received large allotments of arable, meadow, and orchard lands as a result, lands that became increasingly valuable as English settlement expanded. These old proprietors were also, of course, prominent members of Eliot's utopian Christian community there, and many of them also occupied positions of political authority in the town. Finally, some of these families, particularly the large and complex Speen family, were probably recognized as legitimate heirs to sachemships in the region (Bragdon 1981a).

On Gay Head and Nantucket, the Native- and English-language documents associated with sachems and their descendants are different in tone and focus from those of the common people. Several detail the descent of the office of the sachem itself and are also largely concerned with specifying the legitimacy of their control over the great tracts of land that comprised each of the original sachemships. In addition, they include several features not present in other documents, including the archaic speech patterns described above, the use of scribes (when it is clear that the sachems can read and write), the listing of a large number of witnesses, and the use of verbatim quotations (Little 1980b).

The Native-language documents also reflect what appear to be stylized forms of address appropriate to exchanges between people of different status. These forms are particularly marked in

Native language petitions, where expressions such as "we beseech you" reflect forms of address described by Roger Williams in his 1636 Narragansett phrase book, which were, he remarked, how petitioners addressed their sachems when desirous of anything." These petitioners, he added, accompanied their requests by stroking the shoulders of their sachem (Williams 1936:2; see also Bragdon 1996b:154–55, and chapter 1, this volume).

In fact, as I have argued elsewhere, ranking continued even in those Christian communities such as Gay Head, where the office of the sachem was no longer recognized. In the later eighteenth century, for example, a reputation for piety, the ability to host prayer groups, and descent from prominent lineages marked several Native women there as high ranking. It appears, in these instances, that status considerations were more important than gender as a social category (Bragdon 1996a).

It is clear that rank was deeply enmeshed in economic relations. Sachems, the highest ranking individuals in Native societies, granted allotments of land called chippaht8e, or "his/her shares or divisions" (Goddard and Bragdon 1988:613), to their subjects and received tributary payments in return. Tribute took many forms, sometimes labor or foodstuffs, game, or other forms of wealth. The periodic payment of tribute served symbolically to reinforce the social order, and allowed the sachem, whose role was also distributory, to continuously return wealth and food to his followers.

Tribute payments continued well into the eighteenth century, as documented in Native writings from Cape Cod, Martha's Vineyard, and Nantucket, and also among the Narragansett/Niantics during the same period. Elizabeth Little writes of Daniel Spotso, heir of Nantucket sachems Nickanoose and Spotso, for example, that Daniel received land assignment renewal or tribute from English settlers on the island as well (1996:201, 205). At least three accounts recorded in Mary and Nathaniel Starbuck's early eighteenth-century account book refer to labor performed by particular individuals, the payment for which was credited to the account of the sachem Ben Able (Little 1980a:28). At Narragansett, where the followers of Charles Ninegret, Sr., bitterly contested his continuing sale of lands to the English, they nevertheless continued to support him through gifts and services (Plane 1995:170).

The sachem's power to distribute land, and the obligations of his subjects to pay tribute, created and maintained a labor system that was at once economic, spiritual, and social. Those for whom land had been divided owed tribute to the sachems to whom they pledged loyalty. In this way, sachems could be said to acquire "wealth in people" of a type that, according to Carolyn Bledsoe "binds people to their superiors in ties of marriage, clientship, and filial obligation" (1980:1). The sachem's subjects had, in turn, an advocate and insurance against personal or economic hardship. In this way, power was an indigenous concept, also associated with strong ties to the supernatural, and probably did not have the same prerogatives that political power had in English society of the same period, a distinction also evident in other indigenous North American chiefdoms, such as the Powhatan (Williamson 2003).

Nevertheless, the relationship between rank and power was apparent in Native society in southern New England and obvious to the earliest English explorers and settlers, who adapted their own diplomatic efforts to Native preferences in many early encounters with sachems and their courts. Although Native wealth and military strength were cruelly diminished in the later decades of the seventeenth century, the power of elites in Native society to mobilize resistance and to maintain a measure of autonomy continued to be evident in many ways, most dramatically in King Philip's War and in the success of the Mohegan Sachem Uncas and his family in creating and protecting a large preserve on the Thames river that remained largely in Indian hands until the end of the eighteenth century (Weinstein-Farson 1991; Den Ouden 2005).

Philip, son of the sachem Massasoit of Sowams and Pokanoket, was articulate, well educated, bilingual, and a forceful personality, embodying all those skills and attributes required of sachems in the early contact period. The brilliant campaign organized in his name, which required complex negotiations with various Indian communities in southern New England, was made possible by his personal skills, as well as the status and connections he drew upon with consummate skill. The many histories and analyses of this war make clear that the pressures of further English expansion into Indian lands, internal pressures and jealousies dividing progressives from conservatives in all Native communities, and increasingly hostile relations between Indians and non-Indians generally were existing conditions that both influenced Philip's decisions and aided his cause among Natives themselves. However, it is also clear that Philip himself was the touchstone of the war and with his demise the conflict rapidly ended.

Uncas, the subtle and resourceful leader of the Mohegans, formerly tributary to the Pequots, emerged after their defeat (to which he contributed) as the principal Native ruler of the Connecticut coastal region, particularly after his execution of the Narragansett sachem Miantonomi in 1643. The remarkable 1679 document that summarizes Uncas's genealogy stresses marital and kin connections to Pequot, Narragansett, Niantic, and Long Island families (Burton and Lowenthal 1974:595), and it suggests that, although his power was real enough, the condition of royal descent was both the necessary and sufficient requirement for the truly and legitimately great. The biographies of other Native leaders in southern New England during the colonial period confirm this pattern (Little 1996).

The sexual and economic correlates of power and status in Native communities were also marked in the later colonial period. Native rulers were those most frequently found to be polygynous (Plane 1995:159), to have access to education ("King Tom" Ninegret was educated in England), and to have benefited financially from land sales, tributary payments, and access to desirable goods. That these transactions and acquisitions took place within the framework of English land annexation and were overseen by the colonial courts is testimony to the complexity of the cultural adjustments of both groups. Often the sachems worked to consolidate their territories, using a complicated set of transactions based on traditional models of land allotment, to protect their community's corporate holdings.

A great deal of research has documented the history of land cessions from Indian leaders to English settlers during the colonial period (Weinstein 1983a, 1985; Grumet 1980; Thomas 1979). Several studies detail the way the sachem Massasoit and his sons were able to maintain peaceful relations with surrounding English settlers for many decades by ceding or selling only certain tracts within their domains, consolidating their own communities, and distancing themselves from the English, while retaining access to important resource locations. In Pokanoket territories, Massasoit and Plymouth negotiated settlements with the English that placed moratoriums on land sales and required all sales to be negotiated between the sachems and the Plymouth council. In this way, the power of the sachem to distribute lands was employed to prevent indiscriminate land exchanges among individual Indians and Englishmen (Weinstein 1983a). This data seem to suggest that the Native people of the region were able to resist, to some extent, the process whereby labor and its products were separated from community and individual identity in other parts of the world, thereby transforming Indian ideas about personhood (Gewertz 1984).

Elizabeth Little has also documented the successful efforts of the Nantucket sachem Daniel Spotso, who succeeded in acquiring "commons" for Indians in return for sales of land, which guaranteed Indian access to scarce grazing lands on the island. Little notes that some Nantucket English residents were sufficiently familiar with and sympathetic toward the custom of tribute payment that they consented to periodic payments or claim renewals in order to acquire Indian lands (Little 1980b; 1996).

MARRIAGE, ALLIANCE, AND THE ROLE OF WOMEN

All societies organized around lineages or other corporate kin groups work in ways that interweave rights and responsibilities of all groups, especially through time (see the discussion of Annette Weiner's work below). In spite of the fact that leadership was explicitly said to descend from father to son in most Native societies in the region, William Simmons and George Aubin have argued that exogamous (out-marrying) matrilineal clans may also have been operating in some groups, particularly the Narragansett (1975).

Such systems usually have male leaders as well. William Hubbard recorded that leadership passed to the brother of the sachem, and then to the "sons" a pattern often associated with matrilineal organizations (Hubbard 1997:1, 84). Other examples include that of Uncas of the Mohegan, who claimed descent from sachem women from both the Mohegans and the Pequots, and his lineage includes an aunt/nephew marriage as well (Burton and Lowenthal 1974). Simmons and Aubin note that the Narragansetts had a tradition of sibling marriage that founded their sachem's line (1975).

A specific example comes from mid-eighteenth-century testimony regarding the sachemship of Charles Ninegret of the Narragansetts/Niantics. The marriage between Charles and his brother or half-brother Tom Sachem's daughter Betty, negotiated by the prominent female sachem Wootoniske, can be understood as reflecting two possible lineage reconstructions, as shown in figure 4 below.

Assuming the existence of incest taboos that forbid marriages between members of the same lineage, reconstruction #1, a matrilineal reckoning, seems more likely, for even if Tom Sachem and Charles Ninegret do not have the same mother, the fact that they shared a father would make Charles's marriage to Tom's daughter incestuous in a patrilineal system. In a matrilineal system, neither half nor full brothers could have children of the same lineage (which would be those of their wives) and thus their children would be free to marry. Other explanations include a form of royal sibling marriage, not unknown in the area (Simmons and Aubin 1975), or an ambilineal system in which both matrilineal and patrilineal systems were operant and that could be manipulated by elites. These latter explanations, however, as

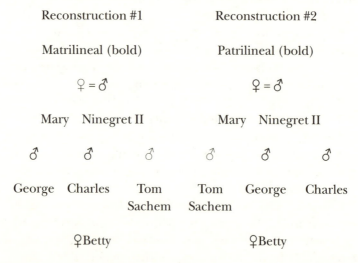

Figure 4. Ninegret's marriage. Comparative reconstructions by Kathleen Bragdon.

Simmons and Aubin have pointed out, still presuppose a matrilineal orientation.

I argue further that matrilineality was crucial in the legitimate possession and transferal of property in all societies in the region and thus the most important organizer of labor. On the islands, moreover, where Native men were often incorporated into the colonial maritime economy, women's rights to property helped to maintain corporate land-holding social groups in the face of pressures toward partible inheritance (the division of land among all heirs equally) in the later colonial period. A central argument of this chapter is that while certain privileges may have been linked to patrilineages, especially the inheritance of leadership positions, descent through women was equally significant in leadership, as well as in other aspects of social life. Indeed, the intimate relations among status, power, and corporate kin group in Native societies in southern New England is nowhere more apparent than in the activities of Native women. Native women were indispensable to social reproduction, as in all societies, but, among the Native people of southern New England, their roles were understood to be derived from their family, rather than their sex. In this, Native societies were in distinct contrast to those of their English neighbors, where women's roles often were submerged within a strongly male-centered political and social system.

"It is the custome of their kings to inherite," wrote William Wood of the "Aberginnians" of northern Massachusetts Bay, "the sonne always taking the kingdome after his fathers death. If there be no sonne, then the queene rules; if no queene, the next to the blood royall" (1977:79). Like Wood, the majority of seventeenth-century observers implied, along with Roger Williams, that these "queens" or sauncksquûaog (1936:141) were women who had sachem status as the agents of men (Winslow 1910:307). Although some women leaders were described as "relicts" of their sachem husbands, there are a number whose authority cannot be explained in that way, including Askamapoo of Nantucket, Wunnatuckquanumow or "Elizabeth Queen sachem" of Martha's Vineyard, and Hepsibah Cagnehew, queen sachem of Chappaquiddick. Scholars have observed that women often participated in land sales or exchanges, and some have concluded that those prominent women came to the fore only after the loss of prominent male leaders from disease or warfare made their leadership necessary. Several seventeenth-century commentators also denigrated these women by labeling them "squaw sachems" (Lechford 1833). But sachem women were powerful in Native society, prior to and throughout the colonial period, because they had always been crucial to the power and authority of men. These women, like others less well known, were also pivotal individuals in the transferal of land, the "social capital," of these communities, the distribution of which was a significant aspect of Native social reproduction in the early colonial period. In addition, since the land of a queen remained her own, it seems likely that in southern New England matrilineal ties and the autonomy of queen sachems made possible the continuity of corporately owned "social commodities" such as land in spite of a strong patrifocal bias in leadership. Because of their prominence, and presence in the records, in analyzing their activities we can extrapolate ideas about women's role in Native society generally. An extended discussion considering the various facets of women's roles in Native societies follows, beginning with an analysis of bridewealth and marital alliance.

Traditionally, discussions about marriage have been concerned with addressing how ideologies of descent and marriage represent "total social systems" (Poewe 1981:55). In this perspective, ideology and social action are treated as an integrated whole. For many feminist scholars, this leads to a new appreciation for how commodities exchanged at marriage give clues to wider conceptual orderings within society. One pertinent example in southern

New England Native societies is the custom of giving bridewealth gifts (often mistermed "dower" payments by the English; see, e.g., M. Mayhew 1694) at marriage. On the mainland, on Martha's Vineyard and Nantucket, and elsewhere in southern New England, marriages were marked by gifts from the groom's family to the bride's family. Edward Winslow recorded this custom among the Pokanokets, and Roger Williams noted a similar practice among the Narragansetts/Niantics. According to the Native minister Samson Occom, among the Natives of eastern Long Island, marriages were arranged between the groom's father (or mother if the father was dead) and the bride's family, and bridewealth was distributed to the woman's kin. Ann Plane notes similar exchanges in the Ninegret sachem family marriages until the mid-eighteenth century (1995).

Bridewealth was one of the ways that families and lineages established ties based on mutual obligations. Although bridewealth gifts were given even by less affluent men to their wife's family at marriage, (Williams 1936:29, 148), other forms of marriage were not accompanied by payments and were said to be less stable (Plane 1995:156). Bridewealth in general is found in both matrilineal and patrilineal societies but is often associated with situations in which the patrisystem requires rights to the children. It follows that in societies with a strong preference for patrilineal succession of leadership, as was the case in southern New England, the bride price gifts for high-status wives would be larger. On the other hand, bridewealth systems can also privilege wife-giving groups, as the substantial wedding gifts enrich the natal families of the brides (Leach 1961:230–31). In the emergent stratified societies of coastal southern New England (Bragdon 1996b), marriage, which involved bridewealth exchanges, ensured that property—both real and moveable—remained within a relatively small group of allied lineages. Representatives of these lineages, the sachems, in turn derived authority and power from this central economic role. An example of family and community involvement in such marriages comes from the testimony of one of Ninegret II's wives:

And when I was married to Ninigret the former sachem all the tribe were come together, and the elders or heads of the tribe were consulted on the matter and the whole tribe consented and contributed and the elders paid the dower and Ninegret gave the same to my mother the old Sunsk Squaw or Queen and the marriage celebrated by all according to Custom. (Miller 1925)

The recorded use of wampum as bridewealth in the early seventeenth century also demonstrates the symbolic importance of women's contributions to marriage. While wampum may have been a form of local currency prior to the arrival of Europeans, it circulated largely among sachem families and was a sign of rank in those societies (Bragdon 1996b:97). Wampum, especially the white form made from the columella of whelk shells, had ritual significance in much of the eastern woodlands. According to Margaret Holmes Williamson, white beads were "symbolically associated with power, access to the supernatural, the sky world, and to fertility" (2003:157). In the first decades of the seventeenth century, wampum would have thus have been an appropriate exchange for women, as cattle were among many African matrilineal systems, because of its interconnectedness with the most central symbolic representations in those societies. Intergenerational exchanges of wampum among sachem wife-givers and wife-takers would serve to symbolically and economically bind these groups together, while at the same time consolidating their moral and economic hegemony over nonparticipating family lines. That wampum was for a time co-opted as a medium of exchange by Dutch and English traders and settlers, led some to believe that Native women could be bought, although this is very unlikely to have been true. Wampum probably remained a restricted form of currency within Native communities in the region and remained linked to larger social and even cosmic concerns. In fact, in most Native language documents, wampum as payment is never mentioned, only English loan words such as "money" and "peny." The symbolic role of wampum was likely revived in the later seventeenth and eighteenth centuries, as it was tied to the powerful Iroquoians and their rituals, with whom the New England peoples continued to trade (see chapters 1 and 5).

As noted above, bridewealth was tied to rank in southern New England. Roger Williams suggested that a larger sum was exchanged for higher-ranking wives among the Narragansetts and Niantics (1936:148), a common situation in bridewealth societies with ranking systems (Collier 1987). Bridewealth in southern New England not only ratified marriages, but also represented part of the social capital of chiefly families. Ann Plane notes that in the eighteenth-century Narragansett/Niantic community, marriage without such payments and the feast that accompanied them failed to legitimize the succession of any children produced from it (1996).

High-ranking women were distinguished not only by the wealth exchanged at the time of their marriage, but by appearance and behavior as well. Low-ranking women worked very hard, and, in polygynous unions, lower-ranking women did the bulk of the domestic work (Winslow 1910:348; Wood 1977:112; Williams 1936:147). High-ranking women, on the other hand, behaved very differently. Mary Rowlandson, captured February 10, 1676 at Lancaster, Massachusetts, by allies of King Philip, described Weetamoo, Philip's sister-in-law, to whom she had been given as a servant:

My master (Quinapin, a Narragansett sachem) had three squaws, living sometimes with one, and sometimes with another one, this old squaw, at whose wigwam I was, and with whom my master had been those three weeks. Another was Wattimore [Weetamoo] with whom I had lived and served all this while. A severe and proud dame she was, bestowing every day in dressing herself neat as much time as any of the gentry of the land: powdering her hair, and painting her face, going with necklaces, with jewels in her ears, and bracelets upon her hands. When she had dressed herself, her work was to make girdles of wampum and beads.

These passages are striking as they also imply that the adornments and the products of high-status women's labor had great symbolic significance as well. Annette Weiner suggests that women's work is intimately linked to a corporate kin groups' spiritual wealth, which is meant to be transferred intergenerationally (1992). This may explain the importance of such belts or girdles manufactured by Philip's wives.

As discussed above, Native language deeds from Martha's Vineyard and Nantucket written on behalf of the queen sachems Wunnatuckquanumow and Askamapoo also reveal differences in discourse styles that presumably marked their high status (Goddard and Bragdon 1988:21). High-ranking women were also different in their status as mothers: Roger Williams wrote "they nurse all their children themselves; yet if she be an high or rich woman, she maintaines a nurse to tend the childe" (1936:40).

According to contemporary testimony, there were also status differences among wives in polygynous marriages. Edward Winslow claimed that the first wife within such a marriage among the Pokanokets was of the highest rank (1910:346–47). On the other hand, Matthew Mayhew of Martha's Vineyard, fully familiar with Native beliefs on the island wrote, "The Blood Royal, being in such veneration that if a prince had issue by divers wives, such succeeded as heir who was royally descended by the mother, although the youngest" (1694:7–8). Elizabeth Little suggests that, on Nantucket, the sachem Nickanoose treated the children of his high-status first wife differently from those of his second, lower-ranking wife. His daughter by the high-ranking wife, Askamapoo (who married the sachem Spotso), also ruled as sachem, as did her sons (1996:203).

Often we learn of the importance of women's rank indirectly. According to contemporary testimony about Ninegret I of the Narragansetts/Niantics:

He left four children one son and three daughters which children he had by two wifes one daughter he had by one of his wives and one son and two daughters by the other. And after the death of the said sachem the tribe of Indians met together in order to choose a sachem or sachems or queen. And when the Indians got together in order to choose one of the said sachems children who was of the most royal blood and upon consulting the affair they agree that his wife by whom he had but one daughter was of the most royal blood her father being a great sachem and her mother also of the royal blood therefore they proceeded & chose his said daughter who was of the most royal blood and made her their sachemess or queen and she continued to be their queen as long as she lived. (PSJ 1734, Deposition of Sompanwat, Kouckeomotonsow and the Old Queen, sister to Old Ninegret)

According to Ann Plane, Ninegret II's four wives may have been of royal Narragansett, Pequot, and Mohegan descent (1995:160). She interprets this passage to mean that the rank of the various wives was crucial in determining the succession of leadership. In fact, as Plane argues, "many colonial court actions over the disposal of land (and sometimes, office) turned on disagreements over who was the legitimate heir to a man who had been polygynously married" (161).The dispute over the leadership of the Sakonnet community was also about legitimacy. Two sons of Awashunks, by another husband, found themselves in conflict with the children of another of Sakonnet's leaders over who should rule. In a letter written to Awashunks by Thomas Prince on October 20, 1671, he reminded her that he "could have wished that [your followers] had been wiser themselves, especially your two sons, that may probably succeed you in your government, and your brother also, who is so nearly tied to you by nature" (Shurtleff and Pulsifer. 1855, 5:75).

Recent feminist scholarship suggests that while descent and marriage are central to social reproduction, the transactions that take place as a result of social transitions within a generation are also significant. In southern New England documented land transfers among Native people are a source of information about such transitions. According to Elizabeth Little, on Nantucket alone, hundreds of deeds were recorded, some of which were written by Indian people themselves in their Native language (Little 1996:200), and a similar number were recorded on Martha's Vineyard. A smaller, but significant number also derive from the Sakonnet and Nauset regions on the edges of Buzzard's Bay. These documents link individuals from several sachemships, hinting at marriage ties not otherwise recorded (Bragdon 2007) and reminding us that land, the principal social commodity, was central to community life.

Since Native land allotments and sales were so commonly the subject of English attention and documentation (Bragdon 1996b:138; Bragdon 1981a:109), another approach to uncovering the relative importance of a woman's family background is to track the female donors and recipients of land. A number of women were able to give or sell land on Martha's Vineyard and Nantucket, and they appear to have been members of sachem lineages (Little 1996).

For example, Little argues, Askamapoo, the queen sachem of Nantucket, wielded significant authority over the allotment of land she inherited from her father Nickanoose (1996; 1990a). Her son Daniel Spotso sometimes acted according to her instructions or with her permission (1996:198–99). As noted above, Askamapoo was the daughter of Nickanoose's first and highest-status wife, and it was her son Daniel that became sachem.

Another queen sachem from the island of Martha's Vineyard was Wunnatuckquanumow "Queen Sachem of Nunpaog," also known as Betty Washaman. Wunnatuckquanumow was the granddaughter of the sachem Towanquatuck, and co-heir with her brother Saggeatanumou of all his lands. Certainly Wunnatuckquanumow was the principal actor in land transfers even when her husband, the sachem Jacob Washaman, was present (Goddard and Bragdon 1988:docs. 15, 16, 21, 27, 28, 31, 33, 36, 69). Washaman in turn was the recipient of land from the sachem Nickanoose of Nantucket (Goddard and Bragdon 1988:253).

Hepsibah (Seiknout) Cagnehew was also known as "Queen sachem of Chapoquidick and Mosskeekett." Hepsibah was the wife of the sachem Samuel Cagnehew and the daughter and heir of the sachem Joshua Seiknout. The Chappaquiddick sachem lines demonstrate a number of aspects of a system based on age and gender, and demonstrate how rank interpenetrated the former categories. Queen sachem Hepsibah's grandfather Seiknout was granted land by Nickanoose and Wawinit of Nantucket, who also made alliances with the Nantucket sachem Spotso to whom he married his daughter Askamapoo. As Little argues, the documents suggest that only sachems and their families appeared in deeds and other documents. The documents show that the transferal of property between Nickanoose and Askamapoo was witnessed by two individuals—Papumahteochohoo and Pakeponessoo, who was the sachem of Chappaquiddick. Pakeponessoo's son, Seiknout, became the sachem of Chappaquiddick, as did Seiknout's son and grandson. Curiously, both Seiknout's daughter and Jacob Washaman's wife were known to the English as "Elizabeth" or "Betty." Three other queen sachems were also given this name, as were sachem women in the Ninegret and Pequot lines. Wunnatuckquanumow (Betty Washaman) and Elizabeth Phillips, described above, also fit into this category. Could this be a clue to their status? One wonders whether the English recognized the ruling status of these women and likened it to their former Queen Elizabeth, or whether the queen sachems chose royal names for themselves. Interestingly, even Satasqua, the wife of Thomas Waban (the first leader of the Natick Praying Town, and heir to lands at Nashoba), was called Elizabeth, and one contemporary observer called her a "Queene" (Dunton 1867:217).[1]

Johanah Mokokinnit (or Coshomon), Betty Josnin, and Elizabeth Phillips of Chappaquiddick were also said to have sachem rights. Johanah was "daughter and heir" to Wampamog and a sizeable landholder at Sangekantacket (DCRD 2/285, 3/271). Before her death (ca. 1710–11) she sold this land to the Englishman Benjamin Smith.

Betty Josnin, another daughter of the ruler Wampamog, left Martha's Vineyard with Joseph Josnin (variously called her brother, cousin, or husband), in the early years of the eighteenth century, and was interviewed in 1715/16 at Bridgewater by Benjamin Smith about her sachem rights to another parcel at Sangekantacket (Goddard and Bragdon 1988:204). That Smith felt it necessary to travel across the bay to consult with her shows that her authority as a sachem woman was significant, even in her absence. Elizabeth Phillips was the wife of Beniah Phillips, who may have had ties to the Phillips sachem family of Noman's land. She was also the daughter of Ephraim Naquatim, a "magistrate" on Chappaquiddick (1988:265, 459). More work may link her family with the sachem family of Nickanoose and Spotso. Other records demonstrate strong ties between the sachem line of Nunpaog and Chappaquiddick, as well as links among the sachem families of Nantucket. Papumahteochohoo was also a witness to

---

1. This analysis is different, but not incompatible with that made by Ann Plane (1998), who cites the case Seeknout v. Sassechuammin (Suffolk Files # 12965) to suggest, as she has elsewhere, that in the eighteenth century legal challenges to Native leadership were framed in terms of English, not Native, ideas about marriage and legitimacy.

the transfer of land from the Nunpaog sachem Towanquatuck, and his grandchildren Joel and Wunnatuckquanumow (781).

Native writings from Cape Cod also remind us that high-ranking women there continued to play an important role in the maintenance of land holdings, which was sometimes commemorated with the payment of tribute. An elderly Native from the Sakonnet community, when called to testify about the sachem status of a particular family, reported: "When I was young many years agoe I saw several Indians in the fall of the year carry corn to Simon Wicket's mother then I asked my father wy so many Indians carried corn to that old squaw. Every fall. He told me that Island called Oister Island was hers and that corn they carried to her was to pay her for their planting on her land" (Massachusetts Historical Society, msc. Bd. April 30, 1718, testimony from Joel, "aged about 70 years").

In another example of power over economic resources, at once more rare and more symbolic, rights to "whale" appear occasionally, and only among sachems. Women were involved in these transfers as well. Elizabeth Little and Clinton Andrews argue that rights to drift whales were specially prized "gifts of Moshup" and were understood as belonging exclusively to sachems (1982). For example, Towanquatuck willed to his son Saggeatanumou "half the whale and half the whalebone" (witnessed by Joseph Papumahteochohoo). Queen sachem Wunnatuckquanumow deeded land to Matthew Mayhew and Thomas Daggett in 1696, but reserved for herself from every beached whale "one flook or part of the tayle and one finne to be severed at the bone, and a yard square in the blubber" (DCHS, ms. 1696). Previously she "gave the tayle of my whale for ever" to Matakekin or Petoson of Chappaquiddick and Nantucket in 1685 (Segel and Pierce 2003:297). Matakekin also held property within the dominion of Nickanoose (2003). This "payment" occurred about the time that Nickanoose sickened or died, and Wawinet, Askamapoo's

111

brother, became sachem (Little 1996:196). In turn, Matakekin gave these whale rights to Kishkuhtukquainnit or Cochquadin in 1696 (Goddard and Bragdon 1988:257). Little and Andrews argue that the locations of beachings may have determined the locus of particular sachemships and become central to reinforcing the status and authority of the sachems, both male and female (1988).

Another line of argument emphasizes the important role that sachem women played as siblings. As discussed above, the role of siblings is central to understanding lineal organization, and many examples from southern New England suggest that leadership succession was from sibling to sibling, and then to a member of the descending generation, and that that person had to have royal blood on both sides. Little has argued, for example, that the Nantucket queen sachem Askamapoo was heir to her brother Wawinet, as well as her father Nickanoose, by virtue of the high status of her mother (1990a:198–99). Wunnatuckquanumow of Nunpaog was co-heir with her brother Saggeatanumou as well, but ruled alone after his death. Perhaps this is what Matthew Mayhew meant when he wrote that women could rule "in defect of a Male of the Blood" (1967:7–8).

In sum, kinship, marriage, and rules about the disposition of land, principles of hierarchy, and the principle of co-equal status between men and women operated in Native societies in southern New England long after the arrival of Europeans. In this way, authority was neither monolithic nor enduring, but depended for its reproduction on succeeding generations of successful high-ranked pairings. The islands of Martha's Vineyard and Nantucket were, therefore, not, as the English imagined, "ruled" by sachems who controlled separate territories, but were social territories where rulers were constantly seeking, through marriage alliance, to strengthen their own authority or that of their children, authority that was often expressed in terms of control over land. Power and authority were always in flux, and the English tendency to think hierarchically about power was a constant source of misunderstanding in Native-English relationships. This is not to suggest that various dyads of power did not exist in Native communities, for example, those between sachem and powwaw, sachem and counselor, men and women, and the like, have been documented in many sources. But if a cultural web of meaning can be constructed for these societies, it rests in a general agreement about the legitimacy of marriage relations, and their relations to authority over land use.

However, as Irene Silverblatt and others argue, as societies move toward centralization, gender hierarchies are often undermined (2000). This seems particularly true of matrilineal societies (Gailey 1987; but also see Peletz 1995). Clearly the principles of matrilineal inheritance in Native societies were being tested by the late seventeenth century. For example, a faction of Sakonnets led by Osomehew, Posotoquo and Mamanewet, who opposed the queen sachem Awashunk's rule, decreed that "our Brother . . . Mamanewet should be the true proprietor and disposer of all our lands, and that our brother Mamanewet himself, and his heirs shall be the chief sachem or head over us" (Little Compton Proprietors Records 1672/3:2).

Mamanewet (or Mamanua) was the son of Awashunk's sachem husband Tosoneyin according to a deed that stated, "[Awashunk's] kindred . . . are of the same stock, the more remote" than Mamanua and his "bretheren the sones of Tosoneyin" (Shurtleff 1853–54, 3:286). Awashunks was the mother of Peter Awashunks, and another deed states, "Tatuckamana, Awashunckes and those of that kindred whoe are of the same stock the more Remote may have some right to lands there as they are relations to the above said Mamaneway and have been longe inhabitants of that place" (Shurtleff 1853–54, 3:286).

Other attacks on sachem women's legitimacy are discussed by Plane, who suggests that protests about the type of relationship (e.g., marriage or concubinage), or gifts given at marriage, were pretexts for assaults on women's role in the legitimization of male leadership (Plane 2000).

Nevertheless, continuities in ideas about women's leadership can be documented in the later colonial period as well. In 1736, a group of Mohegan Indians tried to establish Anne, the daughter of the Mohegan sachem Caesar, as sunksqua, against the claims of Ben Uncas II, a direct descendant of Uncas himself. Trudy Lamb Richmond and Den Ouden suggest that, in particular, reservation communities were "possessed of a political and historical consciousness, and were fully engaged in the colonial world precisely because their remaining lands were perpetually threatened by encroachers" (2003:196). In the resulting dispute, Mamohet, a Mohegan leader, petitioned the crown in person to complain of Connecticut's false treatment of the Mohegans. Connecticut's leaders responded by seeking to undermine Mamohet's claims to leadership, in favor of Ben Uncas, Jr. This was because, they claimed, Mamohet II was the son of a "concubine of a mean extract" (211). His daughter Anne was nonetheless confirmed. Lamb Richmond and Den Ouden suggest that her later forced marriage to Ben Uncas, Jr., was a colonial attempt to resolve the issue in their favor, but "reuniting" the loyalist Uncas family with the recognized leader, Anne (211).

A study yet to be done is an investigation of the ways in which women's authority in the old sachem system was transformed into new roles for women in the later colonial period. It appears that rank and family ties remained important in determining women's authority within a community, and that that authority was closely linked to Christianity and its concomitant vernacular literacy. These factors, along with the frequent absence of men, made women's power both central and conspicuous to outsiders.

Land Transfers and Family
in the Later Colonial Period

Unsurprisingly sachems played a prominent role in land cessions and in creating "preserves" in the seventeenth century, but a closer look at the patterns of land loss and consolidation in the region also gives clues about the inner workings of other kinds of Indian communities in later decades. In particular, Native wills and inventories from Natick, a Christian Native community established by John Eliot according to an idealized proprietorship, link the principles of corporate group, rank, and authority, and the daily concerns of Native individuals together.

Inheritance practices, recorded in Native languages or by Indian people themselves in the eighteenth century, reveal the recognition of a wide family network, probably reflecting lineage relationships in Indian societies generally (Bragdon 1997; O'Brien 1998:131). The will of Benjamin Tray of Natick, cited above, for example, leaves property to his mother, his sisters, and his sisters' daughters (MDX docket # 22768). Another Natick woman, Elizabeth Pognit, whose will is dated 1755, left one pound to her husband "if he comes out of the service of his King and Country" and the remainder of her estate to her granddaughter Sarah Waban including "all my lands and Real Estate and appurtenances and privileges thereto belonging, together with all my household goods, pot, whatever else is mine, . . . but if she has no heirs of her body or does not live to need it such part as is left I give to my brother Solomon Wamsquon's heirs" (MDX docket # 17057).

Through time, inheritance practices at Natick and on Gay Head came to favor wives and children over members of the wider kin group. This was especially apparent for those families who had constructed framed or stone houses and barns that, being unmovable, led Natives to claim the land on which they were built for their children, in defiance of community mores

115

(Bragdon 1981a; 1985). The Native-language will of Peter Ohquanhut, Gay Head minister in the mid-eighteenth century, for example, divided his framed house, which had several rooms and a chamber above, "so that his daughter Dorcas owns it." The remainder of his estate, including the rest of the house, "the oxen, and the mare, and the cow's young, when I die all this estate of mine goes into the hand of my wife; she will own it in the same way I owned any of it, and the same way I used it she may use it. She may eat and wear anything from it as long as she lives" (Goddard and Bragdon 1988:169).

This text reflects the longstanding associations between sustenance and land and its products, and also reflects the importance of obligations to women. Peter Ohquanhut was a nonconformist Christian, an Anabaptist minister, but he was also a member of a prominent sachem family whose traditional role was the accumulation and distribution of property.

The Natick land records, written in the local language by Captain Thomas Waban, record the allotments of land to a variety of individuals, both women and men, presumably those who had original "proprietors' rights" in the community (Bragdon 1981a; Goddard and Bragdon 1988). An example is the allotment for Susannoh, wife of Joseph Ephriam:

Then the proprietors jointly and willingly released one piece of land (it lies at the south side of this house and this river) to the one named Muttassonshq, or Susannoh, the wife of Joseph Ephriam. And that land lies between the boundary of Samuell Commacho and the northwestern corner where the fort used to be, to the boundary further on, the boundary of Andrew Ephriam, and between that: that land towards the north up to the river, and 20 acres or perhaps less. And this has been lovingly given to Muttassonshq. She has that property forever. By Thomas Waban, Town Clerk here. (O'Brien 1998:273)

At Natick, as more and more Native men were drawn into military service at midcentury and did not return, women controlled

the large remaining property holdings and their influence, if anything, increased. As Jean O'Brien notes, however, since Native
women at Natick were usually required to choose non-Indian
executors or, if underage, placed under the control of guardians,
their freedom to distribute property was strictly limited (1998).
However, the practice of assigning "shares" in a particular section
was very common in sachemships throughout southern New England; the first examples were recorded in colonial land records in
the mid-seventeenth century. Since the council that approved
these decisions in Natick was composed of locally prominent
men, they represented a joint decision of the town's leaders, as
was true in more traditionally organized sachemships elsewhere.

These patterns reflect the workings of "the political economy
of knowledge" a phrase that recognizes that every social system
incorporates conflicts and contradictions. As social systems repro-
duces themselves through the mediation of rules of customary
behavior that mask or misrepresent conflict, however, more
antagonistic forms of social life can emerge. Marshall Sahlins has
described this process in eighteenth-century Hawaii, where the
control of culturally valued objects was decoupled from political
power, ultimately undermining the Native political order (1985).
For example, a conflict arose on Gay Head in the mid-eighteenth
century, when one man, Elisha Amos, described above,
attempted to purchase or enclose a large portion of the community lands, a process that seemed both a challenge to local political leaders and at odds with the general pattern of using lands in
common. It would be easy to interpret this man's efforts as an
example of English-influenced acquisitiveness. A later description of his activities recorded that he "built a house on the [land]
and prohibited all the Indians, even those who had not conveyed
any part of their rights . . . from making any improvements . . .
(Dukes County Historical Society n.d.). Further research demonstrates that Amos was a descendant of one of the original sachems

at Gay Head, whose claims were in conflict with those of his brothers (Segel and Pierce 2003). Perhaps Elisha Amos was attempting to acquire, by purchase and enclosure, the status and rights of his forebears. The role that English agents or guardians of Indian people in the eighteenth century played in exacerbating these conflicts within Indian communities is another study yet to be done.

In the next chapter, the complexities of family and community values and the ways English people were drawn into Native communities are further examined through a case study linking an English family and a sachem family on Martha's Vineyard.

4.

Complexities of Cohabitation and Race

Status and power are often implicated in relationships between men and women, and those in Native communities during the colonial period in New England were no exception. As the previous chapter indicates, much of what we know about Native women during this period derives from land sales and other agreements between representatives of Native communities and colonial or local English governmental bodies or private individuals. As we have seen, in Native southern New England, men's and women's power was generally due to their families' status and their control over land, but that power could generally only be exercised fully within the context of a powerful marriage. Descent and alliance was what lent authority to rulers and gave them the power to act. This cut both ways; if the son of a sachem could not contract a powerful marriage alliance, his power was likely diminished, and, secondarily, derived only from the authority of his parents. Similarly, daughters who married lesser men appear less often in the records, although their connections with their parents are constantly invoked and their interests in the sachemship are recognized by all.

If the central function of kinship relations is to reproduce the social group though time, then, as Annette Weiner has argued, it is crucial to examine both the male and female contributions to these relationships and how those are recognized by the societies of which they are a part (1992). Furthermore, as chapter 3 makes clear, kinship studies must pay attention to women not only as wives and mothers, but also as sisters. It is, Weiner argues, the pivotal role that women play in sustaining alliances between families, as well as helping to perpetuate those ties between generations through their children, that permits a social group to constitute and symbolize continuity through time. This continuity is of course crucial in the construction of individual identity as well. In southern New England, it also played a central role in the new complexities of local Native communities, whose members often had social ties with non-Indians. This kind of cohabitation entails many conflicts in the lives of specific individuals, and is a common topic in postcolonial studies. This chapter looks at such an intimate relationship through an example from Martha's Vineyard. Native ideas about marriage and family, women and men, emerge from this story that may represent the new Native reality of the colonial period. Here, indigenous ideas about alliance and descent served a role in preserving a Native community in the midst of the upheavals of that period.

As noted above, one English adventurer on Martha's Vineyard was a man named John Daggett, who may have established ties there prior to 1647 (Banks 1966:2:9). Daggett and three others were given township rights on the eastern side of the island, in an area described as "all Towanquatuck's his right, together with all the land as farr as the Easter-Chop of Homses Hole, and also all the Island called Chapquegick, with full Power to dispose of all and every Part of the said land as they see best for their own comfortable Accomodation. The line is to goe from Tequanoman's Point to the Eastermost Chop of Homes Hole" (December 4, 1646, cited in Banks 1966:2:9).

In their grant to Daggett, the Mayhews specified that he must wait until the Mayhews had chosen their farm, and that it must be a minimum of three miles away from the spring that ran close to the harbor (Banks 1966:1:11). The sachem principally affected by this grant was Wampamog, the son of the sachem Attumsquam, whose territories were theoretically included within this large division. We have no information about Attumsquam's mother, but his sister Alice married the sachem whose English name was Thomas Tyler "from the mainland," one of two known to have established themselves on Martha's Vineyard in the early colonial period. The sachem Puttispaquin was probably also a brother, and his name is associated with this region as well.

John Daggett settled permanently on Martha's Vineyard in 1651, along with his wife Alice Brotherton and their son Joseph; Joseph was probably born by 1648, if not before (Pierce 2007:2). Initially John Daggett occupied a home lot in Great Harbor, in accordance with the 1642 agreement. John Daggett's eldest son Thomas, who was born in England, later joined him on Martha's Vineyard, where he married Hannah Mayhew, governor Mayhew's daughter, thus establishing a link between the two prominent English families.

In 1660 John Daggett exercised his right to establish a 500-acre farm through the "purchase" of land from the sachem Wampamog in the area still known as Farm Neck in Oak Bluffs. In spite of their earlier agreement, Mayhew levied the astonishing sum of 5,000 pounds against Daggett because he "hath broken the order of ten pounds upon every acre in purchasing a farm at Sanchekantacket at the hands of the Indians without the town's consent" (Edgartown Records Office, Town order, January 24, 1652). Since Mayhew had granted him the right to establish such a farm in 1642, Daggett was confirmed by the Plymouth court in his possession of the farm, in spite of Mayhew's strong objections. Historians have never discovered a reason for Mayhew's ire. John Daggett died some time before 1674 and left portions of his property at Sangekantacket Neck to his son Joseph. Joseph was active in town affairs and served, among other capacities, on a committee to divide common lands in Tisbury and Edgartown.

Joseph Daggett had made the unusual decision, however, to marry an Indian woman, a "near relation" of the sachems Wampamog and Puttuspaquin in 1666. Historian Charles Banks includes no contemporary commentary on this marriage, but a passage from Samuel Sewall's diary, dated 1706, records the comments of John Bolt, who was living in Edgartown in 1678, and who purchased land in Sangekantacket in 1686. John Bolt had removed to Boston by March of 1686 and in 1703 he sold his land to Israel Daggett. Sewell recorded that "Mr. Bolt mentioned profane courses he had been entangled in [on Martha's Vineyard]" and later Sewell wrote "I mentioned the problem whether [the children of mixed marriages ?] should be white after the Resurrection: Mr. Bolt took it up as absurd, because the body should be void of all colour" (Banks 1966:2:305).

Banks, a long term resident of the island, writing in 1911, claimed that Joseph Daggett's marriage to an Indian woman "placed him in an anomalous social position" vis-à-vis his English relatives, and remarked that "evidence is not wanting to indicate that there was little affection between the descendants of the two island branches for many years" (1966:3:141). Banks noted, too, that there were a number of "irregularities" in the genealogy of Joseph Daggett, published more than a century after his death (Banks 1966:2:44–47; but see Pierce 2007).

The "anomaly" of this marriage has been the stuff of island folklore. However, this view of the history of the Daggett family is derived entirely from English records and reminiscences collected during Banks's long tenure as Clerk of Courts for Dukes County. Records in which Native people had a voice provide a different picture, one in which the families with whom the Daggetts intermarried were not outcasts, but central to the continuity of the Indian community at Sangekantacket into which the Daggetts married.

Most of the evidence for this process comes from the land records, both in Native language and in English. In particular, the documents recording transactions involving land known in the earliest colonial records as Ogkashkuppeh, and later Sangekantacket, tell a complex story of family ties.

THE DAGGETT FARM
AND THE SANGEKANTACKET COMMUNITY

The original purchase of Daggett's farm was in a part of Wampamog's territory known as Ogkashkuppeh, and, later, as Sangekantacket Neck for the pond on the southern border. In a deed dated 1660, "Wabamuck alias Samuel, son of Autumsquum, sachem of Sanchacantacket alias Akeskeppe Neck" sold this land to John Daggett. Wampamog also sold him "a certain tract of land . . . lying upon the east side of the easternmost chap of Holmes Hole, called by the English Quaasquannes, butting down to the sea on the east, on the north with a line running 320 rods into the woods, and 320 rods to the west and (south?)." The other name attached to this property, Qushquannes, referred to Squash Meadow only or to all of John Daggett's farm (Banks 1966:2:3). This land is now known as Farm Neck.

Unkaw Neck on East Chop is also associated with the Daggett farm. This neck was deeded by Joseph Daggett to his daughter Alice and to his granddaughter Hester Cottle in 1715. When the land was sold to Thomas West of Edgartown in 1724, it was then "in the possession of" John Tallman, an "Indian man of Edgartown." Wampamog retained some rights in this area, as is indicated by his sale in 1686 to Richard Sarson of the salt pond adjoining the east side of Holmes Hole harbor and at the place called Onkaw (Banks 1966:2:9).

Wampamog also sold to Joseph Daggett, a certain neck "neer Sahchakantacket harbor" called Ohhomeck or Ahomma. In 1683, the sachem Thomas Sissetom also sold to Joseph Daggett a plot northwest of Watcha pond. Daggett acquired, in 1669, Quinnaamuk (long beach), probably the long strip of sandy beach separating the lagoon and the harbor. Thomas Sissetom also sold to Joseph Daggett twenty acres of Farm Neck and his meadow lying at Sepoisset in the northwest corner of Daggett's existing farm.

In 1689, the sachem Wampamog gave to "Ales Sessetom and Keziah Sessetom . . . the daughters of Thomas Sessetom" some land, and Banks suggests that Puttuspaquin's sale probably was a gift in confirmation to the children of Alice Sissetom of the property originally given to the Indian sisters Alice and Keziah (Banks 1966:2:44). The property adjoined the tract that John Daggett had first acquired from Wampamog at Sangekantacket, described as "straight up from the water up to Deagit's bounds." Later, Puttuspaquin sold "to my cousins Hester and Ellis (Alice) Daggett . . . my near kindred" a tract of land that is now known to be in the present limits of Eastville adjoining the ponds on the east bank of the Lagoon (DCD 1:251). According to Banks, this territory is identical to a tract of land granted sixteen years before by Wampamog.

Detailed genealogical research by Jerome Segel and Andrew Pierce (2003; Pierce 2007) help to make it possible to reconstruct many of the genealogical links that illuminate the marriage alliances and descent of property and the relations between them, links which serve to maintain the community through time. Records for Sangekantacket involve women as grantors or grantees. In every case except one, males "divide" or "give" land to women, and women divide or give or sell land to men. Most of the Native writings also include peoples whose kin relationships can be traced. This data demonstrate the way women's work and women's alliances are related. Many of the women for whom land was divided had male siblings. What, if any, land divided for these men is not mentioned in these records, with the exception of land divided for men by women. When married women divide or sell land, their names are often written first in the Native language records, which may represent, iconically, their social importance (Goddard and Bragdon 1988). All the documents reinforce the notion that women were understood to have authority and influence over land transactions, and were the conduit through which land passed to the next generation. This idea is further supported by kinship data that suggests a strong emphasis on the symmetry of sibling ties.

This story of Joseph Daggett's Native wife is an interesting example of the way the personal became political in the colonial world, and had everything to do with the high status of her family within Native society. The relationship between Joseph and his wife created prominent island families with ties in both English and Indian societies. Joseph Daggett's daughter Hester, for example, married the Englishman Edward Cottle, but his other daughter, Alice, apparently never contracted a formal marriage and later sued three men named Luce, Look, and Allen for the support of her children (Banks 1966:2:46; Pierce 2007). These children were recognized in Alice's will, dated 1711, and one "Black Henry" Luce received the land originally given to his grandmother by the sachem Wampamog, while the other children received movable property. Banks comments on the irregularity of the children of liaisons such as those between Alice Daggett and the Luce, Look, and Allen men, receiving property, but Joseph Daggett executed his daughter's estate and the inheritance stood (Banks 1966:2: 44–47). Banks wrote that "it is not known what became of these children, but the presumption is that they became united with their Indian associates, and finally lost identity among them, if they survived to adult life" (DCP 1:59–60, 73). This statement is undermined by Segel and Pierce's documentation of the career of Joseph Daggett's descendants, through his daughter Hester Cottle and, possibly, his great grandson Shubal Harden. Another granddaughter, Patience Allen, may have married the Indian John Caleb, although only her first name and the dates she appears in the records support this (DCD 8:273–74). There is better documentation for the children of Joseph Daggett's second marriage to another woman, possibly also of Native descent. The daughters married Englishmen, but their son John's children were rumored to be of partly Native descent (Banks 1966:3:142–43; see also Goddard and Bragdon 1988:165). Although little more is known of these people, it is clear that ties to both English and Native families on the island were recognized along with longstanding links to place. This is no doubt only one example among many of the kinds of intimate relations that grew between English colonists and Native people and the way these relationships were viewed by subsequent generations. That these relations were reinterpreted in racialized terms in the nineteenth century does not undermine their significance to colonial Native communities.

CLASS, GENDER, AUTHORITY, AND RACE ON MARTHA'S VINEYARD

As noted in chapter 4, in the early colonial period men's and women's rank was determined by the rank of both parents. The children of the first wife were given precedence, but some contemporary authors suggest that the children of the highest-ranking wife, regardless of her age, might outrank the children of earlier marriages. Another contributing factor was birth order. For both men and women, it was apparently the first born who ranked highest. If legitimacy was derived from all these factors, it is likely that conditions were not always favorable for dynastic marriages to take place, thereby undermining the authority of the ruling elite. It may be that this is why, by the middle of the eighteenth century, the term "sachem right" as used on the island, had come to refer only to rights over land.

While race was to play an increasingly important role in English treatment of Indians, on the island and elsewhere, it is clear that Native people valued kin ties over racial and ethnic affiliations. Family connections and loyalties may be seen in operation in other documents involving Natives: lawsuits among Indians of the area and between the English settlers and the Indians who lived at Sangekantacket. These lawsuits also involve kinship details and illustrate some of the dynamics of land ownership and rights.

The Indian minister Thomas Sissetom owned land near the "wading place at Sanchekantacket" and sold some of this to Joseph Daggett and Joseph Norton. Thomas Sissetom was presented in court in 1688 along with his mother Monchquanum, Alice Sissetom, Kezia Sissetom, (his daughters?), Jonoisquash Sissetom (his brother), for stealing sheep and eating "muttin." Other suits involve trespass and fencing. Clearly the Sangekantacket lands were contested, and the English "block" was hampered both by the documented ownership of the Daggett's property and their "near relations" with the Sissetoms.

The example of the Daggett/Sissetom alliance demonstrates that while pursing their own traditions of alliance, they were not unaware of the class ranking system of the English, one that placed all Indians lower on the scale than they themselves (Kupperman 2000). I suggest that the marriage of the Sissetom woman and Joseph Daggett deliberately subverted these English class distinctions. John Daggett, himself in competition with the powerful Mayhew family, made two important marriages among his children: one between his son Thomas and Hannah, daughter of Thomas Mayhew, and one between his youngest son Joseph and the daughter of an influential member of an Indian sachem's family. His alliance with Wampamog, through which he acquired a large portion of this sachem's territories, served Wampamog and his community as well. As long as there were Indians with claims to English blood involved, their claims in the colonial legal system were held superior to those without such ties. They were thus able to retain land holdings vital to the construction of community. The contrast between what the English records describe and what the Native documents reveal shows the Indians, on the one hand, as humble and helpless, but on the other, effective actors making use of two differing land tenure systems and vastly different power relations.

NATIVES AND GUARDIANS

The intimacies of intermarriage gave rise to ambiguity in social relationships in both Native and non-Native communities in southern New England during the colonial period. The previous discussion reviews what few relations between Indians and English are documented in terms that both would recognize. Another, more common relationship that gave rise to complex interactions was that between English guardians and their families and the Indian communities they oversaw.

Three examples below will serve to illustrate how guardians and their families benefited from their control over Indian communities, and how Native people worked to undermine those gains or to support them when they were beneficial to communities as a whole. This brief overview is only a beginning; further study will help to illuminate these relationships in more detail.

THE EASTERN PEQUOTS

After the return of the eastern Pequot community to Stonington, Connecticut, in the 1650s, their lands were administered by guardians appointed by the colony. Over the course of the late seventeenth and early eighteenth centuries, members of a single, powerful local English family, the Williams, were associated with the Eastern Pequot community in Stonington. Men from this family had power over land, which they leased out at favorable terms to relatives and friends. Commissions to local doctors, craftsmen, and the owners of expensive farming equipment were theirs to award. Guardians also arranged for the apprenticeship or guardianship of Indian children, and took many of them in themselves, where they were expected to serve as domestic servants. Guardians decided which families or individuals were eligible for financial assistance, and often provided such assistance only when Native people were infirm or near death (Eastern Pequot 2000). A cross check with other demographic and public records, however, suggests that only a small percentage of the community was in regular contact with the guardians, and the remainder were both self-sufficient and self-governing. For the Eastern Pequots, this meant a mobile existence, with persons often coming and going from the reserve. This pattern continued with other guardians well into the nineteenth century.

THE MASHPEE

In the mid-eighteenth century, Mashpee residents were organized against their guardians, who persisted in leasing land at easy terms to white farmers in the area and permitted the cutting down of significant portion of the forested parts of their reserve. Among the most egregious exploiters of these privileges were members of the Bourne family, some of whom had once served as missionaries to the Indians on the upper Cape. Indian men who were engaged in the whaling industry were often away for long periods of time, making those people who remained at home more likely to need financial assistance (Nicholas 2002).

Guardians took on a role similar to that described for the Eastern Pequots. However, the Mashpees successfully resisted some of these abuses and learned to work the lines of communication open to them, going over the heads of their guardians straight to the General Court and beyond (see introduction).

THE GAY HEAD INDIANS

Chilmark merchant John Allen was named guardian to the Indians of Gay Head, and was also a High Sheriff of Dukes County from 1714 to 1733. Someone in his family, perhaps his father James Allen, had fathered a child with the woman Alice Daggett, the daughter of Joseph Daggett and his Native wife, who sued for support for a child named Patience Allen (also mentioned earlier in this chapter) (Banks 1966: vol.2). A relative in the Native community was only one of the complexities of his relations with them, which were both part of his official duties and the basis of his livelihood. These latter are illustrated in his account book, which he maintained from the 1730s to the 1760s.

The following Native names appear in the accounts:

Bomet or Pomet	Joel	Sowag
Benis or Demos	Metak	Gershom
Cheeks	Occouch	Daggett
Coomes	Ohomo	Tallman
Elisha	Ossueit	Wimpeny (Ompany)
Eliab	Passuet	

As the other merchants' account books from the Cape and islands show, Native people were often caught up in mercantile ventures, especially the whaling of their creditors, and Allen's 1730 account book also demonstrates this pattern. In addition to whaling services, Allen's Native clients also performed other tasks including hunting and fowling, shepherding, blacksmithing, spinning, and tailoring.

From other records we know that many of these were prominent Native families on Gay Head; some, like the Metaks, were descended from prominent sachem families there. While all these families had accounts with Allen, they also stood up against him when his practices as overseer angered them. For example, a document in Native language written to Allen by the Native inhabitants of Gay Head in the mid-eighteenth century criticizes his appointment of Elisha Amos as judge (Goddard and Bragdon 1988:225).

Thus, while the painful history of exploitation of Indian people should not be discounted, we can also see how Native people, acting as a group, were able to resist exploitation using methods learned from others, as well as their own internally devised social rules. It is this multilayered view that informs the next chapter, which turns to material culture in colonial Native New England. In many ethnographic studies, material culture is described in early chapters to provide a sense of the physical setting in which social action takes place. The following discussion instead treats the material world as thoroughly implicated in Native societies in the colonial period.

5.

Material Life in
Colonial Indian Communities

The material world of Native people during the colonial period was not merely the physical setting for social action; it also contributed to and gave meaning to that action. The most immediate context in which objects were interpreted was the community, one frame for understanding what Arjun Appadurai terms "the social life of things" (1986). Appadurai remarks that "things have no meanings apart from those that human transactions, attributions, and motivations endow them with" (5). In order to get at these meanings, it is also necessary to observe "things in motion" (5), that is, the ways material objects are created, used, and exchanged. The combined use of Native language documents, comparative analysis, and material culture analysis yield substantive results that explain material culture within its social context. Cultural and social principles that are reflected in the use and collection of objects include relationships of hierarchy, marital alliance, and spirituality. Modes and rules of distribution and allocation are also part and parcel of what objects mean. These "structural" principles underlie the inventiveness of the adaptation of new objects and economic relationships entailed by the wider colonial context, "the variety of liaisons men and women can have with things in the conflicted, transcultural history of colonialism" (5).

In addition to documents and linguistic data, there are numerous archaeological sites that date to the colonial period in southern New England and have yielded artifacts used by Native people. Many objects manufactured and used by southern New England Indians also survive in museum collections. Today we acknowledge those surviving objects as "historical narrative-bearing artifacts of social life" (Thomas 1991:24–26). Their stories are embedded in the histories of the their communities. While we know a great deal about the sources of the objects that Europeans brought with them or manufactured themselves in their new colonial circumstances, and, thanks to the work of numerous historians, have a good grasp of the ways mercantile relations linked both sides of the Atlantic, we know much less about how the colonized Natives experienced and understood their changing material world.

The relationship between English clothing and status in Indian communities has not received any consistent attention. Many sachems in the region were offered gifts of coats, waistcoats, and other items of colorful clothing in negotiations or as a token of English recognition of their power (Dillon 1980:104). There is some evidence about the value of such clothing and its symbolic significance. Grave goods at the Burr's Hill cemetery, for example, include several examples of English-derived decorative clothing items, cloth, and clothing ornaments such as brooches and pins. Native clothing of furs and skins was supplemented very early in the contact period by items of European clothing and ornament acquired through trade. Inventories of early seventeenth-century traders included bells, beads, and cloth as trade items. Natives in many parts of southern New England

133

fashioned breastplates and gorgets out of beaten and cut brass. Jesuit rings, pendants, and other jewelry were also widely traded. By the late seventeenth century, grave furniture included trade cloth, especially wool and linen (1980:102), silver and gold trimming or braid called galloon (105), and many kinds of metal buckles, pins, and rings (Groce 1980) (see chapter 3 for a discussion of women's status and its relationship to dress).

Native men of high status were often given coats, especially red coats, by English emissaries in the seventeenth century. Perhaps this is why one of the Narragansett names for the English was wautauconuog (coatmen) (Williams 1936). Other English clothing was acquired through trade. In a letter written in 1654, Roger Williams claimed "I therefore neither brought nor shall sell [the Natives] Loose Coats or Breeches" (LaFantasie 1988:393). Interestingly, Williams was here linking the newer fashion for loose jackets and long trousers with moral degeneracy, but implying that he had previously traded in older-style English clothing (1988:394). Mary Rowlandson, captive during King Philip's War, recalled a group of Native emissaries to Philip with whom she was traveling: "they were dressed in English apparel, with hats, white neckcloths, and sashes about their waists, and ribbons on their shoulder" (Rowlandson 1913:348)." Philip himself appeared in Boston in 1673 wearing a coat, deerskin breeches, beads, and a belt (Josselyn 1833:143).Dress was also a marker for high status women. Sachem women wore furs and jewelry, and painted themselves for beauty.

Daniel Gookin, who traveled among the more remote of the Massachusett, Pawtucket, and Nipmuck Christian communities, recorded that in the late seventeenth century:

they bought a kind of cloth, called duffils, or trucking cloth, about a yard and a half wide, and for matter, made of coarse wool, in the form as our ordinary bed blankest are made, only it is put into colours, as blue, red, purple, and some use them white. Of this sort of cloth two yards make a mantle, or coat, for men and women, less for children. This is all the garment they generally use, with this addition of some little pieces of the same, or of ordinary cotton, to cover their secret parts. . . . Their ornaments are, especially the women's bracelets, necklaces, and head bands, of several sorts of beads, especially of black and white wompom, which is of most esteem among them and is accounted their chief treasure. (Gookin 1972:152)

The mantles described by Gookin were sometimes worn with leggings, called "stockings" by the English (Josselyn 1833). Eighteenth-century inventories from Natick list such leggings, as well as moccasins, in Native inventories (Bragdon 1979).

Documents in Native languages also provide some clues about everyday dress. Table 8 shows a page from John Cotton's 1666 word list, collected on Martha's Vineyard, listing clothing that was familiar to the Indian converts he spoke with there.

The list includes words for several kinds of clothing, some of English origin. However, these items were apparently common enough to have Massachusett names. In the eighteenth century, Christian Indians wore several items of English-style clothing and adopted their names as well. Josiah Cotton's 1709 word list from Plymouth (see table 9) included the following terms for clothing.

Table 8. John Cotton's 1666 Word List of Household Items and Clothing, Martha's Vineyard

Term	Cotton's English Meaning	Comparison with Narragansett	Williams's English Meaning
Ahsh8noque	A hatt	Ashónaquo	hat or cap
Mauhnake	A Coate	Maúnek	cloth, purchased cloth?
Muttasah	Stokins	Muttásash	leggings
Mahkusnah	Shoes	Mokus, mokkussin	Indian shoes

Source: Williams 1936.

Native People of Southern New England, 1650–1775

Table 9. Josiah Cotton's 1709 Word List for Items
of Clothing, Plymouth

A dress	Wawamek
A garment	Auk8onk
A hat, stokins	Onkqueekh8, muttassash
An English shirt	Choquog wittishataneek
A thin pair of breeches	Wussappineesuog etappiyaeo
A coat, a neckcloth	Petushquishauonk, kehkishin
Shoes, a shoestring	Mohkissonash, mattokquonnape

Source: Cotton 1830:16.

A survey of probate records from Native estates in Natick during the early eighteenth century show that Indian people favored garments from a variety of sources. Men wore coats, jackets, gloves, and belts, affected spectacles, and carried snuff boxes; women wore gowns, shifts, aprons, pocket cases, petticoats, and stays. Some items of Native apparel were listed as well. One Natick inventory recorded in this period also lists leggings.

The Native language will of Naomi Ommaush of Gay Head, written in 1749, carefully itemizes dresses and aprons of English cloth, which are given to various female relatives (see below). The clothing styles adopted by Indian people were a colorful and unique mixture of indigenous and adopted items, instantly recognizable, and characteristic of Native dress for the duration of the colonial period and later.

The inventory of Jonathan Micah of Nantucket included a very elaborate wardrobe of English clothing: one great coat, six flannel or quilted coats, one jacket, four shirts, one pair of stockings, six aprons, two caps, three gowns, two women's shirts, one pair of garters, six handkerchiefs, one pocket, spectacles, and one pair of moccasins (Little 1980a:87).

The account book of John Allen of Chilmark (ca. 1730–65), lists many unusual items of clothing and adornment sold to Native clients, including a beaver hat and Basalony, or Barcelona, referring to the silken handkerchiefs imported from Spain in the eighteenth century (Montgomery and Eaton 2007:154).

As English clothing became more common among them, Indian appearance still remained distinctive. Blanket or mantles, skin leggings, and moccasins continued to be common items of Native clothing (Bragdon 1979). The preference for strong colors, especially red, and the tendency to wear several different-colored garments at once was noted by a number of observers (Stiles 1916). Men and women both kept their hair long, and many, male and female, wore stone, metal, and shell jewelry. Although no descriptions of Native people of southern New England during the colonial period mention hair combs, their importance in Native costume or grooming elsewhere and their frequent occurrence with grave goods in colonial period cemeteries (Groce 1980:114) suggests they, too, had importance well into the eighteenth century.

Clothing in the colonial period thus marked several aspects of Native experience: wealth, status and gender differences, relative acceptance of Christianity, and habitual work. Long hair, and perhaps the use of hair combs of Native design, especially for men, had many sacred and secular associations and a continuing preference for distinctive hair styles set Indians apart in more ways than their English neighbors understood. The early use of items of European clothing and other ornaments as wealth to accompany the dead, or as a sacrifice for the health of the living community, suggests that they had important sacred significance, perhaps in both their substance and social associations. That they were so adopted should not be interpreted to signal a loss of Native values, but rather as a sign of complex symbolic importance, to be read only by those who could look beneath the surface. Such signaling is common among colonized people, a convenient camouflage (Comaroff and Comaroff 1991).

DWELLINGS AND OTHER SOCIAL SPACES

The range of Native dwelling types was quite wide in the late seventeenth and eighteenth centuries. In Natick, Indian's houses were described variously as huts, tents, hovels, and wigwams. William Sturtevant's reconstruction of a Niantic wigwam described by Ezra Stiles in 1764 illustrates one variation in which the Native wetu was furnished with English furniture, including a chest, chair, and table (fig. 5).

Elizabeth Little suggests that, on Nantucket, framed dwellings with open fireplaces whose smoke passed through a hole in the roof were typical of the eighteenth century, and some, notably the house at Sconset, survive in altered form today. Excavations in Mashpee suggest that some Indians living there occupied dwellings indistinguishable from earlier Native houses well into the eighteenth century. Lastly, Kevin McBride's work on the Mashantucket reservation suggests that at least some Pequots lived in English-style houses with dry laid cellars, stone animal pens, and exterior stone or brick chimneys (2005:20–21). This vernacular dwelling style survived well into the nineteenth century on Gay Head, Nantucket, and in Narragansett country (McBride and Chereau 1996; Little 1981).

Single-room dwellings, such as those described among the Niantics, and suggested in the Natick inventories, imply that Native women "kept house" as their mothers and grandmothers had done, keeping stews on the fire for any who were hungry and doing some of their cooking and food preparation outdoors.

We can arrive at some appreciation for what home meant by examining the furnishings of Native homes during the colonial period. Probate inventories from several Native communities list

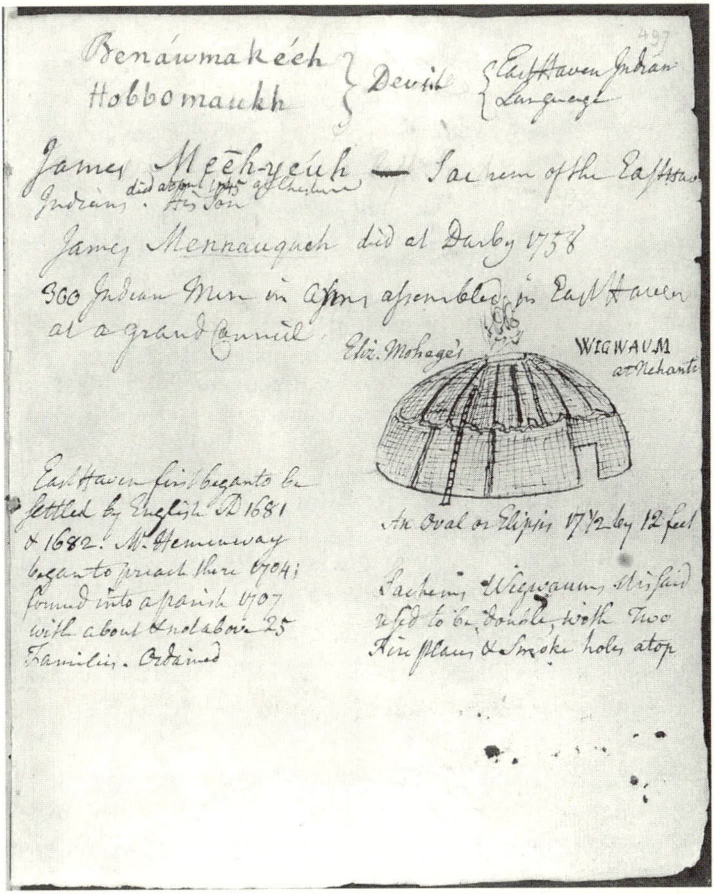
497

Benáwmakéch
Hobbomaukh } Devil { EastHaven Indian Language

James Meēh-yeuh — Sachem of the EastHaven Indians. died about 1745 at Cheshire. His Son

James Mennaugach died at Darby 1758

300 Indian Men in Arms assembled in East Haven at a grand Council.

Eliz. Mohege's WIGWAUM at Nehantic

An Oval or Elipsis 17½ by 12 feet

Sachems Wigwams tis said used to be double, with Two Fire places & Smoke holes atop

EastHaven first began to be settled by English AD 1681 & 1682. Mr. Hemmenway began to preach there 1704; formed into a parish 1707 with about & not above 25 Families. Ordained

Figure 5. Ezra Stiles's sketch of Niantic wigwams (Courtesy of the Bieneke Library, Yale University).

metal kettles, hook and tongs for hanging pots over the fire, some pottery vessels, glass bottles, and, occasionally, bags and baskets.

For example, the estate of Captain Thomas Waban of Natick, taken in 1727, with a total value of 138 pounds, lists the following:

Imp:	To Some Small Indian Books in Octavo five in number And a Salter in the English and Indian tonge Contayning the Psalms and the gospel according to St. John
Item	To a Brass kettle at 20
Item	To an Iron porrage pot with the pothooks
Item	To the wooden dishes and wooden spoons
Item	To an old barrel and two old small barks
Item	To a lott of thirty acres of land being the homestead consisting of arable land orcharding and medow and Swampie land
Item	To fifteen acres of rough, wild land
Item	to two acres of medow lying in a place called Waban medow
Item	To a grant of six acres not yet laid out
Item	to the rights in common

The "barks" listed in this and other Natick inventories were likely the boxes of birchbark described by Gookin (1677) and still made and used by many Native people in the northeast as late as the early twentieth century.

The predominance of hollow-formed ceramic vessels in inventories and on archeological sites (Savulis 1990) and the continued use of open-fire cooking suggest that roasted meats and stews were still common foods in Native communities, and most of the ceramics were used for food preparation and storage.

Spoons are the only eating utensils mentioned in the Natick inventories, and spoons of bone, antler, and wood, of trade metal, and of European manufacture, are also very common as seventeenth- and early-eighteenth-century grave offerings. They appear to have been considered valuable in Native communities, as is suggested by the 1749 will of Naomi Ommaush, who left

Zachary Hossueit, the leader and minister of the Gay Head community, seventeen pewter spoons (punneter kunnomaog). Spoons also suggest the consumption of stews and porridges, probably the common fare, as was the case in the early contact period

Merchants' account books on Martha's Vineyard and Nantucket in the early eighteenth century also indicate that Natives there traded for or purchased small tools, flour and molasses, cloth, and fishing tackle (Bragdon 1979) and owned "calashes" or boxcarts, and horses and oxen to pull them (Little 1980b).

The range of material surroundings, occupations, and subsistence practices of Native people in the colonial period in southern New England is hinted at by the three examples listed above. These solidly Native communities looked different from one another, yet shared a number of underlying similarities, which were part of what made Native life so distinctive at that time.

Archaeological evidence of domesticity and diet in Native communities indicates that shellfish remained an important food and that wild animals were hunted or caught and eaten, and the skins of deer, beaver, and other furbearing animals were processed for sale or trade. Ellen Savulis found that a Mashpee homestead site dating to the early eighteenth century included among its material remains both European and Native domestic items (1990). The Simons site, which dates from 1710–50, contained a midden and two "wigwam-like" structures and is located between two streams, on a well-drained terrace. Freshwater wetlands and inland ponds are nearby. Although glass and redware were in use, most of the tools were of stone, clearly of Native manufacture. Savulis found evidence of hearths and "food processing areas" outside the dwellings, where the remains of clam, quahog, turtle, flounder, sturgeon, and pig and bird bones were found (1990).

In nearby Hingham, the Town Brook site also shows remarkable continuity between the prehistoric settlement of the area and the early historic period. Archaeologists have discovered glass containers, smoking pipes, ceramics and beads, English flint, glass, and the remains of baskets (Mulholland, Barker, and Binzen 2005).

Analysis of the faunal remains, especially the shellfish at the Simons site suggests that it was occupied only during the summer months (Mulholland, Barker, and Binzen 2005:8). That Native people occupied the southern parts of the Massachusetts Bay and western Cape Cod area seasonally is also suggested by John and Josiah Cotton's journals. These ministers, who lived in Plymouth but preached a circuit in the Plymouth/Taunton area, also remarked the seasonal comings and goings of several groups of Native people, some of whom worked on their farm as well (Cotton 1733–48).

The concreteness and sedentism suggested by the Native inventories and deeds, and some of the archaeological remains, are belied by other descriptions of Indian life at the period. Looking back to his own childhood in the Mohegan community in the 1720s and 1730s, Samson Occom recalled that:

My parents Liv'd a wandering Life, as did all the Indians at Mohegan; they Chiefly Depended upon Hunting, Fishing, & Fowling for their Living and had no Connections with the English, excepting to Traffic with them, in their Small Trifles; and they Strictly maintained and followed their Heathenish Ways, Customs, and Religion, though there was some Preaching among them. (Blodgett 1935:27)

How to reconcile this view with the community-centered approach taken in this study will be discussed in chapter 7.

Eighteenth-century Native language deeds from Martha's Vineyard document some changes in Native land use and economy, reflected in the words introduced into the language for new concepts, animals, and plants. English loanwords include those for cows, sheep, and horses, barley and wheat, land measurement

142

(bounds, acres, meadows, commons, and shares) and money (Bragdon 1981a:67–68). Elizabeth Little has shown, however, that Nantucket sachems were successful in preserving Indian lands from encroachment by the English by adopting the concept of commons and shares so that Indians retained grazing rights even on land that had been sold to the English (Little 1996).

While the nature of Native landholding in the period prior to English colonization is still much debated, it is clear that all colonial Native communities sought land over which they had sovereignty as a community and it was rarely subdivided. This open system allowed for seasonal movement and for unlimited access to all resources. It is possible, in fact, that communal land tenure was an adaptation to increasingly limited territories, which encouraged the continuing preference for single-sex work parties over nuclear-family based production.

WOMEN'S SPACE, WOMEN'S WORK

A visitor to Mashpee in 1809 remarked that the houses and outdoor spaces of wigwam compounds seemed to be occupied exclusively by women and girls (Kendall 1809:179–80, 182). Women's work spaces in Native southern New England were generally described as domestic, and their work revolved around the gathering and processing of foods, especially shellfish, wild plants, berries, and nuts, and the maintenance and harvesting of corn. If, as Mary Beth Williams and Jeffrey Bendremer suggest, movements to different resource locations were determined by women's work schedules (1997) in the late Woodland period, this pattern appears to have continued in the colonial period as well.

Steven Mrozowski's excavations at the Sandy's Point site on Cape Cod, with material dating to the first half of the seventeenth century, fit Champlain's descriptions of scattered summer dwellings surrounded by corn fields (Mrozowski 1994). Savulis's excavations at Mashpee, for a site dating at least a century later, show similar seasonal patterning (1990). These outdoor work spaces are also significant in the distribution and amount of lithic scatter, as if tools were being manufactured on the site. While most analyses assume men fashioned tools, their frequency at these two summer sites suggest women may also have knapped stone.

Among the most significant of women's work was the processing of plants for food and medicine. Much of this work involved the use of mortars and pestles, the quintessential women's tools. Depressions in prominent rocks near many prehistoric sites in southern New England were used for mortars. Movable mortars were also made of steatite and accompanied by heavy stone mortars. Surviving historic period mortars from southern New England are all of wood, carved out of log sections, and workable from a standing position (Willoughby 1935). These mortars and the pestles used with them are of serviceable and sturdy design.

The ground stone and explicitly phallic effigy pestles found exclusively with women in historic period cemeteries also suggest the symbolic importance of women's work, which was transformative as well as nurturing (Nassaney 2004). The transformative theme in women's work in southern New England is also marked in the production and use of rush mats, used to cover wigwams, decorate their interiors, and to wrap the dead, and the richly symbolic shells from which wampum and other "wealth" was made. These effigy pestles also had an obvious association with fertility, both in their phallic shape and in their use with seeds. The effigy heads also linked women's work to the supernatural realm of manitou, who were said to include a "Woman's God" (Williams 1936:124).

In the Christian communities, women were also associated with the homesteads, although it is unclear whether women continued to be the primary caretakers of gardens. In Natick, for example, both male and female proprietors were allotted fields, swamp, and meadow land, and some were distant from the dwellings.

In common with other women in the colonial New World, the estates of women of Natick were not often inventoried apart from those of their male relatives. Hannah Speen, heir of proprietor Samuel Will and wife of John Speen, a member of an "old proprietor" family of Natick, had the following items in her estate upon her death in 1742:

books
wearing apparel
bedding
pewter
earthenware and glass bottles
iron ware
woodenware
one old berth (*sic*) mettal skillet
baskets and bookes, brombs and brombsticks
one knife
two old chests
6 chairs
Wampan and suckonhock [purple or "black" wampum]
(MDX docket #00016)

Some of these same items (chests, chairs, and wampum) appeared in the inventory of Moses Speen, a kinsman of John's who died in 1749 (MDX docket #21036). As Jean O'Brien points out, John Speen and his wife lived in an "English-style house" (1998:136–37). But the curation of wampum also resonates with more traditional associations with other high-status Indians.

Perhaps more representative of a Native woman's estate in Natick was that of Mary Pognit, who died in 1760. She owned a Bible and other books, a blanket, a shift, an apron, an old pot, and an old chest (MDX 1760).

Natick women in the eighteenth century supported themselves and their families by making and selling baskets and brooms, and through the rental on land holdings elsewhere. Women could and did own land in Natick and had access to shares in orchards, meadow, and "unimproved" properties within the town boundaries. In the absence of husbands, brothers, and sons, or if the men declined to work in the fields, women were probably the farmers in Natick as well, although some also leased out their Natick holdings to non-Indians, or left their holdings fallow (O'Brien 1998:132).

Foodways

Among those aspects of culture most persistent in the face of assimilative pressure are foodways, "the whole interrelated system of food conceptualization, procurement, distribution, preservation, preparation, and consumption shared by all members of a particular group" (Anderson 1972:2). Scholarship in anthropology and folklore has drawn attention to the importance of foodways in the dynamics of ethnic identity and ethnic group boundary maintenance (Keller Brown and Mussell 1984). Thus this important dimension of cultural tradition provides a logical point of departure in examining the question of Native cultural distinctiveness in southern New England during the late seventeenth and eighteenth centuries.

At least eighty species of fish and shellfish were mentioned in seventeenth-century descriptions of Native fauna in southern New England, many of which the Indians exploited for food (Bennett 1955:385–86). Thirty kinds of birds and at least ten types of animals were also part of the Native diet (1955:386). The period of greatest scarcity would have been late spring and early summer, although shellfish and fresh-water fish should still have been plentiful in most areas (1955). Stored grains and dried legumes and squash compensated for shortages of other foods in most coastal regions, and some Native communities had enough stored surplus to trade (Winslow 1624:133; Williams 1936:95).

146

Yet the extent to which the Natives of the region continued to rely on horticulture in the later colonial period is unclear. The island soils, primarily of glacial till, could never have been as productive as those of the mainland, where the established presence of Native agriculture is also problematic (Bragdon 1996; Williams and Bendremer 1997).

Surviving Native probate records suggest that many aspects of the transplanted English agricultural complex were ignored. Dairying, for example, was not a large part of the Christian Native economy, nor was the keeping of poultry or swine (Little 1980a). Evidence from several sources suggests that the Natives raised sheep, kept horses, and in general maintained small gardens for their own use in which traditional Native crops such as corn, squash, pumpkins, tobacco, and beans were grown (Freeman 1807a:35, 93; Allen 1730; Macy 1835:35).

As in the early contact period, Native diet on the islands in the eighteenth century was heavily dependent on fish, both fresh and salt, shellfish, wild animals, and plants, all of which supplemented the cultivated crops and, later, purchased foodstuffs. These food sources were of course available only seasonally, and their continued use ensured that the Native subsistence practices resembled in many ways the pattern of the early historic period.

Some documentation for this pattern is in the form of account books from Nantucket and Martha's Vineyard.[1] Beginning in the 1670s and 1680s, merchants on both islands employed Indians to

1. For this study, five account books were examined, three from Nantucket (Barnard 1706)—Mary and Nathaniel Starbuck (1662–1757) and Richard Macy (1714–33)—and two from Martha's Vineyard—Allen (1730) and Look (1780–1820).These account books were chosen both for their early dates (1660–1820) and because each was primarily concerned with Indian accounts. They describe accounts with roughly three hundred individuals, many recorded by both month and year.

147

provide commodities such as fish, feathers, and grains, which they in turn sold to English residents and off-islanders. The account books also demonstrate, albeit in a negative manner, that the Natives had little dependence on purchased foodstuffs during the late seventeenth and early eighteenth centuries, and then only seasonally.

Most food purchases were of fresh meat in the fall and winter, and the heaviest purchases of grain were in the spring, presumably both seed grains and stores to tide them over until the first harvest. Beef and mutton provided additional animal protein to the Native diet, which may have been deficient as early as 1680 as the supply of wild game on the island, never plentiful, diminished. Joanne Bowen's study of account books from Suffield, Connecticut, identified similar patterns of food purchase and exchange, and she argues that these reflect adjustment to seasonal availability of resources as well as a form of community insurance against times of scarcity (Bowen 1984).

RESIDENCE AND COMMUNITY

Although community life for Native people varied throughout the colonial period for some, it came to focus on the otanash (towns) into which they were born or married, or were drawn to out of religious conviction or for asylum. The towns themselves were also variable, some only temporarily occupied, others taking shape slowly over time, while a few were the creations of colonial officials who "granted" land to certain groups, wherein Indian occupation was grudgingly tolerated.

Much of what we know about these Indian towns is derived from archaeological data, most of which was collected after 1980. This data raises many questions about the nature of cultural and social change and the way it is reflected in material remains.

As discussed in the introduction to this volume, John Eliot's energetic missionary program included the establishment of a number

148

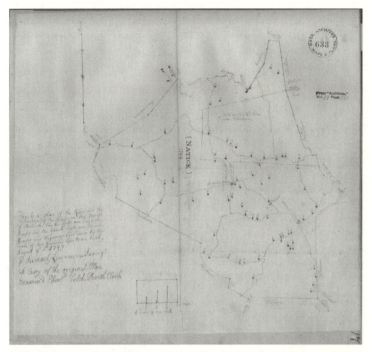

Figure 6. Livermore's map of Natick, 1749, vol. 33: 17, Massachusetts State Archives (Courtesy of the Commonwealth of Massachusetts).

of "praying towns"—mission settlements where Indian converts to Christianity might live. Seven of these were established between 1651 and 1660, including Natick, Punkapoag, Hassanamesitt, Okommakamesit, Wamesit, Nashoba, and Magunkaquog (Carlson 1986). However, Catherine Carlson suggests that "the model English-style Indian town envisioned by Eliot, consisting of neatly laid out streets aligned with English frame houses in a nucleated village pattern, may have been largely unachieved [at Natick]" (Carlson 1986:26) (fig. 6). Extensive archaeological survey of Eliot's first utopian Indian community, as well as extensive documentary

149

research, give us important insights into the appearance of Natick and the daily life of its inhabitants (Bragdon 1979, 1981a, 1988; Brenner 1984; Mandell 1997; O'Brien 1998).

In 1651, the settlement of Natick was laid out near the bridge over the Charles River built by Indian converts the previous year. According to Daniel Gookin's account, Natick was laid out with:

three long streets; two on the north side of the river; and one, on the south; with house lots to every family. There is a handsome large fort, of a round figure, palisaded with trees; and a foot bridge over the river, in the form of an arch, the foundation of which is secured with stone. There is also one large house built after the English manner. The lower room is a large hall, which serves for a meeting house, on the Lord's Day, and a school house on the week days. The upper room is a kind of wardrobe, where the Indians hand up their skins, and other things of value. In a corner of this room Mr. Eliot has an apartment partitioned off, with a bead and bedstead in it. (Gookin 1972:181)

Gookin added further, "their other houses in this town are generally after their old mode" (1972:181). Natick Indians laid out plots according to an open field plan (Bragdon 1981a), including planting fields, and orchards (Eliot 1671). Contemporary descriptions and the so-called Cheney map indicate that dwellings and planting fields were located on both sides of the Charles River (Carlson 1986:31) and the meeting house was along the easternmost boundary between Natick and the neighboring town of Dedham. A burial ground was also located adjacent to the meeting house, much disturbed in the nineteenth century (Brenner 1980). Archaeological testing in the vicinity of the meetinghouse has not uncovered any wigwam or other dwelling remains. Elise Brenner, in particular, suggests that this absence implies Native resistance to conversion, or deliberate falsehood on the part of Eliot and other English apologists for the missionary program in southern New England. An alternative explanation, of course, is that Native dwellings were located near planting fields and away from the burying ground as they were in traditional communities. Wigwams built "without a single nail" are also less visible archaeologically (Carlson 1986:33–34). As Carlson also points out, several likely areas of settlement have not yet been tested, and much disturbance in the area of the old town may also have destroyed such evidence.

After King Philip's War, those Indians who survived incarceration on Deer Island returned to Natick, where they again erected mat-covered wigwams (Dunton 1867:108–9) and resumed planting. Native population at Natick fluctuated during the next half century and gradually became dispersed as English settlers acquired Indian lands in the old town. Probate records and Native-language town records dating to the first quarter of the eighteenth century illustrate that the Native residents were participating in social networks that revolved around land, its allotment, and the church, and they were governed by a group of prominent Christian leaders (Bragdon 1979, 1981a, 1988).

Natick town records begin in 1700, forty years after King Philip's War. In the hand of Captain Thomas Waban, they detail many aspects of life in that community. Landmarks including the stone fort, the meeting house, the spring, and the river orient the allotments, and the proprietorship structure, established in the 1660s, is still functioning, as allotments are passed from father to son back, in some cases, to the original members of the community. It is important to note, however, that these allotments continued to be approved by the community as a whole.

Scholars including Daniel Mandell (1997) and Jean O'Brien (1998) have described the gradual decline of the Natick population and their victimization by English settlers and colonial administrators. However, town records in the Native language, as well as probate records of the Native inhabitants of Natick, provide an intimate glimpse of Natick life in the late seventeenth and early eighteenth centuries that suggests that some aspects of

151

Natick Indian life were still lived on Native terms. Land was laid out for planting, for orchards, and for pasturage. The small number of cattle listed in the inventories suggests that plows and draft animals were shared or that some land was cultivated in the old way, using only hoes. The palisaded fort was evidently allowed to fall into disuse, but the bridge was maintained, probably by the Englishmen who operated the nearby grain mill. There are also several mentions of the weir, still an important community asset. By the mid-eighteenth century, the settlement was more dispersed. The Livermore map of 1749 (see fig. 6, p. 149) clearly locates the positions of Native dwellings and suggests that Indian settlement had scattered as English landholders gained more influence in the community. The so-called meeting house dispute wrested the church from Native control, and the Indians found themselves resented guests in their own church. While this enabled the dispossession of some land holders, it is also true that many Native families represented at Natick had ties to other communities in Worcester County and near Woodstock, Connecticut. Natick should be understood as a physical locality, not necessarily a social one; that community in part rematerialized elsewhere in the mid-to-late eighteenth century.

The extensive excavations carried out by Kevin McBride on the Mashantucket reservation also document a range of housing types, as well as a mixed subsistence with reliance on wild food and game (1994a). McBride documents two distinctive domestic patterns on the reservation. One, associated with the part of the reservation known as "Indiantown," had framed houses resembling English settlements of the period. The other, linked to a more diffuse settlement, was made up of wigwams, underground storage pits, and other indigenous features. This fascinating difference clearly reflects differing attitudes toward the adoption of English material goods and, no doubt, ideologies as well. McBride reports that many of the inhabitants of

Indian town left Connecticut to follow Samson Occom in 1775 (McBride 2005).

In contrast to Natick, the frontier praying town of Magun-kaquog, occupied between 1660 and 1750, appears to have been little more than a frontier "beach head" in the still largely Native-occupied territory of what is now central and western Massachu-setts. Recent documentary work on this town suggests, however, that it served also as an outpost of the Natick community (Herb-ster 2002), perhaps providing Natick residents with access to game and fish unavailable within the settled bounds of that Chris-tian community. Archaeological excavations there in 1997 and 1998 reveal a single cellar hole with the ruins of an exterior chim-ney associated with artifacts dating to the late seventeenth and early eighteenth century. These included items of both English and Native origin, such as gunflints reused as strike-a-lights, nat-ural crystals, pendants, repaired metal pots, and reworked metal tools. Interestingly, the majority of European materials postdate King Philip's War, a time when many of the outlying Native pray-ing towns are thought to have been abandoned (Mrozowski et al. 2005).

The praying town at Hassanimisco, the third praying town established by John Eliot, was located in an area of Native settle-ment, and it was also resettled after King Philip's War. Prelimi-nary archaeological investigations conducted in 2003 identified a terraced cobblestone feature, which may have been an animal pen, as well as a cellar hole similar to that excavated at Magun-kaquog. Alternatively, the cobblestone feature may have served a public function, perhaps as a meeting house, possibly John Eliot's Church, the second one established in a Native praying town (Bonner and Herbster 2005).

Native settlements were tied to the westernmost region of the New England mission outpost at Chabunagungamaog through-out the eighteenth century, and the Society for the Propagation of the Gospel continued to fund a Native teacher and, later, an English minister. This community also had ties to Hassanimisco and Natick, particularly through the Peagan family (Baron, Hood, and Izard 1996).

When Ezra Stiles visited Mashpee in 1762, he found a population of about 250 people, in seventy-five families, living in sixty wigwams and six houses. Jack Campisi notes that settlement at Mashpee clustered at Ashumuit Pond, Santuit Pond, and South Cape (1991:86). Campisi also notes that "the dwellings on the map closely approximate the location of the so-called ancient ways, the early pathways used by the Mashpee" (86). But by 1767, the number of English-style houses had greatly increased. Mark Nicholas attributes this to the earnings of Native men in the whaling industry and their efforts to assert their independence from overseers who tried to determine their fate. Nicolas also notes that Mashpees refused to allow whites to dominate their meetinghouse and paid for pews near the front. Gideon Hawley wrote that they would "give anything for the privilege of a pew because they elevate them to the highest status in the meeting house" (cited in Nicholas 2002:180).

Likewise, the Native community at Gay Head was not a centralized village in the late seventeenth and early eighteenth centuries. Samuel Sewell, who visited the community in 1709, described it as "Orderly settled, a school kept, and God's Word preached to them every Lord's Day" (Kellaway 1961:219).

There were fifty-eight dwellings there, mainly wigwams, along with some framed houses, barns, and animal pens. A 1776 map of the community (DesBarres 1776) shows clusters of settlement including one east of Occouch Pond, and another further to the south (McBride and Cherau 1996). Suzanne Cherau speculates that such clustering was part of a "highly dispersed pattern of small clusters of dwellings on relatively large tracts of land" (McBride and Cherau 1996; see also Freeman 1807a).

Native language deeds, wills, and other documents dating from the eighteenth century indicated that houses, especially framed houses, were passed down between generations, as were particular plots of land. In the early eighteenth century, Indian settlements had consolidated at Christiantown, Gay Head, and Chappaquiddick, where each maintained a meeting house and, usually, a school (see McBride and Cherau 1996; Herbster and Cherau 2002).

By the end of the seventeenth century, Native settlement on Nantucket had coalesced into four communities on the eastern side of the island: Gibbs Pond, Squam, and Polpis, and Miacomet near Sherbourne. These communities contained a mixture of framed houses and wigwams, many of which were transformed into "whaling houses" during the growth of that industry on Nantucket. Little argues persuasively that several such houses survive on Nantucket today (see also Largy and Rainey 2005, and Rainey 2005).

The pattern of dispersed clusters of settlement was repeated with some variations on the Mashantucket and Pequot reservations at Mashantucket and Lantern Hill. As noted above, excavations at the Mashantuck reservation reveal a variety of house types, including wigwams, and framed dwellings with half cellars, animal pens, and a number of other features, hearths, and pits (possibly for storage). Among the most interesting aspects of the Indian Town excavations are the food remains, which include a variety of wild and domesticated animals, and an unusually large proportion of remains of edible roots and tubers (McBride personal communication 2000).

At Mohegan, Jeffrey Bendremer excavated the Uncas's spring cabin site, said to be the residence of the renowned sachem Uncas, dating to the end of the seventeenth century. Bendremer found evidence of continued occupation of that site throughout the eighteenth century as well. Unlike many of the dwellings excavated elsewhere in New England, the Uncas's spring cabin site was unquestionably a framed dwelling, with window glass, nails, and other building materials dominating the material assemblage (Williams and Bendremer 1997).

ENTANGLED OBJECTS: BEYOND ACCULTURATION

The facts of possession as reflected in probate inventories and other historical documents do not, as was implied in earlier acculturation models, tell us much about the cultural and social significance such objects had. Nor do occupational patterns necessarily imply a single pattern of social relationships among Native peoples. Local language communities also had a local materiality that can be investigated in similar ways. Nicholas Thomas's idea of "entangled objects," which places objects at the center of social webs that emerged during colonial encounters or subsequent cohabitation, will be employed in this section. The following case study illustrates the complexities of the Native entanglement with English objects, and the social life of the objects in Indian communities (1991).

The aforementioned will of Naomi Ommaush, a woman with ties to several important families on Gay Head in the eighteenth century, illustrates the complex relations among family and leadership in the Indian community on Gay Head and nicely links these relationships with material life. This will, probated in 1749, is written for Naomi Ommaush by Zachariah Hossueit, minister of the Gay Head Congregational church, who was fluent in English and Massachusett, who himself was part of the family of the principal sachem of Takemmey and of the sachem Mittark of Gay Head.

Naomi Ommaush's spouse was Nehemiah Ommaush, otherwise known as Nehemiah Able, one of many in that prolific and prominent family who shared both a sachem family heritage and a place in the newer Christian community. Nehemiah was the minister and teacher on Slocum's island and an employee of the

Society for the Propagation of the Gospel. He died in 1744 at an advanced age. Naomi's family name is uncertain, but the people she lists in her will show many connections to one another and reflect a tightly linked set of families, among whom leadership was equally dependent on status within the Native Christian church and to ties to hereditary sachem lines. This will and one other are the only two Native-language wills from Gay Head, and each is concerned with moveable property. Naomi Ommaush's will is interesting because it contains reference to three different classes of kin relationships, none of which can be identified with certainty (see chapter 1). The genealogical relations described in Naomi Ommaush's will suggest that while she appears to have been childless, she was nevertheless linked to several families through ties of kinship and affect.

Among these linkages are four principal extended families or lineages. Each of these lines is headed by a man who was tied directly to the two principal sachem lineages of the western end of the island, the Ompahinnit and Keateanum lines. Two others are linked to prominent ohtaskouau (councilors), especially Abel Wauwompaquin and Yonohomoh. These four lines are also interconnected. Abel Wauwompaquin and Ompahinnit were brothers, sons of the Massachusetts Bay sachem Nohtooksaet (Segal and Pierce 2003:602). Another brother, Mittark, was sachem of Gay Head. Keteanumun was the son of the sachem Maukutoquet and ruled over the Takemmey region of Martha's Vineyard. Kishquish (or Kesuckquish) was a sachem at Chilmark, as was his brother Towtooe, whom he succeeded.

Naomi Ommaush left three dresses (nuttogk8), one of blue calico (oneyeu Conneko), and a petticoat (patukkoot) to female relatives, and some red cloth or a coat (numonag ne masquaq) to a male kinsman (Goddard and Bragdon 1988:53–55). The most valuable gift, however, was a collection of pewter spoons, which she left to the minister Zachary Hossueit.

Looking at the document that is the will, we can see it, too, as representative of the social ties that bound these Christian Natives in the mid-eighteenth century. Store-bought clothing and blankets, relatively expensive items on store inventories of that period, were also personal and intimate gifts. According to the will above, it would seem that they were distributed widely among various classes of relatives, none of them direct. The relatives in this category were known as "nuttawam." Another category, perhaps included in her natal family line, was known as "nuttawaeh" (see chapter 1). It thus appears that both extended families and lineages were significant to Naomi socially, and those linkages were part of what animated and maintained this community.

Among the English residents of Martha's Vineyard, as elsewhere in New England, pewter objects were increasingly common in inventories in the late seventeenth century and into the early eighteenth century. Ann Smart Martin estimates that the American market was saturated with pewter products by the mid-eighteenth century (1989:8). Pewter plates and implements had an important role in the foodways complex of the colonial period, and also had a prominent place as displayable goods. In addition, pewter is durable and its value remained relatively stable, even when damaged. Even colonists of the lower economic strata were able to obtain some pewter, which they displayed with pride. A traveler's account from rural Connecticut in 1744, for example, lists a display of pewter in a small log dwelling, indicating, according to the writer "an inclination to finery among these poor people" (cited in Bridenbaugh 1982:55).

However, in fashionable and wealthy households among the English, pewter was gradually being replaced by ceramics, particularly as the tea ritual became important in the social life in the colonies (Bridenbaugh 1982) by the middle of the eighteenth century. Such data suggest that pewter became less valued in English homes through time, and may have "migrated" to food preparation and storage as well as into the hands of servants and slaves (Martin 1989:21–22).

At first glance we might assume that Naomi Ommaush, a well-connected member of the ruling and Christian elite in her community, had kept her spoons as proof of her material success, which reflected her adoption of the standards of her English neighbors. But how did she acquire them? The John Allen account book, detailing hundreds of purchases made by Native residents there during the same period, lists no pewter items of any kind. Furthermore, Naomi Ommaush never appears on the list of Allen's clients. Elizabeth Little notes that, for a similar time period on Nantucket, only one Native man had any pewter in his inventory (1980a).

Evidence from other sources shows that pewter and metal objects such as pots were sometimes given as payment to Native Christian ministers and teachers on Martha's Vineyard, perhaps as the value of such objects declined among the English (Society for the Propagation of the Gospel daybooks 1715–35). It may be that these items came to represent the important role that the Christian missions had in Native life there, as well as marking the status of Native Christian leaders. Unbreakable, nonperishable objects were likewise capable of curation, so that they came to represent a family's longevity. If such objects were no longer to be buried with the deceased, they nonetheless represented links between generations and the spiritual powers represented by people in positions of authority in the Native Christian church. If these spoons had been given to Naomi's husband to mark his role in the Native Christian community, it may be that Naomi's subsequent bequest to Zachariah Hossueit acknowledged Hossueit's similar role. Another interpretation may be that the spoons represented a kind of community wealth, and the gift to the local leader was recognition of his role as representative of the social group.

159

The spoons, although of English origin, were known by a Native term, a term of intimate possession, and one gendered "animate." Other such animate terms included those for "pipe," and "knife." The gender of objects in Algonquian languages is both a formal and a cognitive category, reflecting the widespread belief in a physical world endowed with power and life. Items of intimate ownership were also frequently gendered animate perhaps to reflect the extension of one's own being. The possibility that this animateness was also referenced in Naomi Ommaush's gift to Zachariah Hossueit illustrates the many ways that objects are entangled in social relationships and belief systems. This reinforces our sense that, while the content of Native wardrobes and households changed, the underlying principles of organization did not.

RECIPROCITY, EXCHANGE, AND OTHER ECONOMIC RELATIONSHIPS

The patterns of pre-contact labor and economic relationships glimpsed in the earliest descriptions of southern New England Native life began to change everywhere within years or decades of the first trading contacts. The labor system based on kin ties and the authority of sachems was undermined because of severe disruptions due to heavy population loss. The loss of territories also destroyed the principal foundation of the sachem's power and influence. Native men and women were drawn into the maritime trades that brought so much wealth to English settlers and, in some cases, made English success at these endeavors possible. One of the most dramatic examples of this comes from Nantucket and, to a lesser extent, from Martha's Vineyard, during the developmental period of the deep-sea whaling industry. Native labor became highly desirable for the long voyages and for the more menial of the tasks associated with whaling. To conscript Native labor, Nantucket and Martha's Vineyard merchants resorted to many stratagems, fair and foul (Vickers 1983:571–74;

Byers 1987:95–96). During this period, Native labor was also put to use for other purposes, with merchants "trading" Native laborers among themselves. Mary and Richard Starbuck's account book, for example, documents an almost yearly round of day labor, sandwiched between whaling voyages, for several Natives during the period 1726–60.

The changes in Nantucket whaling technology and in the market for its products were responsible for the change in the relationship between the Natives and the merchants, both because Native labor was now more valuable than the previous products of that labor had been and also because the merchants themselves became more specialized, concentrating more of their resources in the maritime industries and less on the sale of goods to the islanders. The specialized nature of the Nantucket economy in the eighteenth century severely affected the Natives' ability to maintain a traditional seasonal subsistence pattern. After 1726, there is little evidence that any Natives were employed regularly in supplying fish, feathers, and grain. At the same time, the Indians were enmeshed in debt peonage to the merchants and were forced to depend to a greater extent on purchased food supplies as well as upon hired labor to plow and tend their own fields.

The disruption of the Native economy, especially on Nantucket, resulting from these changes was exacerbated by concerted efforts on the part of the English to dispossess the Indians and to circumscribe their mobility and independence. Native men were forced to endure long absences from home and women were also forced into domestic servitude in expiation of debt and misdemeanor. Inability to maintain a balanced, mixed subsistence base year round led to increased dependence on purchased goods, driving many unfortunate Natives further into debt.

The effects of these economic changes on the Native community on Nantucket must have been severe, although they are not easy to document. Men's absence for long periods left families to

161

fend for themselves. Heavy farm work and fishing, two male tasks in the seventeenth century, were necessarily neglected or left to hired help. Women's absence from the home put a strain on their ability to provide clothing for their families, resulting in greater dependence on purchased goods. As historian Daniel Vickers has noted, the Natives were vulnerable to exploitation and the very nature of their relationship with non-Natives reinforced their domination (1983:581).

Vickers's convincing analysis of the institutionalization of debt peonage among the Indians of Nantucket, emphasizing the strategies employed by the English, is less complete in describing Native response. For many of the Natives of Nantucket and Martha's Vineyard, life during the great expansion of deep sea whaling probably continued much as before. Even at the peak of Native participation, no more than one out of three adult males among the Native Nantucketers appears to have been actively engaged at sea, with the others participating in ancillary industries on shore.[2] Based on the surviving account books from Nantucket during that period, the absolute number of Indians associated with particular traders decreased through time, even as the percentage of time spent in expiating debt increased per individual. Table 10 summarizes the numbers of Natives recorded in Mary and Richard Starbuck's account book by decade.

Part of this decrease reflects the general decline of population among the Indians, from approximately eight hundred in 1700 to 358 in 1763 (Macy 1835:58). Yet it also seems to reflect the increased specialization of the whaling merchants and their decreased involvement with the wider Native population.

2. This figure is based on surviving records of whaling crews prorated by total Native populations on the islands for the period 1730–1800. Sources include: Freeman 1807:94, Macy 1792b:159, as well as Vickers's own figures (1981:569).

Table 10. Number of Natives Recorded
in Starbuck's Account Book by Decade

1680–1700	122
1700–20	34
1722–40	17
1740–60	12

Coincidental to this process was the development of patron-client relationships between the wealthy whaling merchants and a number of Natives, such that some were able to maintain long overdue debts that the traders forbore to collect on, no doubt because of their desire to control the skills of the Natives involved. The accounts of the Native Eben Smugg, for example, were often as much as 40 pounds overdue per year, a situation which Starbuck seems to have tolerated in exchange for control over Smugg's skills as a joyner and carpenter (Starbuck and Starbuck 1662–1757:19, 37). This personalized form of clientage was, as Stephen Innes found in seventeenth-century Springfield, "restrictive, but not destructive" (1983:66), and allowed the client Natives some latitude in debt.

Even in the face of great economic pressure, strategies employed by the Natives to maintain a measure of autonomy, to preserve a sense of community identity, and to resist absorption into the lower classes of Anglo-American society included the maintenance of traditional foodways. Account books from Martha's Vineyard document the continued use of Native crops (Allen 1730), and probate records list a varied inventory of "productive goods" employed by the Natives in the mid-eighteenth century in the pursuit of fish, game, and wild foods (Little 1980a; Bragdon 1979).

While most histories of the colonial period focus on economic relations between Indians and non-Indians and on the frequently destructive effects of those relations, the exchanges between and among the Natives themselves are less well studied. These relations must have structured daily life in colonial Native communities, and both mediated and naturalized the material effects of colonization. This book differs from others that describe the place of Native people in the proto-capitalist economy of the region in that the focus is on the "experience" of capitalist relations within Native communities.

While most Native people chose or were forced to work for English employers (see also chapter 6), at least on a part time basis, a small number of Native men kept account books, from which we can learn something about Indians as employers. It appears that ranking individuals in the early contact period had servants and slaves (Williams 1936) and that captives served that purpose in the later seventeenth century (Rowlandson 1682), and while to be a sachem's man was to be his or her assistant, counselor, and factotum, employment and exchange relationships between men and women of equal rank is an aspect of Native social relations about which very little is known.

The lost diary of Paul Mannasses (ca. 1718), for example, recorded payments in foodstuffs to Native day laborers. On Nantucket, the weaver and tailor Netowah's journal lists several Indian clients or debtors to whom he sold or exchanged power and shot, woven cloth, or plowing hard ground in exchange for feathers (Manasses ca. 1718) (fig. 7). These diaries and journals suggest that some economic relationships were modeled after English apprenticeships, indentured servitude, and day employment, rather than according to older models of kinship obligations and joint work parties that varied seasonally. These relationships (now referred to in terms of debt and payment) had previously been framed using metaphors of family and affection. However, the system hinted at in these documents still existed simultaneously with patterns of tribute payment and lineage exchange networks.

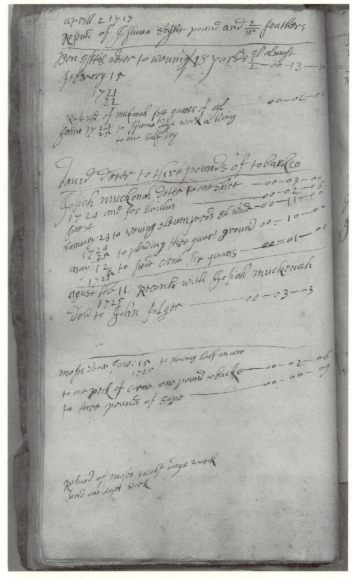

Figure 7. Netowah's 1719 journal (Courtesy of the Nantucket Historical Association).

A number of Native men on Nantucket were engaged in trades that brought them into contact with both Indians and English-men and women. Elizabeth Little identified ten individuals who were engaged in such trades as carpentry, weaving, teaching, and both whale fishing and heavy agricultural work (1980a).

In order to protect themselves from the exploitative terms required by whites in the whale fishing industry, some Indians tried to establish their own businesses. A pair of Potawaumacuts petitioned the General Court for the right to run their own boats from Billingsgate. One of these, Samuel Cooke, oversaw white crewmembers (Nicholas 2002:171).

Claims by English missionaries that shamanic practices had dis-appeared in Christian communities were common by the end of the seventeenth century (Mayhew 1694), yet Native people in those communities, both men and women, continued to effect cures.

A Native language document written in 1763, for example, reads:

I, Jonahauwossuit, and my wife began attending on March 29, regarding Moses Bomut being medicated concerning his gonor-rhea. Every day in April, except two he went elsewhere. Next the month of May also, all of it, we attended to the medicating of Moses, every day with enough medicines until the end of May. Next in June, . . . we cured Moses Bomut. (Goddard and Bragdon 1988:221)

Jonahawossuit and wife charged 6L sterling for this cure (God-dard and Bragdon 1988:221).

The will of Natick man John Wamsquon left five acres of meadow, his household belongings, and the pay for half a mare, in addition to twelve acres of land "where my wigwam stands" to his daughter Elizabeth Pumhammon alias Runnimarsh "partly in consideration of her nursing me" (MDX 23688:1746).

The downward spiral of Native populations in the colonial period left many people without heirs, close family members, or means of support in their old age or illness. However, there is no evidence that either Bomut or Wamsquon were indigent or alone during their illnesses. Records from the New England Company in the colonial period list several payments to white doctors for visits to ailing Natives (Kellaway 1962:235). As well, it remains likely that Indians also consulted and paid for cures by specialists in their own communities. This may also explain the widespread evidence for Native doctors and "doctresses" in southern New England in the eighteenth and nineteenth centuries (McBride and Prins 1996).

The things that Indians used and the activities they engaged in during the colonial period were invested with social and cultural meanings as described above. They were implicated in the negotiations and transformations of Native life during the colonial period and representative of social ambiguity and multivocality, also found in linguistic complexity (see chapter 2). In the next chapter, the adoption of Christianity and literacy in some Native communities in southern New England, adds detail to this complex story.

6.

Christianity and Literacy

Many Native people in southeastern New England, principally Pokanokets or Wampanoags and Nipmucks, adopted Christianity in the seventeenth century, and many of them became literate in their own languages. But instead of beginning this study with analysis of the impact of Protestant missionaries in the region, I introduce this topic now, when other dimensions of these communities have been laid out. This is because the emphasis on conversion in previous work implies a widespread cultural transformation that, ironically (in light of the role of introduced Christianity in the adoption of Native language literacy), is belied by the Native writings themselves. This study looks at Christianity and literacy in terms of its role in Native communities, even in those outside the major sphere of English missionary activity.

The mission to the Indians in New England has been the subject of many historical studies (Ronda 1981; Van Lonkhuyzen 1989; Cogley 1999; and others). Scholarly judgments have varied about the efficacy of this effort, but most have focused on the ways the adoption of Christianity undermined Native worldview and community structure. Alternatively, the missionary literature is taken to represent English attitudes toward the Indians, which were predictably ethnocentric. I differ with scholars who argue that Christianity meant the end of "Native" life in the region; much evidence shows that the situation was more subtle and complex than that. This chapter discusses Christianity as it functioned in Indian communities, and, in particular, its role in the spread of Native language literacy. Christianity also became a central factor in community life and the linkages among communities in eastern Massachusetts Bay and Plymouth colonies in the colonial period. Native Christianity is best addressed through the words of converts, in the context of the most remarkable "product" of Christianity, Native vernacular literacy.

Missionary work in New England was funded by an English missionary society known as the Society for the Propagation of the Gospel, or the New England Company (Kellaway 1962; Bragdon 1981a, 1991). Through its support, missionaries were paid to teach and preach, Native converts were paid to govern, and missionary literature, including many linguistic works, was made available.

A complete discussion of the premises of the English mission to the Indians is beyond the scope of this book, and the missionaries' beliefs and work have been thoroughly covered by other authors. The following is only a summary of the ideas expressed in their writings.

John Eliot, the "apostle to the Indians" began missionary work soon after his arrival in Boston, and continued for the rest of his long life to work among Indian communities in the Massachusetts Bay and westward into Nipmuck territories. His writings emphasize his acceptance of the responsibility that Christians felt for the conversion of nonbelievers, which, for Eliot, meant also a transformation of many aspects of Native culture, including marriage, living arrangements, dress and hygiene, government, and gender relations. In the seventeenth century, many Puritans believed that the first impulse toward conversion was initiated through a physical, albeit divinely inspired stimulus. These stimuli were often sermons or participation in the sacraments (Miller 1964:288). Eliot was convinced that conversion could only take place if Native people could be personally touched by the Bible's teachings, by participating in Christian religious services, and by reading and studying Holy Scripture for themselves. Unlike other missionaries who expected their converts to learn English or another European language, Eliot undertook the challenging task of learning the Native languages of the region himself so that he could preach and teach among the Native peoples directly. Eliot was also responsible for training a number of Native preachers and teachers, who spread his influence still further.

Some Native people of southern New England in the seventeenth and early eighteenth centuries were celebrated converts to Christianity, and their stories are as familiar to us as those of prominent English settlers of the same period. Because conversion is fraught with cultural drama, it has also engaged many theorists who see it as another way colonized people were exploited and their societies destroyed. The path that Christianity took among the Native people in southern New England was not a random one; it was directly related to the relative strength of the Native communities and the size of English populations. It depended on the tolerance of sachems and the strength of the powwaws. For some Native communities, Christianity was introduced by Puritans, Baptists, or Quakers. For others, it came with the Great Awakening. Some Native people became zealous converts; some, through Christianity, came to identify with their English oppressors; others incorporated Christianity into a more encompassing cosmology. Especially on Martha's Vineyard and at Mashpee, and later at Narragansett and Mohegan, Christian congregations became the center of Native social life and the source of leadership.

Individual instances from the records seem to support the idea of total transformation, as some Indian people wrote and spoke eloquently about their desire to live "in the English manner" (Bragdon 1981:156) But from a community and regional perspective, these individuals do not seem representative. This is because the way Christianity and literacy were incorporated into Indian communities followed indigenous patterns and reinforced traditional ideas about kinship, leadership, and cosmology.

THE ORIGINS OF VERNACULAR
LITERACY IN MASSACHUSETTS

The tragic losses in the epidemics of 1617–19 and 1633, and the defeat of the powerful Pequots in 1636, caused widespread disruption in all regions of Native southern New England, and some Indian people, particularly those of the interior regions, fled west or northward out of reach of colonial rule. Among those who remained, many adopted, at least nominally, a Protestant Christianity, and settled or were confined to a number of communities, traditionally called praying towns, including Natick, Wamesit, Hassanimisco, and Mashpee, and Christiantown, and Gay Head on Martha's Vineyard (Salisbury 1974).

Although some of the original praying towns were destroyed in the aftermath of King Philip's War, a surprising number of Christian settlements survived, particularly on Cape Cod, Martha's Vineyard, and Nantucket, where Christians and traditionalists lived together in communities organized around old, accepted principles of hereditary leadership, communal land ownership, and shared community resources (Conkey, Boissevain, and Goddard 1978:177; Bragdon 1981a).

The "print" culture of Puritanism in the seventeenth century led John Eliot and other missionaries, funded by the Society for the Propagation of the Gospel, to develop the justly famous

171

"Indian Library" (Kellaway 1962). The entire Bible, translated by Eliot with significant contributions from a skilled Massachusett-speaking consultant, appeared in 1663, with another edition in 1685, and was preceded and followed by translations of at least a dozen significant works by theologians such as Richard Baxter, Lewis Bayley, and John Cotton, a set of dialogues (1671), a primer (1672), and a grammar (1666) (Pilling 1891). Eliot also embarked on a vigorous campaign of education in Native literacy, developing a Roman-based orthography suited to the sound system of Massachusett, which was amenable to rapid learning and easily printed as well. His efforts soon exceeded his own expectations; he wrote in 1651:

It hath pleased God to stir up the hearts of many of them this winter to learn to read and write, wherein they doe very much profit with a very little help, especially some of them, for they are very ingenious. And whereas I had thought that we must have an Englishman to be their Schoole-Master, I now hope that the Lord will raise up some of themselves, and enable them unto that work. (Eliot to Robert Boyle, April 28, 1651, cited in Pilling 1891:127)

In the 1650s and 1660s, most of the people who were to play an important role in the missionary effort in southern New England were educated at Harvard College. They included John Cotton, Jr., John Eliot, Jr., Cotton Mather, and, slightly earlier, Samuel Danforth, Grindal Rawson, and Nathaniel Gookin, Jr. Also present at Harvard in the early 1660s was Caleb Cheeschaumuck, the only Native graduate of Harvard in the seventeenth century, and four other Native students including John Wompas, Joel Hiacoomes, and possibly John Sassiman, King Philip's notorious advisor. The Native students lived separately in the first building erected in Harvard yard, the so-called Indian college, along with an English companion, John Stanton, Jr., son of the famous interpreter to the Pequots. The Cambridge Grammar School, nearby, housed other Native and English students, while still others boarded with ministers and teachers in Boston and Cambridge. According to Harvard's historian Samuel Morison, about twenty Indians were studying under Master Corlet at Cambridge or Daniel Weld at Roxbury between 1655 and 1672 (1936). Corlet's pupils were examined by President Chauncy at Harvard's commencement in 1659 and "gave good satisfaction" to him and the overseers concerning their growth in the knowledge of the "lattin toungue" (Morison 1936:217).

Other Native students studied with Samuel Danforth and some others with a Mr. Wells. There was, interestingly, some concern about their skills in their own language. Morison quotes Harvard President Chauncy, "There are all at present that are maintained at our charge, who have so much exercise of their owne language, as there is no feare or danger of their forgetting it" (Morison 1936:217).

It seems likely that this refers to the presence of a significant group of Native students, who spoke their Native language amongst themselves. Apparently President Chauncy reluctantly instructed Caleb Cheeschaumuck and Joel Hiacoomes, for in 1664 he wrote of the need for a new Indian tutorial system to encourage "schoolmasters and college tutors who 'have to deale with such nasty salvages,'" and suggested that they should have a "fit salary" in return for their "greater care and diligent inspection." Wealthy donors in England also concerned themselves with the Indian mission. For example, Lady Dorothy Cecil left 200 pounds to President Chauncy and John Cotton, Sr., "hoping that they will improve it, to further the conversion of the Indians." Chauncy spent some of it on two students with the stipulation that they study the Algonquian language but reported that "both of them failed me in this great designe" (Morison 1936:217–18).

John Cotton, Jr., and Josiah Cotton, whose word lists were described in chapter 1, worked in Indian communities and both wrote about meetings with Native converts, meetings that included lectures on scriptural passages and a question and answer period. Ministers of the day used these questions to plumb the depths of their catechumen's knowledge and faith; they looked for signs of revelation, and they pondered the truths they believed to be revealed in these exchanges. A number of scholars have tried to analyze the questions put to Cotton and others by Indians as a metacommentary on their own beliefs. Several schools of thought have developed in interpreting Eliot's work and effects within Indian communities. One school suggests that the missionary movement created a group of Native people whose ideologies were transformed by Christianity (Salisbury 1974; Ronda 1981). Others see the process as more syncretic (Van Lonkhuyzen 1989; Plane 1993), while a third sees resistance in Native response (Brenner 1984).

Cotton's journal and wordlist, like that of his son, is valuable not only because of its relatively early date, but its connection to Martha's Vineyard and Plymouth, where many Native language writings survived, providing a counterpoint to the published writings of other missionaries, especially John Eliot.

Clues about Native religious conversion come from the large body of works published on the missions in southern New England, including the translations of the works of John Cotton and Increase Mather into Massachusett. As might be expected, many of these are admonitions to the Indians to behave as the English thought they should. One of Cotton Mather's sermons is entitled, "An Epistle to the Christian Indians, Giving Them a Short Account, of What the English Desire Them to Know and Do" (Pilling 1891:343). Samuel Danforth's *Woful Effects of Drunkeness*, published in 1710, uses the occasion of the execution of two Indians for murder to expound on the evils of intoxication. Other sermons, such as one by Experience Mayhew (1709) and Danforth's translations of Increase Mather's sermons (Pilling 1891:192), are not directed at a specifically Indian audience but, as they were also published in Massachusett, were purchased or given to literate Natives for reading matter. Several Native probate inventories from the early eighteenth century list "a Bible and sermons" as part of the Native's estate (Bragdon 1979; Little 1980a), and storekeepers on Nantucket stocked a set of books and pamphlets in the Massachusett language until the 1750s (Little 1980a).

These translations fall into three categories: basic guides to Christian principals; translations of scripture and related texts, such as the Psalter; and guides to a Christian life, as English missionaries understood it. Many of Cotton's communicants had questions about both the principles of Christian faith and the practicalities of Christian life that show an active grasp of the differences between their perspectives and practices and those of the English. A deeper appreciation of what Indian people were being told in sermons or other teaching events is available by studying published and manuscript sermons, both by English missionaries fluent in Indian languages and by Native ministers themselves.

There are ten manuscript sermons written by Englishmen, nine in the hands of John and Josiah Cotton of Plymouth, and one attributed to Samuel Treat of Eastham, Massachusetts. These sermons, although not composed by Native speakers of Massachusett, were written during the period when Native Christian churches of the upper Cape Cod region were very active and when most, if not all, services were conducted entirely in Massachusett. Treat reported to Cotton Mather in 1693, for example, that:

There are five hundred and five adult persons of Indians within the limits of our township, unto whom these many years past, I have from time to time imparted the gospel of our Lord Jesus in their own language, (and I truly hope not without success,) . . . and I verily do not know of, nor can I learn that there is so much as one of these five hundred Indians that does obstinately absent from, but do jointly frequent and attend on the preaching of the word. (Mather 1852:436)

John Cotton, Jr., a son of the famous Puritan minister, learned Massachusett on Martha's Vineyard before removing to Plymouth in 1669. There he, and later his son Josiah, preached to the local Christian Indians. John Cotton wrote several sermons in Massachusett, served as editor for the second edition of the Massachusett Bible, and was considered a very proficient speaker of the Native language. Josiah Cotton, who was the author of the Indian Vocabulary recorded ca. 1710 (Cotton 1830), was himself missionary to the Indians for nearly fifty years. Entries from his diary and notations on the sermons themselves indicate frequent visits to various Indian communities in the Plymouth area to deliver "Indian Lectures," some dating as late as the 1740s.

No complete history of the Native peoples of the upper Cape, the Pokanoket nation, is available. In the early seventeenth century, the Pokanokets were centered at Sowams, under Massasoit, and later at Mount Hope in what is now Bristol, Rhode Island, but the subordinate sachems of the upper Cape were recognized authorities over the people of that region. By 1665, a large grant of land at Mashpee had been donated by two of these leaders for the use of Christian Indians of the area. In addition, there were communities at Nukkekummees (Dartmouth), Herring Pond (Plymouth), and at Monument (Pocasset). These communities had contact with a number of English missionaries, including members of the Bourne and Cotton families, Eldad Tupper, and, in the 1760s, Gideon Hawley. However, on a daily basis they were governed by Native rulers and instructed by Native ministers and teachers, some of whom were from Martha's Vineyard. Most of the surviving information about the practice of Native Christianity comes from this region and includes a collection of manuscript sermons, delivered to Indian communities on Cape Cod and in Plymouth in the late seventeenth and early eighteenth centuries.

The existing Massachusett manuscript sermons are of two basic types. The first, exemplified by that attributed to Samuel Treat, which dates to 1705, is superficially similar to the accepted format outlined in seventeenth century English sermon manuals. In the left-hand column is the reference to the text to be discussed, for example, Proverbs 9:17–18, Proverbs 5:3–4, and Job 20:12, concerning sin. The Massachusett translation of the text reads: "Lesson . . . Although wickedness is sweet in his mouth, although he hides it under his tongue." Unlike English sermons of the period, this lecture consists of the repetition of a series of scriptural texts, in part copied directly from the Massachusett Bible. The lecture concludes with a reference to Exodus 20:13, "Thou shalt not kill." This lecture is similar in style and content to the sermons delivered by John Eliot and other first-generation missionaries to the Massachusett, full of dire warnings, threats, and open condemnations of Native customs and beliefs (Bowden and Ronda 1980; Salisbury 1974).

Other surviving sermons, in the hands of John and Josiah Cotton, are more informal in style and organization and, although apparently translations from English and tending toward a more English-like word order, seem to reflect the Cottons' better knowledge of the Massachusett language. One example, entitled "On Fasting" contains both English and Massachusett text, on facing leaves. The text appears to have been written out in full, with references to scriptural passages noted interlineally.

These texts, although directed to Native audiences, stress themes common to Puritan sermons of the late seventeenth and early eighteenth century, in particular salvation through faith and prayer. Each point is numbered and illustrated by examples appropriate to the audience concerning daily work, the care of children, and the relationship between husbands and wives and between neighbors and friends. The Cotton manuscript sermons are of interest not only because of their form and content, but because they contain additional notations concerning where and when the particular sermon was delivered. The sermon referred to above, for example, contains references to at least fifteen occasions ranging from "at Monument Ponds, March 8, 1714" through "at Ned Hood's August 17, 1740" (Cotton 1665–1678).

In spite of legislation requiring people to reside within easy traveling distance of a meeting house, the Christian Indians were living in such remote and scattered areas in the mid-eighteenth century that missionaries were forced to travel to them. The Cotton manuscripts also note sermons by other Native preachers in the Plymouth areas, such as one "delivered by Jno. Neesnumun, 1707."

Kenneth Miner has commented on the remarkable efforts of the missionary John Eliot in translating concepts of Aristotelian and Ramist principles of logic into Massachusett, particularly in the *Logick Primer* (1672) and *Indian Grammar Begun* (1666) and suggests that these are significant, not in what they tell us about Native understanding of such concepts, but rather in their use of such "modern" linguistic notions as morphophonemic representation, and the recognition that a "primitive" language such as Massachusett was systematically structured, rather than randomly organized (Miner 1975:178). He noted the interesting fact that, while Eliot often introduced loan words for such concrete terms as "silver, bible, horse," he scrupulously sought Massachusett words for logical terms like syllogism, argument, logic, and proposition (1975:176).

One of the Cotton manuscripts, as well as that attributed to Treat, gives evidence for another common phenomenon in the Puritan preaching tradition, the copying of published texts for private use. Another Cotton manuscript is a copy of a sermon authored by Cotton Mather entitled "Family Religion excited and assisted" (1703) (Pilling 1891:343), and Treat's is probably a copy of the published *Hatchets to Hew Down the Tree of Sin* (1705). On the other hand, these manuscripts may reveal the true authors of these texts, as some, including James Hammond Trumbull, were of the opinion that Cotton Mather was incapable of writing idiomatic Massachusett and employed a translator.

These terms of logic, which date to the earliest period of conversion efforts by Eliot and others, are indicative of their unfamiliarity with the Massachusett people and their insistence, true to Puritan doctrine, that conversion and salvation proceed along universally applicable lines. I have argued elsewhere that, in spite of such rigidity, Native Christianity in the later decades of the seventeenth and eighteenth centuries developed a unique and vernacular style based on Native concepts of religious practice, community solidarity, and accepted Native speech styles (Bragdon 1991).

Certain lexical items occurring in the manuscript sermons, as well as annotations in Massachusett bibles, indicate that while the terminology of logic invented for the Natives was not in common use, certain other Massachusett words for Christian concepts did survive, sometimes having undergone semantic extension or limitation. Very few English loan words referring to religious concepts appear in the manuscript sermons, in Cotton's vocabulary, or in other Native writings. The common use of primarily Massachusett-based terminology is testified to not only in the sermons but also in Cotton's Indian vocabulary published in 1709. Although much of this terminology is Massachusett in origin, its significance for an understanding of Native Christianity is unclear. Was the use of the Native term manit for the Christian God evidence for a continuation of Native beliefs about manitou? Likewise, is the use of the term chepi for "Satan" or "devil," and chepiokomuk for hell evidence for a continuation of Native views about the afterlife?

Translations and sermons written by missionaries, however, are not necessarily indicative of any profound ideological or perceptual differences or continuities among the Native people. Less

179

ambiguous information about Native Christianity comes from annotations in Native-owned copies of the Massachusett bible, of which there exist nearly a dozen examples. These annotations consist of single words, letters, and phrases, often copied directly from the printed text. Here there are no differences in terminology, but some possible differences in content and style. Whereas the Cotton sermons, written in the early to mideighteenth century, reflect the humanistic, intellectual, and remote Christianity of the years preceding the Great Awakening, some of the annotations in the bibles are stern, moralistic exhortations to other Indians, such as "Remember you people, this book is right and you [people] should do good in all your times" (Lev. 7.1–8.2), or lamentations, for example, "Pitiful people [are we]. It is not good. Always falsehood is heard among us all" (Num. 4.1–4.2).

Such writings (and all other evidence for Massachusett thought and feeling), fragmentary as they are, can be construed as evidence for a vernacular Native Christianity in which elements of traditional religious practice were still given prominent place. Oratory, received with respect by silent and attentive audiences, was a well-known feature of Native life and was often highly structured and stylized discourse laden with exhortations, metaphors, and parables. On the other hand, the Native style of petition was equally full of lamentation, self-condemnation, and pleas for pity. In this, as in the preference for monologues to be delivered with emotion and accompanied by gestures, described for earlier Native speech events, the Christian Indians of New England were early practitioners of a kind of Christianity that only became popular among New Light converts nearly a century later.

At the same time, the processes collectively known as the "colonization of languages" (Mignolo 1992; Fabian 1986), including the effects of imposing classical models on new world examples or even the impact of an alphabetized writing system on the discourse repertoire of previously nonliterate societies, is less important than what the available materials tell us about the social world coming into being.

LITERACY AND SOCIETY IN MASSACHUSETT-SPEAKING COMMUNITIES

The small cadre of English missionaries dedicated to introducing vernacular literacy into Native communities were soon joined by a larger number of Native teachers who taught reading and writing skills throughout the region, such that by the end of the seventeenth century nearly 30 percent of the Native population—men, women, and children—could read and write (Bragdon 1981a:55).

The unique coincidence of the Native emphasis on public speaking as an art form and the possible influence of a long tradition of pictographic representation with the Puritan text-dominated missionary effort created the conditions for an "oral literacy" within these Native Christian communities.

Massachusett vernacular literacy embraced several activities, cross-cutting a number of traditional cultural domains. In formal schools and at home, students worked with primers and other teaching aids and studied translated texts. Literate individuals, usually men, kept a variety of records, including marriage records, deeds, and town proprietor's records. Native officials published marriage banns and issued warrants. One diary or account book in Massachusett is known, and letters were also exchanged (Goddard and Bragdon 1988:13–23). The structure and content of the surviving writings in Massachusett suggest that rhetorical style and formal protocol, particularly that demanded when peoples of differing social statuses interacted, was preserved in written form. The Massachusett case appears to support Wallace Chafe and Deborah Tannen's argument that writing was inherently social, and that reading and writing were "inextricably" tied to speech, even in those modes of discourse that seem most exclusively a matter of writing and reading (1987:398).

Literacy's most prominent use in daily life among the Massachusett speakers was associated with the practice of Native Christianity. Much reading and writing were taught within the context of religious instruction or in preparation for it. The Bible, Psalms, and other books were used in religious services. Those literate, bilingual Native students who were educated by private tutors and at Harvard's Indian College were destined for the ministry as well.

Strong evidence suggests such religion-oriented literacy was highly public and social in nature. Native ministers incorporated Biblical texts into their sermons (Howwoswe n.d.). The service itself consisted of reading, response, and textual exegesis (Bragdon 1991). Annotations from the majority of surviving Native-owned bibles indicate that the Bibles themselves were referred to during the service.

Not all church members were literate, but all participated in literacy to the extent that they interacted with a "reader," and were connected to the sermon through references to the written word. This participation was amplified by the frequent use of psalmody and the "lining" of hymns, whereby a singer would sing a line from the text, and the congregation would repeat it, for the length of the hymn (Becker 1982). Native converts on Martha's Vineyard read to one another as part of daily religious practice, often conducted at home, with family members and neighbors.

The links to the past provided by the ritual use of tobacco after a service are described on Nantucket in the mideighteenth century:

A minister is called cooutaumachary and when the meeting was don they would take there tinder box and strike fire and light there pipes a short pipe and maybe would draw three or foure wises and swollow the smook and then blow it oute of there noses and so hand there pipe to there next neighbor and one pipe of tobaco would serve ten or a dosen of them and they would say taw-poot which is I thank yee it seemed to be done in a way of kind-ness to each other. (Z. Macy 1792b)

Christian services also provided a forum for political activities. An excellent example comes from Mashpee, which had a Christian Indian community as early as 1652. At least two churches were built in Mashpee prior to the early nineteenth century, and Mashpee converts were visited by several English missionaries, including Thomas Tupper, John Cotton, and Josiah Cotton. It is clear from surviving documents that the church was the physical as well as the social center of the community, and that the church itself was the setting for some political debate (see figs. 8 and 9, and discussion of this church in chapter 4).

The public nature of literacy is also reflected in the vernacular writings in Massachusett. A brief survey of original documents reveals a number of characteristics that suggest the sociability of the context in which they were created. Many include lists of numerous witnesses, whose verbatim statements are often attached. Petitions, of which four are known, appear to have been read aloud at group meetings and, in three cases, are accompanied by a complete listing of those present.

The inextricability of speech and writing for the Massachusett is further underlined by the immediacy of expression character-istic of many of the vernacular writings. Elizabeth Little has pointed out that most of the Nantucket Native-language deeds are in reality "recorded oral land transfers" (1980b:63). Direct quotation is the standard form of reported speech in Massachu-sett, and these writings preserve direct quotations from principal participants in land transfers or at public confirmations of title.

Petitions also appear to reflect a similar immediacy. Standard expressions of humility, such as, "we beseech you," "we are poor," and so on, are characteristic of the speech of petitioners in the early contact period, and also appear in written petitions. In

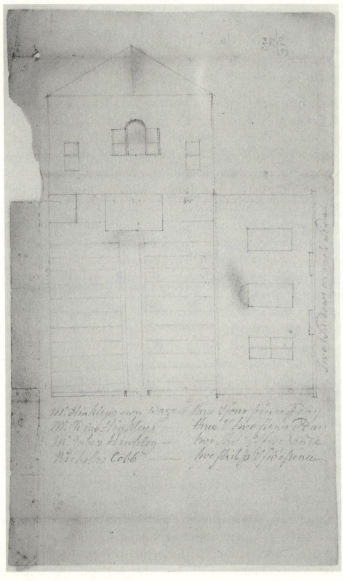

Figure 8. Plan of the Mashpee meeting house (Courtesy of the Massachusetts Historical Society).

Figure 9. Mashpee petition, 1753, vol. 32:427, Massachusetts State Archives (Courtesy of the Commonwealth of Massachusetts).

185

addition, certain rhetorical expressions characteristic of speech were sometimes employed in written petitions, such as the exclamatory "Woj" (Oh!) (Goddard 1993:404). Here it is important to point out that such expressions are not merely remnants of the oral mode surviving into writing, but rather expressions of the ongoing sociability and oralicy of literacy among the Massachusett-speaking people.

The physical condition of these documents and manuscripts and the marginal annotations found in several copies of the Massachusett Bibles and other published books, also suggest that both reading and writing for the Massachusett was a contextualized, community event. Some documents show physical evidence of reuse, of scrutiny by more than one writer, and of revisions, as though the documents were archived as relics or aids to memory. A series of related documents, now located in the Huntington Library, San Marino, California, and transcribed and translated line-for-line, appear in Goddard and Bragdon (1988:60–65) as an example. The documents detail a conveyance of land between two Natives of Martha's Vineyard, Thomas Dila and Nathaniel Cuper, for lands at East Chop (Ogkashkuppeh). It consists of three separate entries, two on one sheet of paper and a third on a separate piece attached to the base of the first. The first, located at the top of the sheet, is dated September 22, 1706, and records the transfer of land from Dila to Cuper. The second document, on the same sheet of paper, conveys the same piece of land from Cuper to John Tallman and is also dated September 22, 1706. The third entry, on the attached sheet of paper, is dated November 14, 1706, and consists of a confirmation of the conveyance to Tallman on behalf of Samuell Makkinnit, and Qunnagkoo who name themselves "defenders of the sachemship" (1988:63, 65). The writer of the third document has added lines to both the previous documents. In the first, the writer added the words "I Thomas Tilla, this land that I convey cost three pounds, which I let

Nathaneill Cuper have. I Nathaneill Cuper say it was done; I bought it for three pounds." The same writer added similar statements to the second document. These conveyances, to which were appended the evidently important verbatim verbal exchanges of the buyers and sellers, document the continuing importance of oral agreement, the presence of numerous witnesses, the archiving of written records, and the participation of several writers and readers in the creation of the manuscripts (20–22).

Particularly interesting examples of the ways Native people used writing and books to reinforce or create a sense of community are the annotations in several copies of Massachusett Bibles owned by Native speakers of that language. The largest percentage of surviving copies of the Bible are what were known as presentation copies, specially bound or with distinctive title pages in English, designed as gifts to benefactors of the missionary work in New England, or for clerics and other interested English scholars. Very few Indian-owned bibles are known to have survived but, of these, eight have annotations and other marginalia in Massachusett (Pilling 1891). Two other books, one a copy of Experience Mayhew's *Massachuset Psalter* (1709) and the other Lewis Bayley's *Manitowompae Pomantamoonk* (1685), were also annotated in Massachusett.

Surviving Bibles and other books with annotations in Massachusett show evidence of multiple owners. The annotated *Psalter*, for example, contains the names of at least two Native writers of Martha's Vineyard, Solomon Omppan and Benjamin Job, and marginal notes dating to 1720 and 1732 (Goddard and Bragdon 1988:466–68). The Bible owned by the Pilgrim Society contains several hands, including those of Benjamin Kusseniyeutt, Francis Ned, and Josiah Ned or Attaunit, presumably of Plymouth. One passage, written on February 15, 1715, reads in part "it's a storm . . . But we Indians still survive well on this morning" (1988:447).

Annotations are often messages, as if to other readers, such as the admonition in the Bible owned by the Native minister Joseph Papenau of Falmouth and Bourne (later owned by the minister Zachary Hossueit of Gay Head: "This is your book, you Papenau. Read it with concentration. Your God will bless you" (423). Other Native-owned Bibles contain endpages with annotations in many hands, creating the impression of a cacophony of voices, or a continuous "conversation" between writers in and readers of these books.

Prior to the publication of Eliot's earliest translations, there is evidence that handwritten versions were passed from hand to hand in Indian communities (Pilling 1891:127). The book and other printed or written matter functioned as a focus for discussion and shared religious practice, rather than as a source of private instruction. In those Massachusett-speaking communities where vernacular literacy was common, those at the interstices of literacy participated in many activities in which the use of documents and books both signified and reinforced the importance of community action and understanding. Reading and writing functioned as ritual actions that both the literate and the nonliterate could share. Books, many of which were in the Massachusett language, also appear to have been prized objects in otherwise sparsely furnished Native homes. Late seventeenth- and early eighteenth-century inventories of Native decedents' belongings from Natick, Massachusetts, and Nantucket frequently mention books (Bragdon 1979), and storekeepers on Nantucket and Martha's Vineyard were still selling copies of works in the Native language in the 1740s (Little 1980a).

The importance of books and writings to the Christian Indians was not lost on others, and their acquisition of literacy did not endear them to many English settlers. Indian students at Harvard were subjected to the ridicule of their English classmates, as mocking annotations in Indian-owned exercise books makes clear (Morison 1936). During King Philip's War, nearly all copies of the Bible, most of which were owned by noncombatants, were destroyed by English soldiers (Gookin 1972). Jill Lepore suggests that part of the motivation behind King Philip's War was a rejection of literacy, and that those Natives who were literate were marked as enemies by Philip and his allies (1998:46–47). The symbolic authority that books had in the seventeenth century (Joyce et al. 1983), in the hands of Indians, was perhaps threatening to those English settlers who were determined to draw sharp boundaries between themselves and the Native "other" (Murray 1996; Lepore 1998). Some Indians, within Christian territories and outside them, also appear to have been suspicious of books, reading, and writing (LaFantasie 1988). It is possible that some Native people linked books and the ability to read to the perceived power of Europeans and to their seeming immunity to disease (Axtell 1985). Others may have rejected these objects as symbolic of a way of life and of a people so threatening to their own. Francis Jennings has suggested that the murder of one of the two Native students to graduate from Harvard in the seventeenth century was motivated by such perceptions (1975).

On the other hand, Native literacy also facilitated the English efforts to undermine Native sovereignty and to acquire Native lands through quasi-legal means. For example, a principal actor in land sales and resettlements in what was to become Worcester County was John Wompus, who may have been the same John Wompus who attended Harvard in the early 1660s and was called a "sachem of Hassanamesit" (Massachusetts, Colony of 1704). This man, also known as John White, must have migrated to London, where his will was recorded on October 1, 1679. In it he left his "estate" to three kinsmen, John Awansamock, Pomhamell, and Norwarunnt. John Awansamock was also a noted resident at Natick (Bragdon 1981a; Goddard and Bragdon 1988). In addition to this estate, White required that "they and every one of them offering, performing, fulfilling and keeping all such Articles and

189

conditions as my Father and I have or ought to have observed, performed, fulfilled and kept" (Humes 1952:34). Two years later, however, several Natick residents, including the aged Waban, protested this sale on behalf of Anthony Tray and Tom Tray, "uncles by the father's side unto John Woampus deceased" (Massachusetts State Archives 30:260a). Apparently another example of the strategy of dispossession through Indian agents, Wompus's land was fraudulently sold to two Englishmen named Pratt and Blake. His will was overturned after a petition from Indians and English settlers in the region demanded the reestablishment of the 1654 bounds of the plantation, with the Indians occupying a four square-mile tract in its center. This settlement also assured the Indians of all properties between Hassanimisco and Natick, access to Quinsigamond Pond, and "free liberty of fishing in said Pond at all times fore ever" (Humes 1952:36).

Literate Christian people of the region created among themselves a functioning, although dispersed, community where both principles of hereditary sachemships and the institutions favored by missionaries among their converts co-existed. Native writings from the region show both the links to Martha's Vineyard and the ways local rulers and their subjects worked at the social task of reproducing themselves through time. This is reflected in a Cape Cod deed, where a scribe trained on Martha's Vineyard, the son of a prominent sachem and his royally descended mother, served another royal descendant, Sary Sepet, in a land confirmation recorded in the early eighteenth century.

Books and Writings in
Native Rhode Island and Connecticut

The remarkable spread of vernacular literacy among Massachusett speakers was not duplicated by other peoples closely linked to them by ties of language and culture, due to differences in colonial administration, to the continuing power of Native communities, and the lack of a single-minded and tireless missionary such as Eliot. Missionary activity was limited in what is now Rhode Island and Connecticut during the seventeenth century. Much of the country was either too remote from English settlement or the Native peoples successfully resisted Christianity. Among the Narragansetts, their allies the Niantics, and the Native societies of coastal Connecticut, early missionary efforts were less dramatically successful, although short-lived missions were established at Branford and Norwich (Conkey, Boissevain, and Goddard 1978:177); other communities adopted Christianity during the Great Awakening of the 1740s (Simmons and Simmons 1982).

When the Reverend Experience Mayhew, a fluent speaker of the Martha's Vineyard dialect of Massachusett, toured southern Rhode Island and eastern Connecticut in 1717, he found little or any evidence of literacy skills among the Natives he encountered (Mayhew 1896). Yet books, especially the Bible, occupied places of importance even in this region. In the mideighteenth century, an Indian school was established at Farmington, on the middle Connecticut River, where Native students were evidently instructed in Latin and English. Joseph Fish, missionary to the Narragansett in the mideighteenth century, reported that the Native minister Samuel Niles preached with an open Bible in front of him, quoting passages he evidently knew from memory, for it appeared that he could not read (Simmons and Simmons 1982). Eleazer Wheelock's Indian school was responsible for the training of such important Native leaders and ministers as the Mohegan's Samson Occom and Joseph Johnson, both prolific writers, although they apparently left no manuscripts in their own language (Love 1899; Murray 1996). Historical and archaeological evidence suggests, additionally, that books and writings in both English and vernacular took on a number of social and religious functions even among nonliterate Native people who were on the peripheries of literate regions.

191

Several sources document, for example, the theft of English, Greek, and Latin textbooks from English school houses and churches (Bragdon 1981a:49; Hall 1994) throughout the seventeenth century. Such thefts were most frequently said to be committed by non-Christian or "strange" Indians (MacFarlane 1933:564). Several seventeenth-century authors recall remarks made by Indians about the importance of books. Roger Williams recounts with approval the explanation given by the Narragansett sachem Miantonimo to an Indian of Connecticut regarding English knowledge of the afterlife: "He hath books and writings, and one which god himselfe made, concerning mens soules, and therefore may well know more than wee that have none, but take all upon trust from our forefathers" (1936:137).

James Axtell has suggested that in New France writing and its mysteries were part of the perceived powers of the Europeans, who, especially in the guise of missionaries, could influence supernatural powers through writing, a skill they jealously guarded (1985). Archaeological finds in two historic-period graves dating to the midseventeenth century, recently excavated in southern New England, suggest that among the nonliterate, non-Christian people of the Pequot and Narragansett, writing, print, and books were indeed believed to be powerful. These fragments of printed pages were evidently included as grave goods along with items of Native and European manufacture (Amory 1996; Kevin McBride personal communication 1996; Paul Robinson personal communication 1996).

But such a distinction among the Native populations of the region may be exaggerated. The Native community at Farmington produced the scholarly Joshua Metuan, whose letter in Latin was sent to the company's office in England in 1715. The Society for the Propagation of the Gospel regularly funded missionaries in several Connecticut settlements throughout the eighteenth century, including the reverend Joseph Fish, who worked with the

Niantics and Narragansetts in the mideighteenth century (Simmons and Simmons 1982).

The stratagem of using the writings of Native students as exemplars of the success of missionary activities in southern New England also gives us a glimpse of the otherwise obscure workings of the Connecticut valley Native communities such as the Wagunks, and others that were nominally Christian (Szasz 1988:188). A curiosity, it would seem at first glance. But it reflects the great complexity of community relations in this region, where Christianity had only a foothold.

Kevin McBride suggests that literacy was resisted among some Native leaders, although they were aware that accepting some schooling might improve their chances of retaining control over their shrinking reserves. The Pequots wrote to the General Assembly in Connecticut in 1735, for example, that

We see plainly that thare [the English] chiefest desire is to deprive us of the priviledge of our land, and drive us off to our uter ruin. It makes us concerned for our children wht will be come of them for thay are about having the gospel preched to them, and is a learning to read, and all our young men and women that are Capable of lerning it. (McBride 2005:8–9)

At Mohegan, the minister Samson Occom, educated and literate in English, lived among Christian converts in the 1730s (figs. 10 and 11). His dwelling house, in the English style, was a prominent feature of the landscape.

Among the Schaghticokes, conversion came with the "New Light" missions of the Great Awakening in the 1730s. In 1740, Moravian missions to the Mahican were established at Sharon and Shekomeko in New York. Under the Schaghticoke sachem Gideon Mauwee, a mission there was active between 1743 until 1770 (Crone-Morange and Lavin 2004). Other Moravian missions were located among the Pootatucks, Weantinocks, and Pishgatikuks (2004). Language studies of this community are based

THE REVEREND SAMSON OCCOM

The First Indian Minister that ever was in Europe who went to Britain to obtain charities for the support of the Revd. Mr. Wheelocks Indian Academy & Missionaries among the savages of North America in 1768.

Figure 10. Samson Occom (Courtesy of the Connecticut Historical Society).

Figure 11. Samson Occom's house (Courtesy of the Connecticut Historical Society).

on Edwards (whose missionary efforts among the Indian converts echoed that of his predecessors in eastern Massachusetts.

LITERACY AND LANGUAGE LEVELING

Literacy, never common outside of the Massachusett-speaking region, probably did not serve as a dialect leveler even there, as written language may not always have reflected what was spoken. Experience Mayhew remarked:

The Martha's Vineyard Indian Dialect, and that of Natick, according unto which last Mr. Eliot translated the Indian Bible are so very much a like, that without a very critical observation you would not see the difference, Indeed the difference was something greater than now it is, before our Indians had the use of the bible and other Books translated by Mr. Eliot, but since that the most of the litle (*sic*) differences that were betwixt them, have

195

been happily lost, and our Indians, speak, but especially write much as those of Natick do (Mayhew 1885 [1722]).

THE LATER HISTORY OF NATIVE LITERACY IN SOUTHERN NEW ENGLAND

The history of Native literacy becomes more difficult to trace in the last decades of the eighteenth century. Although no Massachusett texts have been located dating to after this period, it seems likely that Native language literacy, or at least the archiving of vernacular texts and books in Massachusett, did not die out in Massachusett-speaking communities until the mid-to-late nineteenth century, as evidenced by the Howowswe Papers and other anecdotal evidence (see fig. 12).

When Reverend Stephens of Martha's Vineyard visited Gay Head in the 1870s, he collected more than fifty documents in the Native language (Pilling 1891). The lack of interference from the English in Massachusett texts dating to the latest decades of the eighteenth century, in spite of increasing evidence of bilingualism among Native speakers of that language, and the evidence these texts provide of the preservation of a highly elaborated written form of Massachusett only decades before the language appears to have gone out of general use, suggests that manuscripts and books in the Native language came to reflect its increasingly limited and symbolic function, a "latinization" of the language that almost always precedes language obsolescence (Dorian 1981; Woolard 1992). While some Englishmen published word lists in the Niantic, Quiripi, and Pequot languages, there is little concrete evidence delineating the history of Native language literacy in Connecticut, although Fidelia Fielding, a woman of Mohegan ancestry, kept a diary in that language in the last decades of the nineteenth century (Speck 1928). How this attenuated but persistent vernacular literacy co-existed with increasing bilingualism in English and the ultimate loss of most

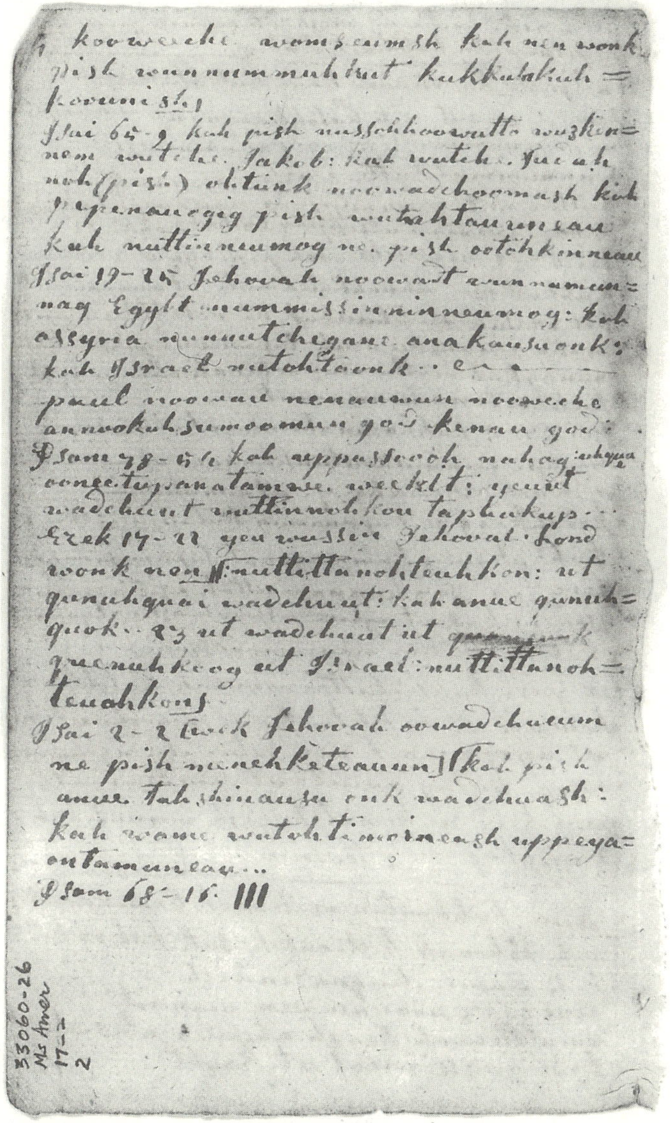
koowecche wamseumsh kah neuwonk
pish wunnummuhkut kukkukkuh=
koonnish;
Isai 65-9 kah pish nussohkoowutto wuzkin=
nom wutche Jakob: kah wutch Juda
noh (pish) ohtunk noowadchoomash kah
pepenaugig pish wutahtauuneau
kah nuttinneumog ne pish ootohkinneau
Isai 19-25 Jehovah noowant wunnamun=
nag Egypt nummissinninneumog: kah
assyria nunnutchegane anakausuonk:
kah Israel nutohtaonk . . . . .
paul noowau nenauwun noowecche
annookuhsumoomun god kenau god:
Psam 78-68 kah uppusseooh nahag uhqua
oonge tupsanatamae. weekit: yeuut
wadchuut nuttinnohkou taphukup.
Ezek 17-22 yeu wussie Jehovah lond
wonk non nuttittannohteuhkon: ut
qunuhquai wadchuut: kah anue qunuh=
quok. 23 ut wadchuat ut ~~qunuhk~~
qunuhkoog ut Israel: nuttittannoh=
teuahkons
Isai 2-2 tuck Jehovah oowadchuum
ne pish nuhkketeauun] kah pish
anue tahshinausu onk wadchuash:
kah wame watohtinnoinnash uppeya=
ontamuneau...
Psam 68-16 III

Figure 12. Page from a 1782 sermon by Zachary Howwoswe (Courtesy of the John Carter Brown Library).

Native languages in the region by the end of the nineteenth century are subjects yet to be examined.

Books and manuscripts were important items of material culture in Native southern New England, objects whose significance lay not merely in their content and origins, but also in their role as one focus for social interaction, as avenues to spiritual power, and as markers of Native identity. The uses for books and writings, and their significance to Native communities both literate and non-literate for two hundred years after contact with Europeans, suggest that our understanding of literacy needs to be broadened further still, to encompass the social and ideological functions of reading and script at the interstices of literate cultures. The linkages created by widespread literacy and Christianity had the unexpected effect of tying even non-Christian communities to those who had many Christian members. But other linkages existed as well, as discussed in the following chapter.

7.

Regional Networks, Itinerant People

James Clifford has recently argued that much of what we understand about community is rooted in our idea of place, that we thereby miss the ways people move through space in cultural ways (1997). He has noted for example, that in the twentieth century, the Mashpee were hampered in their case for federal recognition by "assumptions of rootedness and local continuity, notions of authenticity that denied them the complex agency in an interactive, ongoing colonial history" (Clifford 1988; 1997:3).

Descriptions of Native societies and cultural ideas in the later decades of the seventeenth century were often organized in terms of the Native communities, Christian and non-Christian, which were the concern of English and Anglo-American missionaries and administrators. These communities have been discussed in detail in previous chapters. However, what remains less well-understood are the ways Native communities throughout the region articulated with one another and, perhaps more importantly, how Native people as individuals articulated with these communities (Anderson 1991).

In addition, many scholars suggest that by focusing on communities, we are in danger of ignoring the fact that economic and social forces that shape local events exist far beyond the community. During the colonial period in southern New England, the Indians of the region were affected by forces out of their control. Social relationships in this view are processes in time, and these relationships are also entailed from without.

One way to address the importance of regional relationships is through network analysis. Network analyses trace the activities of individuals as they move through the full range of social relationships (Barnes 1969). In southern New England, there are several kinds of networks that emerge from current descriptions and from other data: intermarriage and other family networks; the Christian Natives, ministers, and teachers network; and the maritime region network (particularly the links forged by the whaling industry and other aspects of the colonial maritime economy). It would be a mistake to visualize Native communities simply as isolated enclaves; their relations over considerable distances explain their effectiveness in the regional colonial contest and their strength through time.

As Ann McMullen has convincingly demonstrated, shared patterns in material culture, especially basketry, are one source of evidence for a regional interpretation (1991) while Kenneth Feder's work at the Lighthouse site, a nineteenth-century community in northeastern Connecticut (1993), shows that people of many different backgrounds have contributed to contemporary "Native" culture in southern New England.

This chapter attempts to uncover the processes by which communities were linked to one another by documenting personal and community networks as they emerge from historical records from the late seventeenth and early eighteenth centuries. These complex sets of relationships, now only partially visible, underlay the larger unities of culture, language, and political affiliation, demonstrating the importance of ties of kinship, friend-ship, and economic interdependency over widespread regions and highlighting the ambiguities of traditional anthropological units of analysis.

At the same time, examples of what Clifford calls "concrete mediations" of the dynamic between dwelling and traveling (1997:24) are common in the historic record of colonial Indian people in New England and suggest that neither mobility nor fix-ity was the norm, but rather that individuals were the nexus between the two.

Another explanation for the complexity of relationships in southern New England during the period when most descriptions were made may lie in the readjustments many Indian communi-ties were making in order to reconstitute themselves after the dis-astrous losses of the 1617–19 epidemic and the equally devastating spread of small pox in the 1630s, which included adopting mem-bers from other regions or coalescing two or more groups into one. Evidence from public records, for example, documents con-nections between peoples of the northern communities of the Pawtuckets, led by Nanepashemet's sons, Wonahaquahan and Montowampate (John and James), and later by Passaconnaway and his sons, Wonalancet and Nanamocomuck, and the Christian towns of Wamesit, Nashoba, Natick, Okomakamesit, and others (Stewart-Smith 1998:454). At the same time, Wonalancet himself had an Abenaki wife and a son fostered in an Abenaki community (Gookin 1972:521).

Linguistic information in Roger William's *Key* suggests the pos-sibility that some communities were multilingual as well. Exam-ples from the *Key* seem to suggest common usage of Narragansett, Cowweset, and Nipmuck terms, as shown in table 11.

Narragansett, according to William's testimony, was character-ized by the "y" reflex, but his own data suggests the presence of "n" as well as "l" speakers among the Cowwesets and Narragansetts.

Table 11. Words for Spouse and Ward in Williams's
A Key into the Language of America (1643)

Term	English Meaning
nullógana	wife
nullóquaso	ward, pupil
pallè nochisquaûaw	he or she has committed adultery
wunnowauntam wulloasin	grieved and in bitternesse
nnowántam, nlôasin	I am grieved for you

Source: Williams 1936:148, 150, 146, 201

Similarly, Loup B, a language related to Mahican and Western Abenaki and possibly spoken in the region extending between the boundaries of these two better-known groups, shows a mixture of n and r (Goddard 1978c: 76).

However, William Burton and Richard Lowenthal (1974) and Paul Robinson (1990) argue that such overarching political distinctions masked a widespread tendency among elite Native families to marry across so-called tribal boundaries and to characterize "royalty" as the product of just such exchanges. This tendency is no better illustrated than in the genealogy of the Mohegan sachem Uncas, recorded in 1679, in which he claims royal descent from Mohegan, Pequot, and Narragansett sachem lineages (Burton and Lowenthal 1974:595–97; also see chapters 2 and 3 of this volume).

In addition, as Robinson argues, the hegemony exerted by certain Native groups, in particular the Narragansetts, was a "construction" of the later seventeenth century, and owed its existence in part to a concerted effort to establish dominance in diplomacy, ritual, and alliances with the English. Part of the strategy also required a deliberate effort at separation and the establishment of distinctive markers of identity, which became, according to Robinson, more overt through time (1990:271).

It seems likely that multilingualism or multidialectism was present in southern New England in the early contact period, a fact unrecognized by English observers due to their general unfamiliarity with the languages and, perhaps more importantly, to the tendency to assume a single-language/single-people model within a given region, as though two or more languages could not occupy the same physical space.

The distribution of place names in southern New England indicates that some resource locations were shared between members of different language groups. Hammond Trumbull notes that "in early deeds and conveyances in the colonial and local records, we find the same river, lake, tract of land or bound-mark named sometimes in the Muhhekan, sometimes in the Narragansett, or Niantic, or Nipmuck, or Connecticut valley, or Quinnipiac (Quiripee) dialect" and that some place names were "extra-limitary" to the tribe that gave them (Trumbull 1881:45). Ten examples, mostly in southern Connecticut and southwestern Rhode Island, are:

1. Teap'anocke (Pequot/Mohegan) Minnebaug (Narragansett), a place in Westerly, R.I. The terms Massachaug, Muschaug, Minnebaug, or Muxquetaug are probably corrupted from the Narragansett equivalent of Pequot/Mohegan muxquataug, from muskechoge (where rushes grow) (Trumbull 1881)
2. Nekkquoweese (Mohegan) Quonaquataug Pond (Narragansett), a place in Charlestown, also called Pespataug, and Wecapaug
3. Pohtaiyomsek (Narragansett) Wattiompsk (Mohegan), a place in Westerly area, possibly refering to a "jutting rock"
4. Puckhunk'onnuck, Pawkhung'ernock (Mohegan) Paukunnawaw-auke (Narragansett), a place in Wyassup region. possibly referring to a "bear place"
5. Quon'acontaug/Conaquetogue' (Narragansett)— (Pespataug and Neekeequowese), Charlestown

6. Ruttawoo (Quiripi) Moosamattuck (Mohegan), a place near New Haven
7. Wequapaug, Wec'apaug (Narragansett), Weexcodowa (Pequot)
8. Aquabapaug or Pesquamscot (Narragansett), a place in Charlestown (possibly Worden's Pond)
9. Mashapaug Pond, also called Pomamganset (Narragansett)
10. Wolopeconnet (Nipmuck), Poncamac (Narragansett), Babcock's Pond in Westerly

The cultural implications of such multilingualism or linguistic cooperation are intriguing. Modern sociolinguists who study multilingual communities note that several strategies exist to determine which language is used in which situation. In some communities, specific languages are used in specific contexts such as in the home, at work, or in the practice of religion. In other communities, languages are restricted by topic. Still other groups engage in what Charles Ferguson (1959) has called diglossic behavior, where one of the languages is treated as the "high" language or dialect and associated with elites and their activities, as well as literature and the arts, while the other "low" language or dialect is employed by lower status individuals, who nonetheless retain it as a marker of group loyalty (Bonvillain 1993:346). These complex linguistic situations are often made more complicated in multilingual regions by the existence of one or more lingua francas, pidgins, or creoles, which facilitate communication across linguistic boundaries. Chapters 2 and 3 address the complexities of regional relationships and local language communities.

Evidence regarding the early and widespread importance of interpersonal networks comes from a variety of sources, including many of the earliest ethnographic descriptions commonly employed to document specific tribal or community histories. Edward Winslow's report (1824), for example, documents ties between the Massasoit and the Massachusett as well as the people of Martha's Vineyard. This suggests the existence of a multilingual or multidialectal community within a broad region.

Such multilingualism was encouraged by Native cultural practices that were well documented in early accounts, including the fostering of high-status children from allied sachemships, intermarriage among the elites of these same groups, and possibly the presence of captives adopted into the community or used there as slaves (Williams 1936; Bragdon 1981a).

As discussed in Chapter 5, another colonial period phenomenon is the deliberate constitution of communities of so-called praying Indians. At Natick, a community seventeen miles southwest of Boston, for which the canonical "n" dialect Bible standard of the Massachusett language was named, there lived many people who spoke other dialects. Thomas Waban, Eliot's stalwart convert and leader of the praying community at Natick, was also called Weegramomenit (MDX 10:557), clearly an "r" dialect name, consistent with other historical evidence that links Waban to the Pawtucket communities of Nashoba and Wamesit. At least three other prominent members of the Natick community also traced their origins to these r-dialect localities. Likewise, several residents came from the west; from l-dialect-speaking areas within Nipmuck territories (Bragdon 1981a:25).

Traditional interpretations of this data tend to treat composite communities as anomalies, or to discount the effects of the multiple backgrounds of community members on the actions or identities of specific communities. Further investigation indicates that membership in many Native communities was fluid and changeable, and that this fluidity must be incorporated into our understanding of the nature of Native society and culture in the colonial period.

The colonial records of southern New England, particularly land and court records, reveal large numbers of Native witnesses and participants in various civil and criminal suits involving both

Indians and non-Indians. They also include local histories, dating mainly from the nineteenth century, and early correspondence, particularly that of colonial officials and missionaries. Extensive records dating to the period of King Philip's War in 1675–76 demonstrate that the political boundaries implied by linguistic differences and reified in early colonial descriptions are more fluid and complex than has been previously understood. Although the records become sparser in the early eighteenth century, they continue to provide consistent support for a regionally based interpretation.

From these records there emerges a series of personal and regional networks, which reflect not only regional connections but linkages through time as well. People known as Quabaugs, although not precisely located, were resident on the middle Connecticut river near Brookfield, Massachusetts, and the term Quabaug is treated by contemporaries and historians alike as both a place and a political entity. Members of this community are shown in figure 13. Prior to 1650, Quabaugs were also associated with the Qussuck, Nonatuck, and Norwottuck communities.

By the 1670s, they had been joined by the Pocumtucks. During and after King Philip's War, residents of Wekabaug, Natick, Pocasset, Matapoiset, Rehoboth, and Pokanoket were also linked to Quabaug families. This dynamic is reflected not only in the fluctuating groupings evident in the records, but also in the personal histories of identifiable persons such as Mettawamppe who, although affiliated with the Pocumtucks in the 1660s, is also connected to Wekabaug and Quabaug in the late 1660s and early 1670s.

In another example, linkages between the Pennacooks and Pawtuckets of the Merrimac drainage of what is now northeastern Massachusetts and southern New Hampshire, show connections ranging as far south and east as Natick and Charlestown (see fig. 14). Other historical evidence shows marriage ties between Pennacooks and Pawtuckets with Niantics and Wamesits as well. The

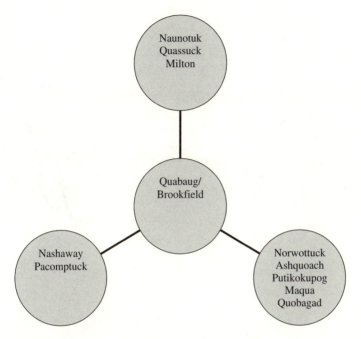

Figure 13. Quabaug community networks

personal linkages of Ahawayet, who died in 1685, are also illustrative. Ahawayet was linked by marriage to the Pawtuckets, had a brother and father both affiliated with the Niantics of southern Rhode Island, both of whom ended up in Saugus, just north of Boston. The reconstructed genealogy of Nanapashemet, said to be the greatest of the early sixteenth-century Massachusett sachems, shows his children and grandchildren associated with communities stretching between Marblehead and Natick.

Similar clusterings and long-distance relationships are found throughout southern New England. The Niantic community, elusive in the historical record and long overshadowed by their powerful neighbors and kin the Narragansetts and Pequot-

207

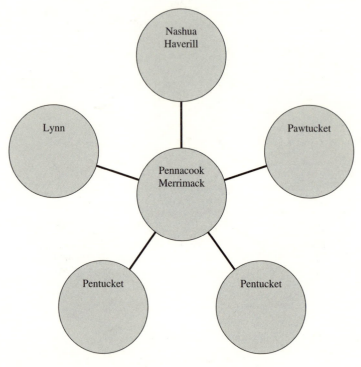

Figure 14. Pennacook community networks

Mohegans, is also of interest. In the late seventeenth century, for example, individuals identified as Niantic claimed relationships with Pequots, Wekapaugs, Pocumtucks, Narragansetts, Wampanoags, and residents of Natick. Similarly, Cowesets, also linked to the Narragansetts and Pequots through sometime tributary status, claimed links to Wampanoags, Agawams, and Pocumtucks (see fig. 15).

Preliminary work on peoples of the lower Connecticut River shows a similar clustering and, importantly, links across what are

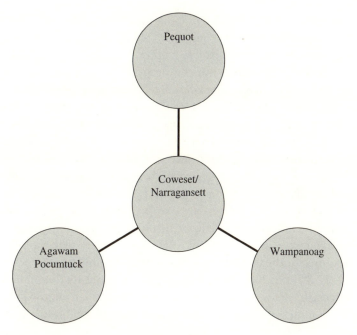

Figure 15. Coweset community networks

now the modern state boundaries; although these modern boundaries are acknowledged by all scholars to be irrelevant to understanding contact and colonial-period Native territories, they often limit investigation of specific communities by default. A reconstruction of the Connecticut River community of Wagunk shows not only strong connections to the upriver groups, but also the important role played by women and their presumed control over land in these connections between communities (Ives 2004).

It has also been possible to create some hypothetical historical/ genealogical networks through time by linking individuals to those associated with them, and then linking their associates to demonstrate not so much a documented chain of kin relations, but an illustration of the complexity of knowledge and relationship that characterized Native communities in the late seventeenth and early eighteenth centuries. Although such linkages are common to all human experience, their concrete expression in this extended chart illustrates dramatically the nature of ties between Native people that transcended both space and time.

The evidence presented here is open to several interpretations. It is consistent with early accounts of marriage exchange, although the mechanics of that exchange are still unclear, particularly the patterning of postmarital residence, descent of political power, and the inheritance of property. However, not all linkages reflected in this data are through marriage, and many of the later seventeenth-century materials suggest that mobility accounts for the majority of multicommunity linkages.

It is also possible to argue that such community fluctuation reflects the disruption that became the status quo in many Native communities in southern New England after the establishment of permanent English settlements there. Direct interference such as that imposed on the residents of Natick by missionaries and colonial officials, and the indirect effects of disease, displacement, and conflicts with rivaling Native groups might all account for the seemingly restless state of Native society in the seventeenth and early eighteenth centuries.

King Philip's War was also clearly responsible for the disappearance and realignment of several Native communities, as Natives loyal to the English disassociated themselves from the rebels, and as communities were displaced or major combatants defeated, dispersed, or imprisoned. After the war, many Natives were displaced and, as Indian communities coalesced in the region, some must have been required to travel in order to maintain ties with relatives and friends. It appears likely, however, that the regional networks clearly established in the early seventeenth century were also instrumental in the continuing survival of Native identity in the postwar period.

Evidence for this comes from several sources. In Windham County, Connecticut, alone, Native peoples of several community backgrounds can be tracked through genealogical and census data (Pasay 2002). Members of the Peagun family of Natick are an interesting example, as they are frequently listed in the Woodstock, Connecticut, and Dudley, Massachusetts, records of the eighteenth century. The Sunsimuns lived variously in Woodstock, Canterbury, Plainfield, and Killingly. Martha's Vineyard and Nantucket public records make note of many Native people who resided on or had interests in communities on both islands (Segel and Pierce 2003). Similar records for southeastern Connecticut and Rhode Island show may links among Narragansetts, Niantics, and Pequots throughout the eighteenth century (Brown and Rose 2001). A letter written by the Reverend Edward Deake in 1765 to the governors of the New England Company noted that among the Narragansetts at Charlestown at that time there were "sundry families of Indians which properly belong to other tribes."

Some of the features of networks described above are clearly related to the connections between the colonies themselves. For example, there are clear links between the communities of Natick, Hassanimisco, and Chaubunagungamaug that are due to the expansion of settlements from Dedham, Massachusetts, to Worcester County, and to the communities of Dudley, Massachusetts, and Woodstock, Connecticut. This feature of Native linkages has yet to be adequately studied.

SERVITUDE AND ENSLAVEMENT

The ordeal of the Pequot Indians after the Pequot War included the enslavement of many of their people by other Indian communities and by the English. Many of those who were not sent out of the colony were distributed among prominent English families, where their circumstances were often harsh and regulated only by tardy colonial court action, especially in Rhode Island and Connecticut. In Middlesex County, a number of such Native servants committed suicide or died of exposure. By the eighteenth century, scholars estimate that nearly one thousand Native people were enslaved or indentured among the English settlers of Rhode Island, Connecticut, and Massachusetts. Among the many hardships associated with this lot, detailed by a number of other scholars, were health hazards. Native people seemed continually subject to ailments that failed to affect the surrounding English throughout the eighteenth century. A glance at Boston church records, for example, lists many Indian servants who died of one complaint or another, such as the 1687 notice concerning the servant Ezbon, an Indian, "hopefully godly, having lived ten years among the English, could read, desired to serve God etc. and dyed" (NEHGS Roxbury Church records, 1738).

The connections of these people to Native communities were various. Robin Cassacinamon, a servant of Wait Winthrop, was later named leader of the reconstituted Pequot community, for example (McBride 1996:81). Others were seemingly placed in English households by their own extended families. In some cases it is difficult to know the status of the individuals who turn up in the English records. A survey of Middlesex County court records (with jurisdiction over most of eastern Massachusetts Bay) listed numerous Native people, both men and women, who were prosecuted in English courts in the late seventeenth and eighteenth centuries. Many of these were prosecuted for proximity to English households and for petty theft, which suggests that these were people who frequented English settlements. Frequently dismissed by contemporaries and more recent scholars as having been "unable to adapt," these were the most troubled survivors of groups whose subsistence base had been destroyed, who had been thrust into dependence and depleted by disease.

A comparison of land records from Middlesex County shows that several individuals prosecuted for theft and other misdemeanors were also witnesses to or participants in land sales and transfers with far flung Native communities. A systematic study of these Native people and the ways they voluntarily, or through force, acted as agents in English land acquisition has yet to be done.

On the other hand, legislation passed between 1670 and 1700 in all New England colonies made it easier for creditors to dispossess or enslave Indian debtors. In addition, between 1696 and 1716, tax codes in all colonies began to categorize servants as personal property. By the mideighteenth century, some of these laws had been relaxed, but the damage was done. John Sainsbury's original study of Indian peoples in the eighteenth century in Rhode Island suggests that close to 37 percent of Native residents of the colony were servants, slaves, or "pauper apprentices" (Sainsbury 1975:379, 392–93; Herndon and Sekatau 1997). At the same time, Native people were increasingly categorized as "negro" or "black," lumping them with enslaved and freed African Americans also becoming more numerous in the colony at that time (Herndon and Sekatau 1997:114–43).

On Martha's Vineyard, by the mid-eighteenth century, several Native persons were listed on "disbursements to the poor." Most of these individuals had family residing in settled communities on the islands (Mayhew n.d.; Segel and Pierce 2003). Among these "poor" was included Zachariah Papemeck, a well-connected, well-known religious leader with family still living. His example, like that of others on the poor list, suggests that disbursements were made to elderly people regardless of their family connections as part of the mission of the Society for the Propagation of the Gospel, and did not necessarily indicate separation from their communities. A similar pattern can be discerned in the guardian's records for the nineteenth century as well (Den Ouden 2005; Doughton 1997).

At Mashpee, Native leaders such as Simon Popmonet, son of the sachem Paupmunnuck of Oyster Island, submitted a petition complaining that local whites were forcing Natives into indebtedness and then forcing them to work or turn over their children for indenture. This pattern was common elsewhere on the Cape as well (Nicholas 2002:169).

An important study that is yet to be done is the relation of these people forcibly enmeshed in colonial society to their families and communities. Ruth Herndon and Ella Sekatau cite several examples of families who "increasingly labored without contracts in the houses and farms of their Anglo-American neighbors." However, as of 1832, the Narragansetts reported that three-quarters of their people were resident on the reservation, so they seem to have had at least vague knowledge of "the rest" (Herndon and Sekatau 1997:160).

ITINERANCY

Josiah Cotton, who had worked among the Christian Natives of the Plymouth area for nearly forty years, wrote in 1756 that "the Native peoples still prefer a wandering life," echoing the sentiments of Daniel Gookin nearly a century before. Are we mistaken in understanding the Native peoples of colonial New England as primarily sedentary, linked by people who moved? Has ethnography "privileged the cultural figure 'Native' over the intercultural 'traveler'" (Clifford 1997:24, 1988)? Appadurai suggests that the notion of "Native" is confining, locating people in space and time (1986), and that ethnography has "localized what is actually a regional/national/global nexus relegating to the margins the external relations and displacements of a 'culture'" (Clifford 1997:24). Thus, in order to understand local/global historical encounters, co-productions, dominations, and resistances, one needs to focus on hybrid, cosmopolitan experiences as much as on rooted Native ones.

Nineteenth-century scholarship documented a network of trails well known to Indian peoples in the colonial period, and some of these are still extant. Tracing the relationship between these trails and Native settlements is a study that is yet to be done, but it is clear that settlement in central Massachusetts was structured along not only waterways, but also by the route along the "great path" that ran west from Boston and split going south to Hartford and west toward Springfield.

There are a number of figures in southern New England Native history that might be termed "travelers." Squanto of Pawtuxet (Clifford 1988) and Epanew of Martha's Vineyard both traveled to Europe and had firsthand knowledge of English life; John Ahatan was a convert who dabbled in the affairs of many Indian communities; John Wompas of Hassanamessit studied at Harvard and died in London, leaving his new world estate to his Nipmuck nephews. One could argue that Uncas, the "first of the Mohegans" made a virtue of cultural flexibility; his ability to work in both English and Indian worlds made him powerful in each.

According to Marshall Sahlins, the idea of the individual as traveler is in part derived from an idea that culture is the abstraction of concrete social structure, that "the notion of social structure was always secreting out pragmatic individuals whose interests and intentions whether for the system or against it, were constituting of it, society was where the action was, and it responded to real politics and real economics" (1999:401). I would add that individuals as travelers played an important role in linking communities together in Native New England, reinforcing regional Native identities and providing a mechanism for flexible choice.

Furthermore, the notion of community does not necessarily require grounding in either space or time; many people understood themselves to be part of communities with whom they had had little physical contact, as Wampas's will (described previously) suggests. Instead, it is possible that community was also a function of shared family, ideas, and experiences, and that Native people in the colonial period came to recognize themselves in these terms.

8.

Being Indian in Colonial New England

English interference in Indian lives took many forms during the colonial period in southern New England. Prior even to permanent settlement, European-derived diseases devastated coastal populations of Massachusett and Pokanoket peoples, depopulating large stretches of fertile, cultivated ground, making English settlement in those areas easier and more rapid than in other parts of the region. English land-use practices also altered the ecology of the region, upsetting seasonal hunting and collecting patterns of the Native inhabitants (Thomas 1979; Cronon 1983). More destabilizing was the relatively rapid spread of English settlement, causing the displacement of Indian communities to the boundaries and less fertile areas of their former territories (Weinstein 1983b). The introduction of English livestock and domesticated crops also affected the ecology and constrained Indian ways of making a living.

Christian missionaries and other colonial officials also interfered with the most intimate aspects of Native life (Salisbury 1974; Axtell 1985). They required the Indians whom they controlled to adopt an English family structure and a moral code that granted dominance to the male head of household; to abstain from polygynous marriages and divorce; and to treat as sinful (and sometimes unlawful) premarital sexual relations and adultery (Plane 1996, 2000). Attacks on Native cosmology, healing practices, and character were common, and alcohol was freely available to the weakened and discouraged of most Indian communities (Cotton 1733–48).

Thomas Mayhew, Sr., assured his readers in 1678 that sorcery had been banished on Martha's Vineyard, and others shared that comfortable assumption. The decline of reported magical practices among the English settlers of southern New England and their descendants by the end of the seventeenth century coincided with the subduing of most of the remaining Indian population of the region. But practices defined and condemned as "magical" were still reported in southern New England in the succeeding century, and practitioners of magic were still sought. The fact that many of these practitioners were Indians, or were said to be Indians, that to be English was increasingly to not be a believer or practitioner of magic, to not be an Indian, raises many questions about English and Indian world views and their relationship to one another. In many ways, Indian and English identity in southern New England was mutually defined, just as their destinies were inextricably linked.

According to William Simmons, a structural model opposing good and evil (Simmons 1981:56) provided Puritans with a framework for explaining cultural differences between them and the Indians they sought to displace. As Simmons notes "The Puritans who settled in Massachusetts, Connecticut, and Rhode Island believed that the Indian inhabitants of these areas worshipped devils, that Indian religious practitioners were witches, and that the Indians themselves were bewitched. These beliefs appear as matter of fact assumptions in the vocabulary of all the

New English who wrote about Indian culture" (56). According to Simmons "Puritan commitment to the devil and witchcraft theory of Indian culture intensified rather than diminished with experience . . . since Puritans perceived the devil and all behavior associated with him as the inversion of godliness, they experienced natural man-Indians as well as English sinners as an inverted expression of their cultural ideal. The belief in witches provided the Puritans with an extremely negative image against which the exemplary citizen and saint could be contrasted" (58). Simmons points out that in contrast to Puritan orthodoxy, revelations were acceptable communications from the supernatural among Indians in the seventeenth century (59–60). Such revelations were viewed by the English as disruptive to ordinary social life, and those who admitted to them were to be shunned or punished.

At the same time, although Puritans noted the existence of Indian witchcraft, they did not fear its effects on themselves (Simmons 1981:64–65) because they felt their God was stronger and the Indian devil weaker. However, "in the New World, Puritan witchcraft beliefs provided a framework for evaluating cultural differences, and through them Indians became mythologized" (65).

This hardening of attitudes also had an impact on Indian lives in many other ways. Land use and customs of inheritance in some communities were transformed. Political organization in others was disrupted, traditional economic relations were upset, and intercommunity ties were severed or strained. Land loss and the disruption of traditional means of providing for community members left many Indians homeless and poverty stricken. Some who were dispossessed through debt or defeat in the Pequot War or King Philip's War were forced into long-term apprenticeship, servitude, or slavery (Sainsbury 1971). Native people began to accept the negative evaluations of their traditional culture. Folk stories and memorates collected among New England's people in the nineteenth and twentieth centuries suggest that the old ways were understood to be forbidden or at least dangerous, that the manitou that infused the world had become embodied in malevolent ghosts (Simmons 1986; Crosby 1988).

While every Native community was different and each Indian person's experience was unique, some patterns emerge with great time depth. Family relationships, kinship, and intermarriage remained distinct from those of the English, a pattern discussed by Plane (1995), whose analysis suggests that initial English interference into Indian family structure and morality gave way in many areas to a dismissive disinterest allowing a variety of domestic and marital arrangements to remain possible in Indian communities.

Lineage strength and elite leadership continued to mark many Indian communities, and further research into the genealogical connections in the longest surviving communities seems to support this pattern. Communities continued to be connected through marriage and kinship, with status considerations continuing in importance in regulating intercommunity relations as well.

Cosmological principles of animatism, supernaturalism, and a belief in portents and dreams were marked in Indian communities. Witchcraft and sorcery, the province of powwaws in the seventeenth century, were practiced on the one hand by healers and herbalists, and, on the other, greatly feared in Indian communities. Ethnographic studies of witchcraft suggest that as communities are embattled or otherwise oppressed, where there are sanctions against open aggression, witchcraft accusations become common. These conditions exactly describe many Indian communities at the end of the eighteenth century. Here, as elsewhere, traditional practices found new or altered meanings within the colonial context

According to Simmons (1986), Indian folk healers served Indian and white clients during the colonial and postcolonial period. An early historian of Natick observed that the town "once teemed with Indian physicians and 'doctresses.'" As late as the 1920s Matthias Amos of Mashpee was well known on Cape Cod as a healer (1986:100–1). In southern Maine, Molly Ockett was a Pigwacket healer in the early years of the nineteenth century (McBride and Prins 1996).

Roy Harvey Pearce, Neal Salisbury, and Richard Slotkin have argued that warfare against Indians was warfare against undesirable aspects of the Puritan self projected on Indians, and, when the Indians had been subdued, those undesirable aspects were seen as the "Indianization" of Puritans themselves (Simmons 1986:70–71). As Simmons argues, the devil-witchcraft dichotomy "provided a moral basis for distancing, depersonalizing, and eventually displacing the Native inhabitants, and when this process was completed, it provided the plot for historical interpretations of these events" (71). Puritans remembered Indians mainly in terms of the "myth by which they accounted for the evil within themselves" (72).

As the frontier moved westward, leaving some Native peoples behind the frontier, it becomes more difficult to find them in historical records. Only occasionally do Native peoples attract the attention of the English colonists, most of whom now saw New England as their ancestral land. Occasionally, descriptions are written of Native people, especially when they came together in groups. Gathering places for the Indians of the region included church grounds, dances, weddings, and funerals. The "frolics" deplored by some whites and Indians were times when Indians sang, danced, and "fittled" and interacted both with neighbors and "strange Indians." These gathering places are also marked on the landscape; dance grounds, meeting grounds, grave yards, and fishing spots, many associated with folklore, have survived to the current day.

These practices had a long life in Indian communities in southern New England. Gladys Tantaquidgeon, the descendant of noted Mohegan Indian women healers, recorded the presence of a several Indian healers on Martha's Vineyard where she did field-work in the early part of the twentieth century. According to Tan-taquidgeon, "there were, it was said, certain of the old women who were more adept in the art of preparing and administering medicines," and who were "herb doctors of great renown" (1928:16). Among the characteristics of these women's work was the tendency to treat cures as "secret property." Women "went out at odd times to places where desired roots and plants grew, when others would not know of their whereabouts." The herb doctors also practiced "certain rules" in the preparation of med-icine, including the use of sun-dried plant materials that partook of the sun's healing power and avoidance of metal implements in their preparation (17). Similar practices were also recorded among the nearby Mohegan (Tantaquidgeon 1972:69). Al-though Tantaquidgeon notes the "absence of magic and ritual" in these cures, in comparison with the sorcery practiced elsewhere in Native North America, she also notes that one healer, the well-known Gay Head woman Tamson Weeks, one of the last fluent speakers of the Massachusett language, often described her own technique as using herbs and medicines to expel the "tcipai," or "devil" that was causing the patient to suffer. Tantaquidgeon also heard of some people who were said to practice the "black arts" such as a woman who was said to be able to transform herself into a bear, a bird, or a white feather, and of others who annoyed peo-ple with their practices (25–26).

Annmarie Shimony, who has studied witchcraft among the Iro-quois, believes that, among these people, the very close connec-tion between witchcraft and the Native medicinal complex is an accommodation to the modern situation (1994:162). Medicine was already linked aboriginally to witchcraft, in that the effects of witchcraft were often evident in illness. And since Native medi-cine has been relatively little affected by acculturation, it is not surprising that it now lends its techniques and its personnel for combating malevolence. In fact, witchcraft and medicine have become merged in many instances.

ETHNICITY AND HISTORICITY:
GHOSTS, SPIRITS, ANCESTORS, AND THE LANDSCAPE

A growing recognition among Native people in southern New England of their ethnic identity as "other" is evident in later Native language documents in which "nissinuog" or "auwaog people" was replaced by "Indiansog." Beliefs in dual souls, culture heroes, and shape changers were told in Native communities as a reflection of the awareness that Native life had been profoundly different prior to the English settlement of their lands. Stories of ghosts and spirits became very common in Native folklore in the nineteenth century, with precedents in Native, African, and English folk culture (Simmons 1986). The brush heaps that marked many Indian trails, the monuments of battles, and the continued isolation of many sacred places in the landscape of Indian people further reinforced the presence of supernatural beings or beings from the past (Crosby 1988). Native people continued to live in what Simmons called "a myth-filled world where old frontier incidents, Indian memories, and stories of Indian ghosts were still in the thoughts of living people" (Simmons 2002:131). Theirs was a magical historicity.

The seamlessness of Indian life during the colonial period was a product of the way daily interactions and seasonal celebrations reinforced basic relationships and truths. Many aspects of symbolic expression and extensions of meaning are lost to us, but it appears that Native symbols, including birds and serpents, continued to play an important role in Native cosmology, and tobacco continued to reflect spirituality and harmony. Supernatural beings, including the Christian God, ghosts, and the Devil were very present in the Native universe, and if the devil came to be associated with paganism, it was "paganism" that many were sure was very near the surface, ready to break forth at any time.

Books and writings in Native languages gained symbolic status in many communities, especially as Native languages were less and less frequently spoken. These books and writings became a kind of community wealth, a preservation of Indian heritage that explains why so many Indians kept such books even when they could not read them.

LANGUAGE CHANGE, LOSS, AND PERSISTENCE

The admittedly sparse evidence suggests that the linguistic landscape in the seventeenth century was enriched and mediated by multilingualism, intermarriage, shifting political alliances, and English patronage. As these social factors changed, a different kind of linguistic complexity may have resulted. Social trends that developed in the late seventeenth and eighteenth centuries included the establishment of permanent Christian communities, the concomitant adoption of vernacular literacy, and the development of self-promoted hegemonies where language itself may have become a marker of local Indian identity.

In this scenario, multilingualism, possibly the norm in southern New England at the time of contact, declined with changing patterns of marriage, alliance, and the increasing isolation of Native communities. At the same time, isolation itself contributed to increasing dialectical differences at the local level, leading in some cases to the isolation of dialects (and ultimately languages) within single households or extended families. Here, the linguistic complexity and declining "cross-communication" increasingly noted by English observers was possibly reflected.

By the beginning of the eighteenth century, Englishmen fluent in the Native languages noted significant linguistic differences within much more limited regions. Plymouth minister Josiah Cotton's wryly humorous dialogue written in 1709, between an English minister and an Indian, reads in part (according to a letter drafted by Cotton Mather to the New England Company in 1710):

The former Editions of the bible were in the Natick Dialect. but if it be done in the Noop dialect, which would best suit the most valuable body of our surviving Indians; those on the Main, and at Nantucket would not understand it so well as they should. The books written by two eminent Preachers in their Tongue, the Indians complain of a Difference in them that is considerable. (quoted in Pilling 1891:157)

There is little doubt that the increasing familiarity of at least some Englishmen with Native languages led to an increased appreciation of their complexity and of the differences between them. Experience Mayhew, a humble and thoughtful man, as well as a fluent speaker of Massachusett, concluded his description of the Indian language by saying: "I shall at present ad no more concerning the Indian language, save in general I think it good and regular. That it may seem otherwise to Some, is as I Judge, because there is yet no good Gramer made for it, nor are the Rules of it fully understood" (1722:17).

Whether such complexity, as observed by sophisticated and fluent eighteenth-century missionaries and scholars, was entirely due to their sensitivity and not (at least in part) to historical and cultural factors that influenced Native language use at that period is unclear. Scattered references to Native language use, in combination with a knowledge of the early-contact linguistic scene, indicates that some part of the changes in Native language use were indeed the result of changing social relations among the Indians themselves, as indicated by Mayhew: "I found that there was so much difference betwixt theirs and that used among us, that I could not well understand their discourses and they much less understand mine, which obliged me to make use of an Interpreter" (Mayhew 1722 cited in Trumbull 1873:146).

While at Connecticut, Mayhew collected a version of the Lord's Prayer, with the help of an interpreter, "in the dialect of the Pequot Indians." Comparing this to Massachusett, Trumbull finds that /y/ appears where /n/ would be expected, and also finds differences in locative endings. Trumbull concluded that this was rather an example of the Niantic dialect (1873:146). Another version of the Lord's Prayer collected in 1721 from Pequots and Mohegans near New London is so corrupted it is impossible to tell how it might have differed from that retrieved by Mayhew (148).

Later in the eighteenth century, however, reportage of dialects and languages emphasized local diversity, with word lists collected by Ezra Stiles, at Narragansett, Naugatuck, and Groton in 1769, 1787, and 1762 respectively, and an Unquachog vocabulary collected by Thomas Jefferson in 1791 (Goddard 1978c:72; Stiles 1787; Cowan 1973b:164). The Naugatuck vocabulary printed in John De Forest's *History of the Indians of Connecticut* (1964:491) indicates that the Paugusset of western Connecticut spoke an "r" dialect, in common with the Schaghticokes, and, like Delaware to the west and south, a contrast in common usage such as the word for bear (awauuso) (see, also, for example, Massachusett mashq) (Speck 1928:215). Thomas Jefferson wrote of the Unquachogs that "the language they speak is a dialect differing a little from the Indians settled Near Southampton called Shinicocks and also from those of Montock called Montocks. The three tribes can barely understand each other" (Jefferson 1791:467–68; Harrington 1903).

Zaccheus Macy of Nantucket, who took a lively interest in the Native people there, reported at the end of the eighteenth century: "They desese [decease] latter years much from there former speach boath in names of places & there common talk and yet all read in one Bibel but cannot understand one another as far as Dartmouth & but very hardly understand the great mash [Mash-

pee] Indians the Vineyard Indians they can make out to understand" (Macy 1792b).

The history of Native languages in southern New England is
more difficult to trace as local communities turned inward, as
missionary efforts diminished, and as Native populations continued to decline. Native language use in the nineteenth century
was confined to increasingly private contexts. Multilingualism
and multidialectism, which might have been encouraged by the
well-documented interactions of Native communities throughout southern New England, instead probably contributed to the
further isolation of speakers as the century wore on.

At the same time, the nature of contact between Native peoples
in the eighteenth and early nineteenth centuries may also have
contributed to the ultimate loss of most of these languages. Such
contact was frequently in the form of visits from itinerant Native
preachers and ministers, who, along with more formally trained
English clerics, regularly visited Native communities and
preached to them in English (O'Connell 1992; Simmons and
Simmons 1982:xxx). As (Biblical) English became associated
with prestigious and highly valued religious activities, it also
became the functioning lingua franca for Natives who undoubt-
edly still spoke their Native language at home.

In sum, the history of language use and the history of linguistic
study of Native languages in southern New England do not tell
entirely the same story. The writings of seventeenth- and
eighteenth-century Englishmen of varying skills and sympathies
are the basis for our knowledge of most of these now extinct languages and how they were used, and more recent writing on the
subject of these languages has tended to reflect their prejudices.
Modern philological analysis and sociolinguistic research provide
additional clues about the rich linguistic environment experienced by the Native peoples of southern New England and also
emphasize the role their own shifting social and cultural identities

and concerns played in the history of language use, a history that we only dimly recognize today.

MOBILITY

In addition to these changes, some communities, especially among the Narragansetts (dispossessed by their sachem Tom Ninegret), took up a mobile way of life, unable to settle and unwilling to abandon each other and their homeland. These people ultimately settled near Charlestown, Rhode Island. Other mobile families and groups were reported for Plymouth, in the area around Worcester, and the middle Connecticut River. These people, who continued a kind of seasonal round, also made a living by day labor and the sale of baskets, brooms, and berries. Ann McMullen's extensive survey of the basket-making tradition in southern New England documents the movements of these communities, with baskets acting as regional/ethnic markers giving sense of place and identity to these itinerant groups (1991).

The mobility associated with occupational preferences and necessities was also a feature of eighteenth-century Indian life. In particular, the whaling industry created a large body of itinerant Indian men who spent months, or even years, at sea, leaving families at home, and friends to protect their property. Several portraits of these whalers and maritime trades are available (Vickers 1981; Nicholas 2002) but their role in the regional linkage of communities is less well known. Among the Eastern Pequots, for example, men were regularly at sea where they served alongside Native men from Gay Head, Nantucket, Dartmouth, and elsewhere.

CRIME AND IDENTITY

On Martha's Vineyard, a study of the eighteenth century English court records identifies a number of persistent petty criminals among the Indians, many of whom were prosecuted for theft or trespass. These same individuals, however, were participants in complex family networks with longstanding ties to particular territories, which suggests that the pattern of theft is really an expression of community boundaries (Bragdon forthcoming). Numerous reported incidents of sheep stealing on Martha's Vineyard are examples of this, and the Native thief and those who were caught eating the "muttin" with him or her were often prosecuted as a group. A study yet to be done is the way Native family groups acted in concert to assert their rights to land or resources in the eighteenth century.

It is almost impossible to read with objectivity the discouraging word-pictures of Indians in New England suffering "the Woeful effects of Drunkeness" and engaging in lengthy card games or gambling matches from which they emerged penniless that come to dominate late eighteenth-century literature on Indians. Several authors have described in detail the many suicides, murders, and ruined lives alcohol claimed in Indian communities (Jennings 1975). Still others note that gambling and other debts made many Indians, especially in Natick, landless and homeless (O'Brien 1999).

At the same time, it is clear that liquor was considered a high-status drink that was associated with a period of great wealth in Native history, and it likely contributed to a kind of out-of-body experience approximating those once sought through trance. It is probably not an accident that several of the most prominent of Indian preachers, especially during the widespread conversions of the Great Awakening, had sometimes been addicted to "strong drink." Gambling had many sacred associations in Native New England (Bragdon 1996b) and was also a feature of nearly all community gatherings in the early contact period. It is also likely, therefore, that gambling and other frolics derived their continuing popularity among Indian people from these older associations, in the same way that traditional Creek church services often ended with a ball game.

Even the practice of Christianity had the ironic effect of reaffirming Native ethnicity through its use of Native language in the service and hymns, its associations with the early history of many communities, and its associations with the Indian bible and Indian language literacy. Thus on Gay Head, even after the majority of the community had become Baptists, the church remained both the physical and symbolic center of the community. Likewise, at Mashpee and Narragansett the Indian churches served a number of community functions and were the location of yearly powwaws or festivals that were surely the continuations of ancient first-fruit or harvest festivals (Willoughby 1935).

Conclusions

The elderly minister of Gay Head, Zachary Hossueit, was said to be the last to preach in the Native language. When asked why he did so he replied "why, to keep up my nation."

—Burgess 1970:22

This book has been about Indians during the colonial period in southern New England. It is not a history, but a cultural interpretation. By focusing on ideas and beliefs, by emphasizing social institutions and practices within Indian communities as well as the historical context in which such social actions took place, it has many of the characteristics (and drawbacks) of a modern ethnography. Presently anthropologists work with people who are most often emerging from the impositions of colonial authority around the world, people whose societies can no longer be understood as isolated entities (if they ever could). Anthropologists now take into account the effects of colonialism and its agents, and their critiques of older ethnographies are part of this process. Writing historical cultural accounts of colonized people is even more difficult because the people one would hope to interview are no longer present, and all that remains are fragments of what must once have been a tremendously complex and confusing array of behaviors and beliefs.

231

Conclusion

However, the overt and implicit use of the acculturative model by most scholars who have tried to explain Indian life in New England during the colonial period has not been successful. In order to fit the analyses into the master narrative of American history, most scholars have, perhaps unwillingly, echoed the findings of earlier racist or triumphalist interpretations, that Indians in New England disappeared or were absorbed or were robbed of any meaningful ways of expressing themselves and their groups' identities.

By taking a language-based perspective, one that looks at how people enacted and expressed ideas and relationships through speech, and the ways varieties of speech reflect the complexities of social relationships in colonial and postcolonial Native communities, this book examines the vibrancy of Indian communities in the past. Indian communities were local language communities, and the ways they created social realities are partly reflected in the documents they left and the words that were recorded in other sources.

Language gives a way into social relationships as well. Recorded land transfers, marriage banns, and petitions are themselves reflections of varying social roles and activities and are immediate evidence of the ways these were negotiated after Christianity and literacy were introduced.

In the absence of first person testimony, we can turn to ethnographic methods for determining patterns of marriage and inheritance to demonstrate that certain cultural principles appear in the patterns we can detect in the surviving records. Careful scrutiny of these records shows that Native people in southern New England were pursing goals that their ancestors would have recognized: to act morally by protecting family and community through sacrifice, risk, and a close relationship to the supernatural world.

Conclusion

The emphasis on Indian communities as moral entities as well as physical ones also allows us to understand the choices individual Native people may have made: to marry non-Indians or to enter into other relationships with them; to acquire or consolidate territories; to adopt new work, and to accept new ideas. It also allows us to see the ways Indians might move from place to place and still identify as Indian. Those working or living away from home were still thought to belong, and they contributed to their communities in a variety of ways, as well as maintaining intercommunity ties for all.

Indian people changed during the colonial period. Grandchildren behaved differently than their grandparents and great-grandparents, just as English children born in the decades after the establishment of Plymouth or Boston were different than their immigrant ancestors. Nevertheless, we characterize the eight generations of Anglo-Americans of the colonial period in New England as participants in a particular cultural style and as sharing a particular world view. New England Indian people, too, had a particular cultural style, and their world view was distinct as well.

We can imagine them in a world filled with objects they did not create, clothed in garments that evolved in another social context, and paying heed to religious ideas that called into question some of their parents' beliefs. But we can also imagine them showing deference to leaders whose parents had been sachems, who descended from men and women who were "rightful" rulers. We can imagine them recognizing the unseen forces of the supernatural world and the need to propitiate them. We can imagine them marrying to keep lineages aligned and to maintain physical connections to various places. And we can imagine them working in the interstices of the colonial economy, showing only the most acceptable face to those who controlled their activities and paid their wages. We know they did this because their writings and speeches have survived. A few observant outsiders pointed it out as well. A cultural account lets us use this information to understand colonial Indian life as it was experienced, not temporally, not through a Euroamerican lens, but according to a Native logic.

As the English frontier moved west, and as the population continued to decline, Native people in New England received very little attention from non-Indians, except when they became burdensome as colonial wards, or irksome, as when they refused to comply with what they considered arbitrary or unjust treatment. The portrait of the Native people in the colonial period presented here is one that depends on ethnographic descriptions of the early contact period, linguistics and archaeology, as well as comparative information about people in similar circumstances. It recognizes that what the Native people of New England became was due to both their past and to the colonial context in which they found themselves. It also recognizes that colonial Native New England was a mosaic of many contexts and experiences. In spite of the many tragedies and injustices that became their lot as a people, this book has tried to demonstrate the remarkable vitality of colonial Native culture. On their journey to becoming modern Americans, they continued to take a different path.

References

Akin, David, and Joel Robbins, eds. 1999. *Money and Modernity: State and Local Currencies in Melanesia*. Pittsburgh: University of Pittsburgh Press.

Ales, Marion Fisher. 1979. "A History of the Indians on Montauk, Long Island." In *The History and Archaeology of the Montauk Indians*, ed. Gaynell Stone, 13–124. Stony Brook, N.Y.: Suffolk County Archaeological Association.

Allen, John. 1730. Account Book. Dukes County Historical Society. Edgartown, Massachusetts.

Amory, Hugh. 1996. "Preliterate Uses of Print: Two Seventeenth-Century Algonquian Fragments." Paper delivered at a symposium entitled "'Communicating with the Indians: Aspects of the Language Encounter with the Indigenous Peoples of the Americas, 1492–1800." John Carter Brown Library, Brown University, Providence, R.I., October 18–20.

Anderson, Benedict. 1972. "The Idea of Power in Javanese Culture." In *Culture and Politics in Indonesia*, ed. Clair Holt, 1–69. Ithaca: Cornell University Press.

Anderson, Benedict, and Richard O'Gorman. 1991. *Imagined Communities: Reflections on the Origin and Spread of Nationalism*. London/New York: Verso Press.

References

Anderson, Virginia DeJohn. 1994. "King Philip's Herds: Indians, Colonists, and the Problem of Livestock in Early New England." *William and Mary Quarterly* 51 (4): 601–24.

Appadurai, Arjun. 1986. *The Social Life of Things: Commodities in Cultural Perspective.* Cambridge: Cambridge University Press.

Archer, Gabriel. [1706] 1902. "Bartholmews Gosnols Reys Van Engeland Na Het Noorder Gedeelte Van Virginien, anno 1602." In *Gosnold's Settlement at Cuttyhunk,* ed. Pieter Leyden Vander Aa. Boston: Directors of the Old South Work.

Attaquin, Helen A. 1987. "There Are Differences." In *Rooted Like the Ash Trees: New England Indians and the Land,* ed. R. G. Carlson, 54–57. Naugatuck, Conn.: Eagle Wing Press.

Axtell, James. 1985. *The Invasion Within: The Contest of Cultures in Colonial North America.* New York: Oxford University Press.

———. 1988. "At the Water's Edge: Trading in the Sixteenth Century." In *After Columbus: Essays in the Ethnohistory of Colonial North America,* 144–81. New York: Oxford University Press.

Ayer, Mary Farwell. 1908. "Richard Bourne: Missionary to the Mashpee Indians'" *New England Historical Genealogical Register* 62:139–43.

Backus, Isaac. 1871. *A History of New England. With Particular Reference to the Denomination of Christians Called Baptists.* 2 vols. Newton, Mass.: Backus Historical Society.

Badger, Stephen. [1798] 1835. "Historical and Characteristic Traits of the American Indian in General and those of Natick in Particular." Massachusetts Historical Society, Boston, Mass. Collections, 1st Ser., Vol. 5:32–45.

Bailey, Christine Ward. 1987. *Kinship to Kingship: Gender Hierarchy and State Formation in the Tongan Islands.* Austin: University of Texas Press.

Baker, Brenda. J. 1994. "Pilgrim's Progress and Praying Indians: The Biocultural Consequences of Contact in Southern New England." In *In the Wake of Contact: Biological Responses to Conquest,* ed. Clark Spencer Larsen and George R. Milner, 35–44. New York: Wiley-Liss.

Banks, Charles Edward. 1966. *The History of Martha's Vineyard Dukes County Massachusetts in Three Volumes.* Dukes County Historical Society. Edgartown, Mass.

References

Barber, John Warner. 1839. *Historical Collections, Being a General Collection of Interesting Facts, Traditions, Biographical Sketches, Anecdotes &c. Relating to the History and Antiquities of Every Town in Massachusetts.* Worcester, Mass.: Dorr, Howland & Co.

Barber, Jonathan. 1733. Letter to Benjamin Colman, October 2, 1733. Benjamin Coleman Papers, Manuscript no. 1013. Massachusetts Historical Society, Boston, Mass.

Barbour, Philip, ed. 1986. *The Complete Works of John Smith.* 3 vols. Chapel Hill: University of North Carolina Press.

Barnard, John. 1706. Account Book. Peter Foulger Museum Library, Nantucket, Mass.

Barnes, J. A. 1969. "Networks and Political Process." In *Social Networks in Urban Situations,* ed. J. Clyde Mitchell, 57–76. England: Manchester University Press.

Baron, Donna Keith, J. Edward Hood, and Holly V. Izard. 1996. "They Were Here All Along: The Native American Presence in Lower Central New England in the Eighteenth and Nineteenth Centuries." *William and Mary Quarterly,* 3rd series, 53:561–86.

Bartlett, John R. 1856–65. *Records of the Colony of Rhode Island and Providence Plantations in New England* (1636–1792). 10 vols. Providence: A. Crawford Greene and Brothers.

Bassett, Benjamin. 1792. "Fabulous Traditions and Customs of the Indians of Martha's Vineyard."' Massachusetts Historical Society, Boston, Mass. Collections, 1st ser., Vol. 1:139–40.

Basso, Keith. 1983. 'Stalking with Stories: Names, Places, and Moral Narratives among the Western Apache." In *Text, Play, and Story: The Construction and Reconstruction of Self and Society,* ed. Stuart Plattner, 19–55. Washington D.C.: American Ethnological Society.

———. 1996. *Wisdom Sits in Places: Landscape and Language among the Western Apache.* Albuquerque: University of New Mexico Press.

Bateson, Gregory. 1958. *Naven.* 2nd ed. Stanford: Stanford University Press.

Baxter, James Phinney, ed. 1890. *Sir Ferdinando Gorges and His Province of Maine.* 3 Vols. Portland, Maine: Hoyt, Fogg, and Donham.

Bayley, Lewis. 1685. *Manitowompae Pomantamoonk.* Transl. John Eliot. 8 vols. Cambridge, Mass.: [Samuel Green].

References

Baylies, William. 1793. "'A Description of Gay Head (1786)." In *Memoirs of the American Society of Arts and Sciences*, Vol. II, Part 1., 150–55. Boston: n.p.

Becker, Laura L. 1982. "Ministers vs. Laymen: The Singing Controversy in Puritan New England, 1720–1740." *New England Quarterly* 55:79–96.

Bendremer, Jeffrey, Elizabeth Kellog, and Tonya Baroody. 1991. "A Grass-Lined Maize Storage Pit and Early Maize Horticulture in Central Connecticut." *North American Archaeologist* 12(4):325–49.

Benes, Peter, ed. 1983. "American Speech 1600—Present." *Annual Proceedings of the Dublin Seminar for New England Folklife*. Boston: Boston University.

———. 1990. "Itinerant Physicians, Healers, and Surgeon-Dentists in New England and New York, 1720–1825." In *Medicine and Healing*, 95–111. *Annual Proceedings of the Dublin Seminar for New England Folklife*. Boston: Boston University.

Benison, Chris. 1997. "Horticulture and the Maintenance of Social Complexity in Late Woodland Southeastern New England." *North American Archaeologist* 18(1):1–17.

Bennet, M. K. 1955. "The Food Economy of the New England Indians 1605–75." *The Journal of Political Economy* 63:360–96.

Berkhofer, Robert. 1979. *The White Man's Indian: Images of the American Indian, from Columbus to the Present*. New York: Vintage.

Besnier, Niko. 1995. *Literacy, Emotion, and Authority: Reading and Writing on a Polynesian Atoll*. Cambridge: Cambridge University Press.

Beth. 1794. "Joseph Nauhaught." *Massachusetts Magazine* 6 (3):150–51.

Bhaba, Homi. 1995. *The Location of Culture*. London: Routledge.

Biglow, William. 1830. *History of the Town of Natick, Massachusetts*. Boston: Marsh, Caper, and Lyon.

Bird, F. W., Whiting Griswold, and Cyrus Weekes. 1849. *Report of the Commissioners Relating to the Condition of the Indians*, Massachusetts House Document no. 46, Boston.

Bledsoe, Caroline. 1980. *Women and Marriage in Kpelle Society*. Stanford: Stanford University Press.

Blodgett, Harold. 1935. Samson Occom. Dartmouth College Manuscript Series no.3. Hanover, N.H.

References

Blu, Karen. 1996. *"'Where Do You Stay At?' Homeplace and Community Among the Lumbee."* In *Senses of Place*, ed. Steven Feld and Keith H. Basso, 197–228. Santa Fe, N.Mex.: School of American Research Press.

Boas, Franz. 1911. *The Handbook of American Indian Languages.* Vol. 1. Bureau of Ethnology Bulletin 40. Washington, D.C.: Government Printing Office.

Boissevain, Ethel. 1959. "Narragansett Survival: A Study of Group Persistence Through Adapted Traits." *Ethnohistory* 6(4):347–62.

Bonner, Jennifer, and Holly Herbster. 2005. "Documenting the Past: Massachusetts 'Praying Indians' in the Eighteenth Century." Paper presented at the Eastern States Archaeological Federation, Williamsburg, Va., November 9–12,

Bonvillain, Nancy. 1993. *Language, Culture, and Communication.* Englewood Cliffs, N.J.: Prentice-Hall.

———. 1997. *Language, Culture, and Communication: The Meaning of Messages.* 2nd ed. Upper Saddle River, N.J.: Prentice Hall.

Bourne, Russell. 1990. *The Red King's Rebellion: Racial Politics in New England 1675–1678.* New York: Oxford University Press.

Bowden, Henry W., and James P. Ronda, eds. 1980. *John Eliot's Indian Dialogues: A Study in Cultural Interaction.* Westport, Conn.: Greenwood Press.

Bowen, Joanne. 1984. "Account Books and the Study of Subsistence on the New England Farm." Paper presented at the Historic Deerfield Colloquium, "Early American Account Books: Needs and Opportunities for Study," Deerfield, Mass., March 24.

Bradford, William. 1970. *Of Plymouth Plantation, 1620–1647.* Reprint. Ed. Samuel Eliot Morison. New York: Knopf.

Bragdon, Kathleen. 1979. "Probate Records as a Source of Algonquian Ethnohistory." In *Papers of the Tenth Algonquian Conference*, ed. William Cowan, 136–41. Ottawa: Carleton University.

———. 1981a. "'Another Tongue Brought In': An Ethnohistorical Study of Native Writings in Massachusett," Ph.D. diss., Brown University.

———. 1981b. "Crime and Punishment Among the Indians of Eastern Massachusetts, 1675–1750." *Ethnohistory* 28: 23–32.

References

————. 1981c. "Linguistic Acculturation in Massachusett." In *Papers of the Twelfth Algonquian Conference*, ed. William Cowan, 121–32. Ottawa: Carlton University.

————. 1986. "Native Economy on Eighteenth Century Martha's Vineyard and Nantucket." *Papers of the Algonquian Conference* 17:27–42.

————. 1987. "Emphatical Speech and Great Action: An Analysis of Speech Events Described in Seventeenth-Century Sources." *Man in the Northeast* 33:101–11.

————. 1988. "The Material Culture of the Christian Indians of New England, 1650–1775." In *Documentary Archaeology in the New World*, ed. Mary C. Beaudry, 126–31. Cambridge: Cambridge University Press.

————. 1991. "Native Christianity in Eighteenth-Century Massachusetts: Ritual as Cultural Reaffirmation." In *New Dimensions in Ethnohistory*, ed. Barry Gough and Christie Laird, 119–26. Hull, Quebec: Canadian Museum of Civilization.

————. 1992. "Language, Folk History, and Indian Identity on Martha's Vineyard." In *The Art and Mystery of Historical Archaeology: Essays in Honor of James Deetz*, ed. Anne Yentsch and Mary Beaudry, 331–42. Boca Raton, Fla.: CRC Press.

————. 1995. "The Shamanistic Text in Southern New England." *The Kroeber Anthropological Society Papers* 79:166–76.

————. 1996a. "Gender as a Social Category in Native Southern New England." *Ethnohistory* 43 (4): 573–92.

————. 1996b. *Native People of Southern New England, 1500–1650*. Norman: University of Oklahoma Press.

————. 1997. "Massachusett Kinship Terminology and Social Organization 1620–1750. *Northeast Anthropology* 54: 1–14.

————. 1999. "Native Languages as Spoken and Written: Views from Southern New England." In *The Language Encounter in the Americas, 1492–1800*, ed. Edward Grey and Norman Fiering, 173–88. Oxford/New York: Berghahn Books.

————. 2002. "The Interstices of Literacy." In *Anthropology, History, and American Indians: Essays in Honor of William Curtis Sturtevant*, ed. William L. Merrill and Ives Goddard, 121–30. *Smithsonian Contributions to Knowledge* 44:121–30.

————. 2007. "The Pragmatics of Learning to Write: Graphic and Linguistic Pluralism on Martha's Vineyard 1660–1720." Paper

References

Presented at the Annual Meetings of the American Society for Ethnohistory, Tulsa, Okla., November 7–10.

———. Forthcoming. *John Cotton's Martha's Vineyard Wordlist.* Massachusetts Historical Society.

Bratton, Timothy. 1988. "The Identity of the New England Indian Epidemic of 1616–1619.'" *Bulletin of the History of Medicine* 62:351–83.

Breen, Louise A. 1999. "Praying with the Enemy: Daniel Gookin, King Philip's War, and the Dangers of Intercultural Mediatorship." In *Empire and Others: British Encounters with Indigenous Peoples, 1600–1850,* ed. Martin Daunton and Rick Halpern, 101–21. London: UCL Press.

Brenner, Elise M. 1980. "To Pray or to Be Prey, That Is the Question: Strategies for Cultural Autonomy of Massachusetts Praying Town Indians." *Ethnohistory* 27(2):135–52.

———. 1984. "Strategies for Autonomy: An Analysis of Ethnic Mobilization in Seventeenth-Century New England," Ph.D. diss., University of Massachusetts, Amherst.

Brereton, John. [1602] 1905. "A Briefe and True Relation of the Discoverie of the North Part of Virginia in 1602." In *Sailor's Narratives of the Voyages along the New England Coast 1524–1624,* ed. George Parker Winship. Boston: Houghton, Mifflin, and Company.

Bridenbaugh, Carl. 1982. *The Pynchon Papers: Letters of John Pynchon, 1654–1700.* Boston: Colonial Society of Massachusetts.

Brightman, Robert. 1995. "Forget Culture: Replacement, Transcendence, Relexification." *Cultural Anthropology* 10(4):509–46.

Brodeur, Paul. 1985. *Restitution: The Land Claims of the Mashpee, Passamaquoddy and Penobscot Indians of New England.* Boston: Northeastern University Press.

Brown, Barbara W., and James M. Rose. [1980] 2001. *Black Roots in Southeastern Connecticut, 1650–1900.* Detroit, Mich.: Gale Research Company

Brown, Jennifer, and Robert Brightman. 1988. "*The Orders of the Dreamed': George Nelson on Cree and Northern Ojibwa Religion and Myth, 1823.*" St. Paul: Minnesota Historical Society Press.

Brumann, Christoph. 1999. "Writing for Culture: Why a Successful Concept Should Not be Discarded." *Current Anthropology* 40(supplement):S1—S27.

Burgess, Edward. 1970. "The Old South Road of Gayhead." *Dukes County Intelligencer* 12:1.

Burton, William, and Richard Lowenthal. 1974. "The First of the Mohegans." *American Ethnologist* 1(4):589–99.

Byers, Edward. 1987. *The Nation of Nantucket: Society and Politics in an Early American Commercial Center, 1660–1820.* Boston: Northeastern University Press.

Callender, John. 1838. "An Historical Discourse on the Civil and Religious Affairs of the Colony of Rhode Island." In *Collections of the Rhode Island Historical Society* 4. Providence: Knowles, Vose, and Company.

Calloway, Colin G. 1997a. *After King Philip's War: Presence and Persistence in Indian New England.* Hanover, N.H.: University of New England Press.

————. 1997b. *New Worlds for Old: Indians, Europeans, and the Remaking of Early America.* Baltimore: Johns Hopkins University Press.

Campbell, Paul R., and Glenn W. LaFantasie. 1978. "'Scattered to the Winds of Heaven'": Narragansett Indians 1676–1880." *Rhode Island History* 47:66–83.

Campisi, Jack. 1991. *The Mashpee Indians: Tribe on Trial.* Syracuse: Syracuse University Press.

Campisi, Jack, James D. Wherry, Christine Grabowski, and Bettina Malonson. 1983. Wampanoag Tribal Council of Gay Head. Summation of the Historical Narrative and Supportive Documentation in Support of a Petition requesting the acknowledgement of the existence of the Gay Head Wampanoag Tribune using Criteria as contained in 25 CFR 83 as recodified April 1, 1983. Submitted to the Federal Acknowledgement Project, Department of the Interior, Bureau of Indian Affairs.

Canup, John. 1990. *Out of the Wilderness: The Emergence of American Identity in New England.* Middletown, Conn.: Wesleyan University Press.

Carlson, Catherine. 1986. *Archival and Archaeological Research Report on the Configuration of the Seven Original Seventeenth-Century Praying Towns of the Massachusetts Bay Colony.* Amherst: University of Massachusetts Archaeological Services.

References

Carlson, Catherine C., George L. Armelagos, and Ann Magennis. 1992. "Impact of Disease on the Precontact and Early Historic Populations of New England and the Maritimes" In *Disease and Demography in the Americas*, ed. John W. Verano and Douglas H. Ubelaker, 141–52. Washington, D.C.: Smithsonian Institution Press.

Carroll, Brian D. 1999. "Patriarchy, Puritanism & Punishment: Native American Women in the Eighteenth Century New England Legal System, 1710–1790." Paper presented at the 1999 Annual Meeting of the American Society for Ethnohistory, Mashantucket, Conn., October 22.

Cave, Alfred A. 1992 "New England Puritan Misperceptions of Native American Shamanism." *International Social Science Review* 67(1):15–27.

————. 1996. *The Pequot War*. Amherst: University of Massachusetts Press.

Ceci, Lynn. 1975. "Fish Fertilizer: A Native North American Practice." *Science* 188 (4183):26–30.

————. 1979–80. "Maize Cultivation in Coastal New York: The Archaeological, Agronomical, and Documentary Evidence." *North American Archaeologist* 1(1):45–74.

————. 1982. "Method and Theory in Coastal New York Archaeology: Paradigms of Settlement Pattern." *North American Archaeologist* 3(1):5–36.

————. 1990. "Native Wampum as a Peripheral Resource in the Seventeenth-Century World System." In *The Pequots in Southern New England: The Fall and Rise of an American Indian Nation*, ed. Laurence Hauptman and James Wherry, 48–64. Norman: University of Oklahoma Press.

Chafe, Wallace. 1998. "The Importance of Native American Languages." The David Skomp Distinguished Lectures in Anthropology, Indiana University, Bloomington, Ind.

Chafe, Wallace, and Deborah Tannen. 1987. "The Relation between Written and Spoken Language." *Annual Review of Anthropology* 16:383–407.

Champlain, Samuel. [1613] 1966. *Les Voyages du Sr de Champlain*. Paris: Jean Berjon. Ann Arbor: University Microfilms.

Chapin, Howard M. 1918. *Rhode Island in the Colonial Wars*. Providence: Rhode Island Historical Society.

References

Child, D. L., H. Stebins, and D. Fellows, Jr. 1827. *Report on the Condition of the Native Indians and Descendants of Indians, in this Commonwealth* Mass. House Report No. 68, 12–13. Boston.

Church, Benjamin. 1975. *A Diary of King Philip's War, 1675–76*, ed. Alan Simpson and Mary Simpson. Chester, Conn.: Pequot Press.

Clifford, James. 1988. "Identity in Mashpee." In *The Predicament of Culture: Twentieth Century Ethnography, Literature and Art.* Cambridge: Harvard University Press.

———. 1997. *Routes: Travel and Translation in the Late Twentieth Century.* Cambridge: Harvard University Press.

Cogley, Richard W. 1986/7. "John Eliot and the Origins of the American Indian." *Early American Literature* 21:210–25.

———. 1991. "Idealism vs. Materialism in the Study of Puritan Missions to the Indians'." *Method and Theory in the Study of Religion* 3:165–82.

———. 1995. "Two Approaches to Indian Conversion in Puritan New England: The Missions of Thomas Mayhew, Jr., and John Eliot." *Historical Journal of Massachusetts* 28:44–60.

———. 1999. *John Eliot's Mission to the Indians before King Philip's War.* Cambridge: Harvard University Press.

Cohn, Bernard. 1985. "The Command of Language and the Language of Command." In *Writings on South Asian History and Society,* ed. Ranajit Guha. *Subaltern Studies* IV: 276–329. Delhi: Oxford University Press.

Collier, Jane F. 1987. "Rank and Marriage: Or, Why High Ranking Wives Cost More." In *Gender and Kinship: Essays toward a Unified Analsysis,* ed. Jane Collier and Sylvia Yanagisako, 197–200. Stanford: Stanford University Press.

Comoroff, Jean, and John Comoroff. 1991. *Of Revelation and Revolution: Christianity, Colonialism, and Consciousness in South Africa.* Vol. 1. Chicago: University Of Chicago Press.

Conkey, Laura E., Ethel Boissevain, and Ives Goddard. 1978. "Indians of Southern New England and Long Island: Late Period." In *Northeast,* ed. Bruce Trigger, 177–89. *Handbook of North American Indians* Vol. 15. Ed. William C. Sturtevant. Washington D.C.: Government Printing Office.

Conkey, M. W., & S. H. Williams. 1991. "Original Narratives: The Political Economy of Gender in Archaeology." In *Gender at the Crossroads of Knowledge: Feminist Anthropology in the Postmodern*

Era, ed. M. di Leonardo, 102–39. Berkeley: University of California Press.

Connecticut. *Public Records of the Colony of Connecticut.* 1850–1890 [1636–1776]. 15 vols. Ed. J. H. Trumbull, vols. 1–3; C. J. Hoadley, vols. 4–15. Hartford: (Press of) Case, Lockwood & Brainard.

Connecticut State Archives. Indian Papers. 1647–1789 (1st series) and 1666–1820 (2nd series). *Early General Records of Connecticut: Papers and Correspondence of the General Assembly, the Governor and Counsel, and other Colony or State Officials.* Connecticut State Archives, Hartford.

Cook, S. F. 1973. "The Significance of Disease in the Extinction of the New England Indians." *Human Biology* 45:485–508.

Cotton, John R. 1665–1678. *Journal and Vocabulary of the Indians (at Martha's Vineyard).* Manuscript. Massachusetts Historical Society, Boston, Mass.

Cotton, Josiah. 1726–1748. *Memoirs of Josiah Cotton 1726–1756.* [ca. 1732.] Ed. John Middleton and E. H. Winter. Massachusetts Historical Society, Boston, Mass.

———. 1733–1748. *Diary.* Collections of the Pilgrim Society, Pilgrim Hall. Plymouth, Mass.

———. [1707] 1830. *Vocabulary of the Massachusetts (or Natick) Indian Language.* Massachusetts Historical Society, Boston, Mass. Collections, 3rd ser., Vol. 2:147–257.

Cowan, William. 1973a. "Narragansett 126 Years After." *International Journal of American Linguistics* 39(1):7–13.

———. 1973b. "Pequot from Stiles to Speck." *International Journal of American Linguistics* 39(3):164–72.

Crèvecoeur, J. Hector St. John de. [1782] 1971. *Letters from an American Farmer.* New York: Everyman's Library.

Crone-Morange, Paulette, and Lucianne Lavin. 2004. "The Schaghticoke Tribe and English Law: A Study of Community Survival." *Connecticut History* 43(2):132–62.

Cronon, William. 1983. *Changes in the Land: Indians, Colonists, and the Ecology of New England.* New York: Hill and Wang.

Crosby, Alfred W. 1976. "Virgin Soil Epidemics as a Factor in the Aboriginal Depopulation in America." *William and Mary Quarterly* 33:289–99.

References

Crosby, Constance. 1988. "From Myth to History, or Why King Philip's Ghost Walks Abroad." In *The Recovery of Meaning: Historical Archaeology in the Eastern United States*, ed. Mark P. Leone and Parker B. Potter, Jr., 183–210. Washington D.C.; Smithsonian Institution Press.

———. 1993. "The Algonkian Spiritual Landscape." In *Algonkians of the Past and Present*, ed. Peter Benes, 183–209. *Annual Proceedings of the Dublin Seminar for New England Folklife*. Boston: Boston University.

Cuffee, Paul. 1839. *Narrative of the Life of Paul Cuffee, a Pequot Indian, During Thirty Years Spent at Sea, and in Traveling in Foreign Lands*. Vernon, Conn.: Horace N. Bill.

Danforth, Samuel. 1710. The Woful effects of Drunkenness. A Sermon at Bristol, October 12, 1709, when two Indians, Josias and Joseph were Executed for murther. Boston: B. Green.

Deetz, James. 1996. *In Small Things Forgotten: An Archaeology of Early American Life*. Exp. and Rev. Ed. Garden City, N.Y.: Anchor Press.

De Forest, John W. [1851] 1964. *History of the Indians of Connecticut: From the Earliest Known Period to 1850*. New York: Archon Books.

Delabarre, Edward B. 1917. "Early Interest in Dighton Rock." *Publications of the Colonial Society of Massachusetts*. Boston, Mass.

———. 1928. *Dighton Rock: A Study of the Written Rocks of New England*. New York: Walter Neale.

De Laguna, Frederica. 1972. *Under Mount Saint Elias: The History and Culture of the Yakutat Tlingit*. Washington, D.C.: Smithsonian Institution Press.

Dempsey, Jack, ed. 2000. *New English Canaan by Thomas Morton of "Merrymount": Text, Notes, Biography & Criticism*. Scituate, Mass.: Digital Scanning Inc.

Den Ouden, Amy E. 2005. *Beyond Conquest: Native Peoples and the Struggle for History in New England*. Lincoln: University of Nebraska Press.

Des Barres, Joseph F. W. 1776. Chart of Cape Cod. Original in the Massachusetts Historical Society. *The Atlantic Neptune*. London: The Admiralty.

References

"A Description of Mashpee in the County of Barnstable, September 16, 1802." 1802 [1815]. Massachusetts Historical Society, Boston, Mass. Collections, 2nd ser., Vol. 3:1–17.

Dexter, Franklin Bowditch, ed. 1901. *The Literary Diary of Ezra Stiles*. Vol. 1. New York, Scribner's Sons.

————, ed. 1916 *Extracts from the Itineraries and Other Miscellanies of Ezra Stiles 1755–1794*. New Haven: Yale University Press.

Dickason, Olive P. 1984. "Amerinds in Europe." In *The Myth of the Savage and Beginnings of French Colonialism in the Americas*. Edmonton: University of Alberta Press.

Dillon, Phyllis. 1980. "Trade Fabrics." In *Burr's Hill: A Seventeenth-Century Wampanaog Burial Ground in Warren, Rhode Island*, ed. Susan Gibson, 100–107.

Dincauze, Dena. 1997. "Centering." Introduction in *Proceedings of the Massachusetts Archaeological Society* 66(2):1–4.

Dorian, Nancy. 1981. *Language Death: The Life Cycle of a Scottish Gaelic Dialect*. Philadelphia: University of Pennsylvania Press.

Dorson, Richard. 1946. "Comic Indian Anecdotes." *Southern Folklore Quarterly* 10(2):113–28.

Doughton, Thomas L. 1997. "Unseen Neighbors: Native Americans of Central Massachusetts, a People Who Had Vanished." In *After King Philip's War: Presence and Persistence in Indian New England*, ed. Colin G. Calloway, 207–30. Hanover, N.H.: University Press of New England.

Drake, James D. 1995. "Symbol of a Failed Strategy: The Sassamon Trial, Political Culture and King Philip's War." *American Indian Culture and Research Journal* 19:111–41.

————. 1999. *King Philip's War: Civil War in New England, 1675–1676*. Amherst: University of Massachusetts Press.

Drake, Samuel G. 1854. *History of the Early Discovery of America and Landing of the Pilgrims. With a Biography of the North American Indians*. Boston: Higgins and Bradley.

Dubuque, Hugo A. 1907. *Fall River Indian Reservation, Fall River, Mass. With "a schedule of the Lotts of the Indians Land and to whom they Severally Belong lying in Freetown in the County of Bristol,"* vol. 33, 269–73. Original in the Massachusetts State Archives, Boston, Mass.

DCCR. Dukes County Court Records, 1671–1775. Edgartown, Mass.

References

DCD. Dukes County Deeds. Registry of Deeds, Dukes County Court-house, Edgartown, Mass.

DCHS. Dukes County Historical Society, Edgartown, Mass. Manu-scripts.

DCP. Dukes County Probate Records, Registry of Probate, Dukes County Courthouse, Edgartown, Mass.

Dukes County Land Records, 1655–1775. Edgartown, Mass.

Dunford, Frederick J. 1993. "Territory and Community: The Spatial Dimensions of Ceramic Design Variability on Cape Cod, Mas-sachusetts (1000–4000 Years BP)," Ph.D. diss. prospectus, Department of Anthropology, University of Massachusetts.

Dunton, John. 1867 [1686]. Letters Written From New England, a.d. 1686. Boston: The Prince Society.

Earle, John Milton. 1861a. Indian Commissioner. Private papers. Dukes County Record Office, Edgartown, Mass.

———. 1861b. *Report to the Governor and Council, Concerning the Indi-ans of the Commonwealth, Under the Act of April 6, 1859.* Senate Document No. 96. Boston: William White.

Eastern Pequot Tribe of Connecticut. 2000. "Being an Indian in Con-necticut." Submitted to the Department of Acknowledge-ment and Recognition, Bureau of Indian Affairs, U.S. Department of the Interior, Washington, D.C.

Eliade, M. 1960. *Myths, Dreams, and Mysteries: The Encounter Between Con-temporary Faiths and Archaic Realities.* New York: Harper & Row.

Eliot, John. 1663. *The Holy Bible. Containing the Old Testament and the New.* Cambridge: Samuel Green and Marmaduke Johnson.

———. 1666. *The Indian Grammar Begun; or, An Essay to Bring the Indian language into Rules for the Help of Such as Desire to learn the Same for the Furtherance of the Gospel Among Them.* Cambridge: Samuel Green and Marmaduke Johnson.

———. 1669. *The Indian Primer; or the Way of Training up of our Indian Youth in the good knowledge of God.* Cambridge, Mass.

———. [1670] 1810. Letter to Robert Boyle, September 30, 1670. Massachusetts Historical Society, Boston, Mass. Collections, 1st ser., Vol. 3:177–88.

———. [1671]a 1868. *A Brief Narrative of the Progress of the Gospel amongst the Indians in New-England in the year 1670, 1671.* Boston: J. K. Wiggin & W. P. Lunt.

———. 1671b. *Indian Dialogues.* Cambridge: S. Green.

248

References

————. 1672. *The Logick Primer.* Cambridge: S.Green.

————. [1651] 1834. Strength out of Weakness. Massachusetts Historical Society, Boston, Mass. Collections, 3rd ser., Vol. 4:149–96.

Eliot, John, and Thomas Mayhew, Jr. 1653. Tears of Repentance. Massachusetts Historical Society, Boston, Mass. Collections, 3rd ser., Vol. 4:197–260.

ER. Edgartown, Massachusetts. Records. Record Office, Edgartown, Martha's Vineyard.

Erhardt, John G. 1982–2001. *Plymouth Colony 1645–1912. A History of Rehoboth, Seekonk, Swansey, Attleboro & No. Attleboro, Mass., and East Providence, Barrington, & Pawtuket, RI.* 4 vols. New England Historical Genealogical Society Library, Boston, Mass.

Fabian, Johannes. 1986. *Language and Colonial Power: The Appropriation of Swahili in the Former Belgian Congo, 1880–1938.* Cambridge: Cambridge University Press.

Fawcett, Melissa Jayne. 1995. *The Lasting of the Mohegans: The Story of the Wolf People.* Ledyard, Conn.: Pequot Printing.

Fawcett-Sayet, Melissa. 1988. "Sociocultural Authority in Mohegan Society." *Artifacts* 16(3–4):28–29.

Feder, Kenneth L. 1993. *A Village of Outcasts: Historical Archaeology and Documentary Research at the Lighthouse Site.* Mountain View, Calif.: Mayfield Publishing.

Feit, Harvey A. 1991. "The Construction of Algonquian Hunting Territories: Private Property as Moral Lesson, Policy Advocacy, and Ethnographic Error." In *Colonial Situations: The Contextualization of Ethnographic Knowledge,* ed. G. W. Stocking, Jr. *History of Anthropology Series,* Vol. 7. Madison: University of Wisconsin Press.

Feld, Steven, and Keith H. Basso. 1996. *Senses of Place. Advanced Seminar Series.* Albuquerque, N.M.: School for Advanced Research Press.

Ferguson, Charles A. 1959. "Diglossia." *Word* 15:325–40.

Fitts, Robert K. 1998. *Inventing New England's Slave Paradise: Master/Slave Relations in Eighteenth Century Narragansett, Rhode Island.* New York: Garland Publishing.

Fogelson, Raymond, and Richard N. Adams. 1977. *The Anthropology of Power: Ethnographic Studies from Asia, Oceania, and the New World.* New York: Academic Press.

References

Forbes, Harriette Merrifield. [1923] 1967. *New England Diaries 1602–1800: A Descriptive Catalogue of Diaries, Orderly Books and Sea Journals.* New York: Russell and Russell.

Ford, John W. 1896. *Some Correspondence Between the Governors and Treasurers of the New England Company in London and the Commissioners of the United Colonies in America, the Missionaries and Others Between the years 1657 and 1712.* London: Spottiswoode and Co.

Foreman, Carolyn Thomas. 1943. *Indians Abroad, 1493–1938.* Norman: University of Oklahoma Press.

Frazier, Patrick. 1992. *The Mohicans of Stockbridge.* Lincoln: University of Nebraska Press.

Freeman, Frederick. [1858] 1965. *The History of Cape Cod: The Annals of Barnstable County and Its Several towns, Including the District of Mashpee.* 2 vols. Yarmouth, Mass.: Parnassus Imprints.

Freeman, James. 1776. A Description of the East Coast of the County of Barnstable. Manuscript. Massachusetts Historical Society, Boston, Mass.

———. 1807a. Description of Dukes County. Massachusetts Historical Society, Boston, Mass. Collections, 2nd ser., Vol. 3:38–94.

———. 1807b. Notes on Nantucket. Massachusetts Historical Society, Boston, Mass. Collections, 2nd ser., Vol. 3:19–38.

Gailey, Christine Ward. 1987. *From Kinship to Kingship: Gender Hierarchy and State Formation in the Tongan Islands.* Austin: University of Texas Press.

Galloway, Patricia. 1995. *Choctaw Genesis, 1500–1700.* Lincoln: University of Nebraska Press.

———. 1997. "Where Have All the Menstrual Huts Gone? The Invisibility of Menstrual Seclusion in the Late Prehistoric Southeast." In *Women in Prehistory: North America and MesoAmerica,* ed. Cheryl Claassen and Rosemary A. Joyce, 47–64. Philadelphia: University of Pennsylvania Press.

Gardner, Russell Herbert. 1970. "My Sanchekantacket."' *Dukes County Intelligencer* 12(2):47–67.

———. 1994. "The Cape Cod-Nantucket-Martha's Vineyard Connection: A Traditional Lineage from Sachems of the Cape and Islands." *Nantucket Algonquian Studies* 15. Nantucket: Nantucket Historical Association.

References

Gay Head, Massachusetts. 1870. *Report of the Committee of the Legislature of 1869, on the Condition of the Gay Head Indians.* Senate Doc. No. 14. Boston.

Geertz, Clifford. 1973. "Deep Play; Notes on a Balinese Cockfight." In *The Interpretation of Cultures: Selected Essays,* 412–53. New York: Basic Books.

Gewertz, D. 1984. "The Tchambuli View of Persons: A Critique of Individualism in the Work of Mead and Chodorow." *American Anthropologist* 86:615–29.

Ghere, David L. 1997. "Myths and Methods in Abenaki Demography: Abenaki Population Recovery 1725–1750." *Ethnohistory* 44:511–34.

Gibson, Susan, ed. 1980. *Burr's Hill: A Seventeenth-Century Wampanoag Burial Ground in Warren, Rhode Island.* Providence: Haffenreffer Museum of Anthropology, Brown University.

Giddens, Anthony. 1990. *Central Problems in Social Theory: Structure and Contradiction in Social Analysis.* Berkeley: University of California Press.

Goddard, Ives. 1973. "Delaware Kinship Terminology." *Studies in Linguistics* 23:39–55.

————. 1975. "Indian Names in Connecticut by James Hammond Tumbull." *International Journal of American Linguistics* 43(2):157–59.

————. 1977. "Some Early Examples of American-Indian Pidgin English from New England." *International Journal of American Linguistics* 43(1):37–41.

————. 1978a. "A Further Note on Pidgin English." *International Journal of American Linguistics* 44(1):73.

————. 1978b. "Central Algonquian Languages." In *Northeast,* ed. Bruce Trigger, 583–87. *Handbook of North American Indians* Vol. 15. Washington D.C.: U.S. Government Printing Office.

————. 1978c. "Eastern Algonquian Languages." In *Northeast,* ed. Bruce Trigger, 70–77. *Handbook of North American Indians* Vol. 15. Washington D.C.: U.S. Government Printing Office.

————. 1993. "Two Mashpee Petitions, from 1752 (in Massachusett) and 1753 (in English)." In *American Indian Linguistics and Ethnography in Honor of Laurence C. Thompson,* ed. Anthony Mattina and Timothy Montler, 397–416. *University of Montana*

References

Occasional Papers in Linguistics, No. 10. *International Journal of American Linguistics* 63:4.

————. 1996. "The Use of Pidgins and Jargons on the East Coast of North America." Paper presented at a symposium entitled "Communicating with the Indians: Aspects of the Language Encounter with the Indigenous Peoples of the Americas, 1492 to 1800." John Carter Brown Library, Providence, R. I., October 18–20.

Goddard, Ives, and Kathleen Bragdon. 1988. *Native Writings in Massachusett.* American Philosophical Society Memoir #188. Philadelphia: American Philosophical Society.

Goody, Jack. 1990. *The Oriental, the Ancient, and the Primitive: Systems of Marriage and the Family in the Pre-Industrial Societies of Eurasia.* New York: Cambridge University Press.

Gookin, Daniel. 1677. An Historical Account of the Doings and Sufferings of the Christian Indians in New England. *Transactions and Collections of the American Antiquarian Society,* Vol. II, 423–534.

————. 1806. "Historical Collections of the Indians in New England." Reprinted in Massachusetts Historical Society, Boston, Mass. Collections, 3rd ser., vol.1:141–229.

————. [1836] 1972. *An Historical Account of the Doings and Sufferings of the Christian Indians in New England in the Years 1675, 1676, 1677.* New York: Arno Press.

Grabowski, Christine. 1994. "Coiled Intentions: Federal Acknowledgement Policy and the Gay Head Wampanoags." Ph.D. diss., City University of New York.

Gregory, C. A. 1982. *Gifts and Commodities.* London: Academic Press.

Groce, Nora. 1980. "Ornaments of Metal: Rings, Medallions, Combs, Beads and Pendants." In *Burr's Hill: A Seventeenth-Century Wampanoag Burial Ground in Warren, Rhode Island,* ed. Susan Gibson, 108–18. Providence: Brown University Press.

Grumet, Robert S. 1980. "Sunksquaws, Shamans, and Tradeswomen: Middle Atlantic Coastal Algonkian women During the Seventeenth and Eighteenth Centuries." In *Women and Colonization: Anthropological Perspectives,* ed. Mora Etienne and Eleanor Leacock, 145–89. New York: Praeger Publishers.

References

————. 1995. *Historical Contact: Indian People and Colonists in Today's Northeastern United States in the Sixteenth Through Eighteenth Centuries.* Norman: University of Oklahoma Press.

————. 1996. *Northeastern Indian Lives 1632–1816.* Amherst: University of Massachusetts Press.

Haas, Mary. 1967. "Roger Williams's Sound Shift: A Study in Algonkian." *To Honor Roman Jakobson: Essays on the Occasion of His Seventieth Birthday, 11 October, 1966.* Volumes I–III. *Janua Linguarum Series* Major, 31, 32, 33. The Hague/Paris: Mouton and Co.

Haefeli, Evan, and Kevin Sweeney. 1993. "Wattanummon's World: Personal and Tribal Identity in the Algonquian Diaspora, c. 1660–1712." In *Proceedings of the 25th Algonquian Conference,* ed. William Cowan, 212–24. Toronto: Carleton University.

Hall, David D. 1994. "Books and Literacy in Colonial New England." Paper presented to the Institute of Early American History and Culture, College of William and Mary, Williamsburg, Va.

Hall, Robert. 1977. "An Anthropocentric Perspective for Eastern United States Prehistory." *American Antiquity* 42(4):499–518.

Hallowell, A. Irving. 1928. "Recent Changes in the Kinship Terminology of the St. Francis Abenaki." *Proceedings of the 22nd Americanist Conference* 19(2):99–145.

————. 1955. "Spirits of the Dead in Saulteaux Life and Thought." In *Culture and Experience,* 151–71. Philadelphia: University of Pennsylvania Press.

Hamell, George R. 1987. "Mythical Realities and European Contact in the Northeast During the Sixteenth and Seventeenth Centuries." *Man in the Northeast* 33: 63–87.

Handsman, Russell G., and Trudie Lamb Richmond. 1995. "The Mahican and Schaghticoke Peoples and Us." In *Making Alternative Histories: The Practice of Archaeology and History in Non-Western Setting,* ed. Peter R. Schmidt and Thomas C. Patterson, 87–117. Santa Fe: School of American Research Press.

Hare, Lloyd C. M. 1932. *Thomas Mayhew: Patriarch to the Indians, 1593–1682.* New York: D. Appleton and Company.

Harrington, M. R. 1903. "Shinnecock Notes." *Journal of American Folklore* 16(60):37–39.

Harris, Nathaniel. 1893. *Records of the Court of Nathanile Haris. One of his Majesty's justices of the Peace within and for the County of*

References

Middlezes holden at Watertown. 1734–1761. Historical Society of Watertown, Conn.

Hauptman, Laurence, and James Wherry, eds. 1996. *The Pequots in Southern New England.* Norman: University of Oklahoma Press.

Hawley, Gideon. [1743–1806] 1809. Letters and Journal. 4 vols. Congregational Library, Boston, Mass.

Heath, Dwight. 1963 *Mourt's Relation: A Journal of the Pilgrims at Plymouth.* Bedford, Mass.: Applewood.

Herbster, Holly. 2002. "Contexts for Contact: The Documentary Archaeology of Magunkaquog." Paper presented at the annual meeting of the American Society for Ethnohistory, Quebec City, Quebec, October 16–20.

Herbster, Holly, and Elizabeth Chilton, eds. 2002. *Native Coastal New England. Northeast Anthropology* 64.

Herbster, Holly, and Suzanne Chereau. 2002. "Past to Present: Archaeology and the Ahquinnah Wampanoag." In *Native Coastal New England,* ed. Holly Herbster and Elizabeth Chilton, 43–54. *Northeast Anthropology* 64.

Herndon, Ruth Wallis. 1996. "The Domestic cost of Seafaring: Town Leaders and Seamen's Families in Eighteenth-Century Rhode island." In *Iron Men, Wooden Women: Gender and Seafaring in the Atlantic World, 1700–1920,* ed. Margaret S. Creighton and Lisa Norling, 55–69. Baltimore: Johns Hopkins Press.

———. 1999. "Racialization and Feminization of Poverty in Early America: Indian Women as 'the Poor of the Town' in Eighteenth-Century Rhode Island." In *Empire and Others: British Encounters with Indigenous Peoples,* ed. Martin Daunton and Rick Halpern, 186–203. London: UCL Press.

———. 2001. *Unwelcome Americans: Living on the Margin in Early New England.* Philadelphia: University of Pennsylvania Press.

Herndon, Ruth Wallis, and Ella Wilcox Sekatau. 1997. "The Right to a Name: The Narragansett People and Rhodes Island Officials in the Revolutionary Era." *Ethnohistory* 44 (3): 433–62.

———. 2003. "Colonizing the Children: Indian Youngsters in Servitude in Early Rhode Island," in *Reinterpreting New England Indians and the Colonial Experience,* ed. Colin G. Calloway and Neal Salisbury, 137–73. Boston: Colonial Society of Massachusetts.

References

Hicks, George, and David I. Kertzer. 1972. "Making a Middle Way: Problems of Monhegan Identity." *Southwest Journal of Anthropology* 28(1):1–24.

Hill, Jane, and Bruce Mannheim. 1992. "Language and World View." *Annual Review of Anthropology* 21:381–406.

Hill, Jane, and Kenneth C. Hill. 1986. "Honorific Usage in Modern Nahuatl: The Expression of Social Distance and Respect in the Nahuatl of the Malinche Volcano Area." *Language* 54(1):123–55.

Hoadly, Charles J., ed. [1643–1709] 1932. Hoadly Memorial: Early Letters and Documents Relating to Connecticut. In *Collections of the Connecticut Historical Society* Vol. 24. Hartford: Connecticut Historical Society.

Hocart, A. M. 1970. *Kings and Councilors: An Essay in the Comparative Anatomy of Human Society,* ed. Rodney Needham. Chicago: University of Chicago Press.

Holmes, A. 1804. Additional Memoir of the Moheagans, and of Uncas, their Ancient Sachem. Massachusetts Historical Society, Boston, Mass. Collections, 1st ser., Vol. 9:75–99.

Holmes-Williamson, Margaret. 2003. *Powhatan Lords of Life and Death: Command and Consent in Seventeenth-Century Virginia.* Lincoln: University of Nebraska Press.

Hough, Franklin B. 1856. *Papers Relating to the Island of Nantucket, with Documents Relating to the Original Settlement of that Island, Martha's Vineyard, and Other Islands Adjacent, Known as Dukes County, While Under the Colony of New York.* Albany, N.Y.: Weed, Parsons, and Company.

Howwoswee, Zachariah. n.d. Papers. MS America, John Carter Brown Library at Brown University, Providence, R.I.

Hubbard, William. [1677] 1997. *A Narrative of the Indian Wars in New England, From the First Planting Thereof in the Year 1607 to the Year 1677.* Hanover, N.H.: University Press of New England.

Humes, John Fred. 1952. "John Wampas and the Beginning of Sutton." In *History of the Town of Sutton,* Vol. 2:19–40. Sutton Massachusetts Historical Society.

Humins, John H. 1987. "Squanto and Massasoit: A Struggle for Power." *New England Quarterly* 60(1):54–70.

Hurd, D. Hamilton. 1882. *History of New London County, Connecticut.* Philadelphia. J. B. Lippincott and Co.

References

Hutchins, Francis G. 1979. *Mashpee: The Story of Cape Cod's Indian Town.* West Franklin, N.H.: Amarta Press.

Innes, Stephen. 1983. *Labor in a New Land: Economy and Society in Seventeenth-Century Springfield.* Princeton: Princeton University Press.

Ives, Timothy. 2004. "Expressions of Community: Reconstructing Native Identity in Seventeenth-Century Central Connecticut through Land Deed Analysis." Paper presented at the Fifth Annual Alqonquian People's Conference, Albany, N.Y., March 14.

James, Sydney V., ed. 1963. *Three Visitors to Early Plymouth.* Plymouth: Plimoth Plantation.

Jefferson, Thomas. [1791] 1982. Vocabulary of Unquachog. Manuscript no. 1289 in the Library of the American Philosophical Society. Philadelphia. Reprinted in *The Papers of Thomas Jefferson*, vol. 20, ed. Julian P. Boyd, 467–70. Princeton: Princeton University Press.

Jennings, Frances. 1971. "Goals and Functions of Puritan Missions to the Indians." *Ethnohistory* 18:197–212.

———. 1975. *The Invasion of America: Indians, Colonialism, and the Cant of Conquest.* Chapel Hill: University of North Carolina Press.

Johnson, Eric S. 1993. "'Some by Flatteries and Others by Threatenings': Political Strategies among Native Americans of Seventeenth-Century Southern New England," Ph.D. diss., Department of Anthropology, University of Massachusetts, Amherst.

———. 1996. "Uncas and the Politics of Contact." In *Northeastern Indian Lives, 1632–1816*, ed. Robert S. Grumet, 29–48. Amherst: University of Massachusetts Press.

———. 1998. "Released from Thraldom by the Stroke of War: Coercion and Warfare in Native Politics of Seventeenth-Century Southern New England." *Northeast Anthropology* 55:1–13.

Johnson, Margery Ruth. 1966. "The Mayhew Mission to the Indians, 1643–1806," Ph.D. diss., Clark University.

Johnson, Richard R. 1977. "The Search for a Usable Indian: An Aspect of the Defense of Colonial New England." *Journal of American History* 64:623–51.

References

Jones, Douglas Lamar. 1975. "The Strolling Poor: Transiency in Eighteenth-Century Massachusetts." *Journal of Social History* 8(3):28–54.

Josselyn, John. 1833. An Account of Two Voyages to New-England 1675. Massachusetts Historical Society, Boston, Mass. Collections, 3rd ser., Vol. 3:211ff.

Joyce, William L., David D. Hall, Richard D. Brown, and John B. Hench, eds. 1983. *Printing and Society in Early America.* Worcester: American Antiquarian Society.

Kawashima, Yasuhide. 1969. "Legal Origins of the Indian Reservation in Colonial Massachusetts." *American Journal of Legal History* 13:42–56.

———. 1986. *Puritan Justice and the Indian: White Man's Law in Massachusetts, 1630–1763.* Middletown, Conn.: Wesleyan University Press.

———. 1988. "Indian Servitude in the Northeast." In *Handbook of North American Indians: History of Indian-White Relations.* Vol 4, ed. Wilcomb E. Washburn, 404–406. Washington, D.C.: Smithsonian Institution Press.

Keesing, Roger, and Andrew Strathern. 1998. *Cultural Anthropology: A Contemporary Perspective.* New York: Harcourt, Brace and Co.

Kellaway, William. 1961. *The New England Company, 1649–1776: Missionary Society to the Indians.* New York: Barnes and Noble.

Keller Brown, Linda, and Kay Mussell, eds. 1984. *Ethnic and Regional Foodways in the United States: The Performance of Group Identity.* Knoxville: University of Tennessee Press.

Kences, James E. 1984. Some Unexplored Relationships of Essex County Witchcraft to the Indian Wars of 1675 and 1689. *Essex Institute Historical Collections* 120:179–212.

Kendall, Edward Augustus. 1809. *Travels Through the Northern Part of the United States in the Years 1807 and 1808.* 2 Vols. New York: I. Riley.

King, H. Roger. 1994. *Cape Cod and Plymouth Colony.* Lanham, Md.: University Press of America.

Koehler, Lyle. 1979. "Red-White Power Relations and Justice in the Courts of Seventeenth-Century New England." *American Indian Culture and Research Journal* 3:1–31.

References

Kroskrity, Paul V. 1984. "Negation and Subordination in Arizona Tewa: Discourse Pragmatics Influencing Syntax." *International Journal of American Linguistics* 50(1):94–104.

Kuper, Adam. 1988. *The Invention of Primitive Society: Transformations of an Illusion.* London: Routledge.

Kupperman, Karen. 2000. *Indians and English: Facing Off in Early America.* Ithaca: Cornell University Press.

Laet, Johan de. 1909. "Extracts from the 'New World' 1625, 1630, 1633, and 1640." In *Narratives of New Netherland, 1609–64,* ed. J. Franklin Jameson, 29–60. New York: Charles Scribner's Sons.

LaFantasie, Glenn W., ed. 1988. *The Correspondence of Roger Williams, Volumes I (1629–1653) and II (1654–1682).* Hanover, N.H.: University Press of New England.

Lamb Richmond, Trudie. 1994. "A Native Perspective of History: The Schaghticoke Nation, Resistance and Survival." In *Enduring Traditions: The Native Peoples of Southern New England,* ed. Laurie Weinstein, 103–12. Westpoint, Conn.: Bergin & Garvey.

Lamb Richmond, Trudie, and Amy E. Den Ouden. 2003. "Recovering Gendered Political Histories: Local Struggles and Native Women's Resistance in Colonial Southern New England." In *Reinterpreting New England Indians and the Colonial Experience,* ed. Colin G. Calloway and Neal Salisbury, 174–231. Boston: The Colonial Society of Massachusetts.

Largy, Tonya, and Mary Lynne Rainey. 2005. "Poverty or Natural Wisdom: Native Home Solutions in Eighteenth-Century Nantucket." Paper presented at the Eastern States Archaeological Federation, Williamsburg, Va., November 9–12.

Leach, Douglas. 1958. *Flintlock and Tomahawk: New England in King Philip's War* New York: W. W. Norton & Co.

Leach, Edmund. 1961. *Rethinking Anthropology. London School of Economics Monographs in Social Anthropology* 22. London: Athlone.

Leacock, Eleanor. 1954. *The Montagnais 'Hunting Territory' and the Fur Trade. Memoirs of the American Anthropological Association* 78. Menasha, WI.

Lechford, Thomas. [1642] 1833. "Plaine Dealing: or News from New England." Reprint. Massachusetts Historical Society, Boston, Mass. Collections, 3rd ser., Vol. 35: 53–128.

References

Lepore, Jill. 1998. *The Name of War: King Philip's War and the Origins of American Identity.* New York: Knopf.

Lescarbot, Marc. [1618] 1907–1914. *The History of New France.* Reprint. Ed. and trans. W. L. Grant. Toronto: The Champlain Society.

Leveillee, Alan, Joseph Waller, Jr., and Donna Ingham. 2006. "Dispersed Villages in Late Woodland Period South-Coastal Rhode Island." Paper presented at the 72nd annual meeting of the Eastern States Archaeological Federation, Williamsburg, Va., November 9–12.

Levermore, Charles Herbert. 1912. *Forerunners and Competitors of the Pilgrims and Puritans.* Brooklyn: The New England Society of Brooklyn.

Lincoln, Charles H. 1913. *Narratives of the Indian Wars, 1675–1699. Original Narratives of Early American History.* New York: American Historical Association.

Lindholdt, Paul J., ed. 1988. *John Josselyn, Colonial Traveler: A Critical Edition of Two Voyages to New England.* Hanover, N.H.: University Press of New England.

Little Compton Proprietors Records. 1672/3. Transcription. Town Clerk's Office, Little Compton, R.I.

Little Doe, Jessie. 1998. "Report on the Wampanoag Dictionary Project." Paper presented at the 25th Algonquian Conference, Cambridge, Mass., October.

Little, Elizabeth. 1980a. *Probate Records of Nantucket Indians. Nantucket Algonquian Studies* 2. Nantucket: Nantucket Historical Association.

———. 1980b. "Three Kinds of Deeds at Nantucket." In *Papers of the Eleventh Algonquian Conference,* ed. William Cowan, 61–70. Ottawa: Carleton University.

———. 1981a. "Historic Indian Houses on Nantucket." *Nantucket Algonquian Studies* 4. Nantucket: Nantucket Historical Association.

———, ed. 1981b. "The Writings of Nantucket Indians." *Nantucket Algonquian Studies* 3. Nantucket: Nantucket Historical Association,

———. 1990a. "Indian Horse Commons at Nantucket Island, 1660–1760." *Nantucket Algonquian Studies* 9. Nantucket: Nantucket Historical Association.

————. 1990b. "The Nantucket Indian Sickness." In *Papers of the Twenty-First Algonquian Conference*, ed. William Cowan, 181–96. Ottawa: Carleton University Press.

————. 1996. "Daniel Spotso: A Sachem at Nantucket Island, Massachusetts, circa 1691–1741." In *Northeastern Indian Lives 1632–1816*, ed. Robert Grumet, 193–207. Amherst: University of Massachusetts Press.

————. 1997. "Nantucket Indian Place Names." *Historic Nantucket* (fall):9–16.

Little, Elizabeth, and J. Clinton Andrews. 1982. "Drift Whales at Nantucket: The Gift of Moshup." *Man in the Northeast* 23:17–38.

Look, David. 1780–1820. Account Book. Dukes County Historical Society. Edgartown, Mass.

Love, William DeLoss. 1899. *Samson Occam and the Christian Indians of New England.* Boston: Pilgrim Press.

Luedtke, Barbara. 1980. "The Calf Island Site and the Late Prehistoric Period in Boston Harbor." *Man in the Northeast* 20:25–76.

MacCulloch, Susan. 1966. "A Tripartite Political System Among the Christian Indians of Early Massachusetts." *Papers of the Kroeber Anthropologic Society* 34:63–74.

MacFarlane, Ronald. 1933. "Indian Relations in New England, 1620–1760: A Study of a Regulated Frontier," Ph.D. diss., Harvard University.

Macy, Obed. 1835. *The History of Nantucket.* 2nd ed. Mansfield, Mass.: Macy and Pratt.

Macy, Richard. 1714–1733. Account Book. Peter Foulger Museum Library, Nantucket, Mass.

Macy, Zaccheus. 1792a. A Letter from Zaccheus Macy forwarding to the Historical Society an account of the former Indian divisions of the Islands, &c. Reprinted in *The History of Nantucket*, by Obed Macy, 253–54.

————. 1792b. A Short Journal of the Island of Nantucket, with some of the most remarkable things that have happened since, to the Present Time. Massachusetts Historical Society, Boston, Mass. Collections, 1st ser., Vol. 3:157–65.

————. n.d. Manuscript account of the Indians of Nantucket. Collections. Nantucket Historical Association, Nantucket, Mass.

References

Malonson, Donald. 1992. Invocation. Presented at the Gay Head Wampanoag History Conference, Edgartown, Mass., November 11–12,

Manasses, Paul. ca. 1718. Diary. Manuscript copy in the collections of the Tozzer Library Rare Books Division, Harvard University.

Mandell, Daniel. 1997. *Behind the Frontier: Indians in Eighteenth-Century Eastern Massachusetts.* Lincoln: University of Nebraska Press.

Martin, Ann Smart. 1989. "The role of Pewter as a Missing Artifact: Consumer Attitudes Toward Tableware in Late-Eighteenth-Century Virginia." *Historical Archaeology* 23(2):1–27.

Marx, Karl, and Friederick Engels. "The Eighteenth Brumaire of Louis Bonaparte." In *Selected Works*, Karl Marx, 97–108. New York: International Publishers.

Massachusetts, Colony of. 1704. Records of the General Court.

———. 1765. Census making in Massachusetts, 1643–1765, with a reproduction of the lost census of 1765. Boston: Charles E. Goodspeed.

Massachusetts, Commonwealth of. Records on Microfilm. Indian Records, Vols. 30 and 31. Massachusetts Archives, Boston.

Massachusetts Historical Society. Manuscripts. Boston, Mass.

Massachusetts House Journals. 1919–1973. *Journals of the House of Representatives of Massachusetts 1715–1766.* 43 vols.

Massachusetts State Archives. Manuscript Collection. Indian Volumes 30–33.

Massachusetts, State of. 1869–1922. *The Acts and Resolves, Public and Private, of the Province of the Massachusetts Bay.* 21 vols.

Massachusetts Superior Court of Judicature at Barnstable. Suffolk Files. Barnstable, Mass.

Massachusetts, University of. n.d. Survey of Archaeology of Eastern Massachusetts, for the National Park Service.

Massachusetts. Unpassed Legislation Relating to Indian Affairs, Massachusetts State Archives, Boston, Mass.

Mather, Cotton. 1689. *Memorable providence relating to witchcrafts and possessions.* Boston: R. P.

———. [1702] 1852. *Magnalia Christi Americana, or The Ecclesiastical History of New England, From its First Planting, in the year 1620, Unto the Year of Our Lord 1698,* ed. Thomas Robbins. 2 vols. Hartford: Silas Andrus & Son.

————. 1703. "Family Religion Excited and Assisted." In *Bibliography of the Algonquian Languages*, by James Constantine Pilling (1891), p. 343).

————. 1712. Drawing of Dighton Rock. *Publications of the Colonial Society of Massachusetts*, Vol. XVIII. Transactions 1915–1917 (1917) p. 246. Boston: Colonial Society of Massachusetts.

————. 1716. Letter to John Woodward, 12 July, 1716, transcribed in G. L. Kittredge, "Some Lost Works of Cotton Mather," in *Proceedings of the Massachusetts Historical Society* 45 (1911–1912), p.422. Boston, Mass.

————. 1663–1728. Mather Ephemera: Vol. 62. Microfilm. American Antiquarian Society.

Mavor, James W., Jr., and Byron E. Dix. 1989. *Manitou: The Sacred Landscape of New England's Native Civilization*. Rochester, Vt.: Inner Traditions.

Mayhew, Experience. 1709. *Massachuset Psalter*. Boston: Nathaniel Green.

————. 1720. *A Discourse Shewing that God Dealeth with men as With Reasonable Creatures . . . with a brief account of the State of the Indians on Martha's Vineyard*. Boston: B. Green.

————. [1722] 1885. "Letter of Experience Mayhew, 1722, on the Indian Language." *New England Historical Genealogical Register* 39:10–17.

————. 1727. *Indian Converts or some Account of the Lives and Dying speeches of a Considerable Number of Christianized Indians of Martha's Vineyard*. London: J. Osborn and T. Longman.

————. 1896. *A brief Journal of my Visitation of the Pequot and Mohegan Indians, at the desire of the Honourable Commissioners for the Propagation of the Gospel*. London: Spottiswoode.

————. n.d. Experience Mayhew Papers. Massachusetts Historical Society, Boston, Mass.

Mayhew, Matthew. [1694] 1967. "A Brief Narrative of the Success which the gospel hath had among the Indians of Martha's Vineyard." In *Magnalia Christi Americana*, by Cotton Mather, Vol. II:423. New York: Russell and Russell.

McBride, Bunny, and Harald E. Prins. 1996. "Walking the Medicine Line: Molly Ockett a Pigwacket Doctor." In *Northeastern Indian Lives 1632–1816*, ed. Robert Grumet, 321–48. Amherst: University of Massachusetts Press.

References

McBride, Kevin. 1994a. "'Ancient and Crazie': Pequot Lifeways During the Historic Period." In *Algonkians of New England: Past and Present*, ed. Peter Benes, 63–75. *Annual Proceedings of the 1991 Dublin Seminar*. Boston: Boston University.

———. 1994b. "Cultures in Transition: The Eastern Long Island Sound Culture Area in the Prehistoric and Contact Periods." *Journal of Connecticut History* 35(1):5–21.

———. 1994c. "The Source and Mother of the Fur Trade: Native-Dutch Relations in Eastern New Netherland." In *Enduring Traditions: Native Peoples of New England*, ed. Laurie Weinstein, 31–52. Westport, Conn.: Bergin & Garvey.

———. 1996. "The Legacy of Robin Cassacinamon: Mashantucket Pequot Leadership in the Historic Period." In *Northeastern Indian Lives 1632–1816*, ed. Robert Grumet, 74–92. Amherst: University of Massachusetts Press.

———. 2005. "Transformation by Degree: Eighteenth-Century Native American Land Use." Paper presented at the 72nd Annual meeting of the Eastern States Archaeological Federation, Williamsburg, Va., November 9–12.

McBride, Kevin, and Suzanne Chereau. 1996. "Gay Head Aquinnah Wampanoag Community Structure and Land Use Patterns." *Northeast Anthropology* 51:13–39.

McMullen, Ann. 1991. "Native Basketry, Basketry Styles, and Changing Group Identity in Southern New England." *Annual Proceedings of the Dublin Seminar for New England Folklife* 16:76–88.

———. 1994: "What's Wrong with this Picture? Context, Conversion, Survival and the Development of Regional Native Cultures and Pan-Indianism in Southern New England." In *Enduring Traditions: The Native Peoples of New England*, ed. Laurie Weinstein, 123–50. Westport, Conn.: Bergin & Garvey.

———. 1996. "Culture by Design: Native Identity, Historiography, and the Reclamation of Tradition in Twentieth-Century Southeastern New England." Ph.D. diss., Brown University.

McMullen Ann, and Russell G. Handsman, eds. 1987. *A Key into the Language of Woodsplint Baskets*. Washington, Conn.: American Indian Archaeological Institute.

MDX. Middlesex County, Cambridge, Mass. nd. Court Records.

Mignolo, Walter D. 1992. "On the Colonization of Amerindian Languages and Memories: Renaissance Theories of Writing and the Discontinuity of the Classical Tradition." *Comparative Studies in Society and History* 34(2):301–30. Society for the Comparative Study of Society and History.

Miller, Jay. 1974. "The Delaware as Women: A Symbolic Solution." *American Ethnologists* 16(4):786–96.

Miller, Perry. 1954. *The New England Mind: The Seventeenth Century.* Cambridge: Harvard University Press.

———. 1964. *Errand into the Wilderness.* New York: Harper & Row.

Miller, William Davis. 1925. Dr. Joseph Torrey and his Record Book of Marriages. Church of Christ. South Kingston, R.I.

Miner, Kenneth. 1975. "John Eliot of Massachusetts and the Beginnings of American Linguistics." *Historiographica Linguistica* 1:169–83.

Monaghan, E. Jennifer. 1990. "'She Loved to Read in Good Books': Literacy and the Indians of Martha's Vineyard, 1643–1725." *History of Education Quarterly* 30(4):492–521.

Montgomery, Florence, and Linda Eaton. 2007. *Textiles in America, 1650–1879.* New York: W. W. Norton.

Morgan, Philip. 1999. "Encounters Between British and Indigenous Peoples." In *Empire and Others: British Encounters with Indigenous Peoples, 1600–1850,* ed. Mary Daunton and Rick Halpern, 42–78. London: UCL Press.

Morison, Samuel Eliot. 1936. *Harvard College in the Seventeenth Century.* Cambridge: Harvard University Press.

———. 1971. *The European Discovery of America: The Northern Voyages, a.d. 500–1600.* New York: Oxford University Press.

Morrison, Dane. 1995. *A Praying People: Massachusett Acculturation and the Failure of the Puritan Mission, 1600–1690.* New York: Peter Land.

Morse, Jedidiah. [1822] 1972. A Report to the Secretary of War of the United States on Indian Affairs, Comprising a Narrative of a Tour Performed in the Summer of 1820, Under a Commission of the President of the United States, for the Purpose of Ascertaining, the Use of the Government, the Actual State of the Indian Tribes in our Country. St. Clair Shores, Mich.: Scholarly Press.

Morton, Thomas. 1632. "New English Caanan." In *Publications of the Prince Society* 14 (1883), ed. Charles F. Adams. Boston: The Prince Society.

References

Mrozowski, Stephen A. 1994. "The Discovery of a Native American Cornfield." *Archaeology of Eastern North America* 22:47–62.

Mrozowski, Stephen A., Holly Herbster, David Brown, and Katherine L. Priddy. 2005. "Magunkaquog: Native American Conversion and Cultural Persistence." *Mashantucket Pequot Museum and Research Center Occasional Paper. No. 1*. In *Eighteenth Century Native Communities in Southern New England in the Colonial Context*, ed. Jack Campisi, 57–71. Mashantucket, Conn.: Mashantucket Pequot Museum and Research Center.

Mulholland, Mitchell, T. F. Timothy Barker, and Timothy Binzen. 2005. "Rhyolites, Flints, Pots, Baskets and Beads: A Historic Period Native American Site in Hingham, Massachuetts: A Work in Progress." Paper presented at the Eastern States Archaeological Federation, Williamsburg, Va., November 9–12.

Murray, Laura J. 1996. "The Diaries of Joseph Johnson and Peter Jones." Paper presented at symposium entitled "Communicating with the Indians: Aspects of the Language Encounter with the Indigenous Peoples of the Americas, 1492 to 1800." John Carter Brown Library, Providence, R. I., October 18–20.

Naeher, James 1989. "Dialogue in the Wilderness: John Eliot and the Indians' Exploration of Puritanism as a Source of Meaning, Comfort, and Ethnic Survival." *New England Quarterly* 62:346–68.

Nassaney, Michael. 1989. "An Epistemological Enquiry into Some Archaeological and Historical Interpretations of Seventeenth-Century Native American—European Relations. In *Archaeological Approaches to Cultural Identity*, ed. S. J. Shennan, 76–93. London: Unwin Hyman.

———. 2004. "Native American Gender Politics and Material Culture in Seventeenth-Century Southern New England." *Journal of Social Archaeology* 4(3):334–67.

New England Company. New England Company Records, Guildhall Library, Corporation of London, Great Britain.

NEHGS. New England Historical Genealogical Society. Manuscripts. Boston, Mass.

Nicholas, Mark A. 2002. "Mashpee Wampanoags of Cape Cod, the Whalefishery, and Seafaring's Impact on Community Development." *American Indian Quarterly* 26(2):165–97.

References

Noyes, James. 1690. *Pequot Indian Glossary*. Beinecke Library, Yale University, New Haven, Conn.

Oberg, Michael Leroy. 1999. *Dominion and Civility: English Imperialism and Native America, 1585–1685*. Ithaca: Cornell University Press.

———. 2003. *Uncas, First of the Mohegans*. Ithaca: Cornell University Press.

O'Brien, Jean. 1996. "Divorced from the Land: Accommodation Strategies of Indian Women in Eighteenth-Century New England." In *Gender, Kinship, Power: A Comparative and Interdisciplinary History*, ed. Mary Jo Maynes, Ann Waltner, Brigitte Soland, and Ulrike Strasser, 144–61. New York: Routledge.

———. 1998. *Dispossession by Degrees*. Cambridge. Cambridge University Press.

———. 1999. 'They are so Frequently Shifting Their Place of Residence; Land and the Construction of Social Place of Indians in Colonial Massachusetts." In *Empire and Others: British Encounters with Indigenous People, 1600–1850*, ed. M. Daunton and R. Halpern, 204–16. Philadelphia: University of Pennsylvania Press.

Occom, Samson. 1809. An Account of the Montauk Indians of Long Island. Massachusetts Historical Society, Boston, Mass. Collections, 1st ser., Vol. 10:106–10.

O'Connell, Barry. 1992. *On Our Own Ground: The Complete Writings of William Apess, A Pequot*. Amherst: University of Massachusetts Press.

Ortner, Sherry. 1973. "On Key Symbols." *American Anthropologist* 75:1338–46.

Parry, Jonathan P. 1989. *Money and the Morality of Exchange*. Cambridge: Cambridge University Press.

Pasay, Marcella. 2002. *Full Circle: A Directory of Native and African-Americans in Windham County, Connecticut and Vicinity, 1650–1900*. 2 vols. Houle-Pasay Memorial Project. Westminster, Md.:Heritage Books.

Pearce, Roy Harvey. 1988. *Savagism and Civilization: A Study of the Indian and the American Mind*. Berkeley: University of California Press.

Peletz, Michael. G. 1995. "Kinship Studies in Late Twentieth-Century Anthropology." *Annual Reviews in Anthropology* 24:343–72.

References

Perley, Sidney. 1912. *The Indian Land Titles of Essex County, Massachusetts*. Salem Mass.: Essex Book and Print Club.

Pestana, Carla Gardina. 1993. "Religion and the Persistence of Magic: Puritanism, Magic, and Witchcraft in New England." *Reviews in American History* 21:13–18.

Peters, Russell. 1994. "Foreword." In *Enduring Traditions: The Native Peoples of Southern New England*, ed. Laurie Weinstein, ix–x. Westpoint, Conn.. Bergin & Garvey.

Peterson, Jaqueline. 1982. "Ethnogenesis: The Settlement and Growth of a 'New People' in the Great Lakes Region, 1702–1815." *American Indian Culture and Research Journal* 6:23–64.

Peterson, Mark A. 1993. "The Plymouth Church and the Evolution of Puritan Religious Culture." *New England Quarterly* 66:582–91.

Pfeiffer, John. 1996. "Post-Contact Populations on the Nehantic Reservation of Lyme, Connecticut." *Bulletin of the Archaeological Society of Connecticut* 59:78.

Philbrick, Nathaniel. 1998: *Abram's Eyes: The Native American Legacy of Nantucket Island*. Nantucket: Mill Hill Press.

Pierce, Andrew. 2007. Joseph Daggett's Native American Wife. And their Descendants. *New England Historical and Genealogical Society Register*, vol. 161, \#641.

Pierson, Abraham. 1658. *Some Helps for the Indians*. Cambridge: Samuel Green.

Pilling, James Constantine. 1891. *Bibliography of Algonquian Languages*. Bureau of American Ethnology Bulletin 13. Washington, D.C.: Government Printing Office.

Plane, Ann Marie. 1992. "Childbirth Practices of Native American Women of New England and Canada, 1600–1800." In *Medicine and Healing*, ed. Peter Benes, 13–24. *Annual Proceedings of the Dublin Seminar for New England Folklife*. Boston: Boston University.

———. 1993. "'The Examination of Sarah Ahhaton': The Politics of 'Adultery' in a Seventeenth-Century Indian Town of Massachusetts." In *Algonkians of New England: Past and Present*, ed. Peter Benes, 14–25. *Annual Proceedings of the Dublin Seminar for New England Folklife*. Boston: Boston University Press.

———. 1995. "Colonizing the Family." Ph.D. diss., Department of History, Brandeis University.

References

————. 1996. "Putting a Face on Colonialism: Factionalism and Gender Politics in the Life History of Awashunkes, the 'Squaw Sachem' of Saconet." In *Northeastern Indian Lives, 1632–1816*, ed. Robert S. Grumet, 140–65. Amherst: University of Massachusetts Press.

————. 2000. *Colonial Intimacies: Indian Marriage in Early New England.* Ithaca: Cornell University Press.

Plane, Anne Marie, and Gregory Button. 1993. "The Massachusetts Indian Enfranchisement Act: Ethnic Contest in Historical Context, 1849–1869." *Ethnohistory* 40(4):587–618.

Poewe, Karla. 1981. *Matrilineal Ideology: Male-Female Dynamics in Luapula, Zambia.* New York: Academic Press.

Porterfield, Amanda. 1992. "Witchcraft and the Colonization of Algonquian and Iroquois Culture." *Religion and American Culture* 2(1):103–25.

Prince, J. Dyneley. 1907. "Last Living Echoes of the Natick." *American Anthropologist* 9(3):493–98.

Prince, J. Dyneley, and F. G. Speck. 1903. "The Modern Pequots and Their Language." *American Anthropologist* 5(2):193–212.

Prince, Thomas. 1727. Some Account of those English Ministers who have successively presided over the work of gospelizing the Indians on Martha's Vineyard and Adjacent Islands. In *Indian Converts or some Account of the Lives and Dying speeches of a Considerable Number of Christianized Indians of Martha's Vineyard*, by Experience Mayhew, 277–310.

Pring, Martin. [1603] 1906. "A Voyage Set Out from the Citie of Bristoll with a Small Ship and a Barke for the Discoverie of the North Part of Virginia. In *Early English and French Voyages Chiefly from Hakluyt 1534–1608*, ed. Henry S. Burrage, 341–52. New York: Charles Scribner's Sons.

Prins, Harald. 1993. "To the Land of the Mistigoches: American Indians Traveling to Europe in the Age of Exploration." *American Indian Culture and Research Journal* 17:175–95.

PSJ. Pawtucket Superior County Judicial Records. 1734. File papers, Pawtucket, R.I. Deposition of Sompanwat, Kouckeomotonsow, and the Old Queen, sister to Old Ninegret.

Pulsipher, Jenny Hale. 1996. "Massacre at Hurtleberry Hill: Christian Indians and English Authority in Metacom's War." *William and Mary Quarterly* 53:459–86.

References

———. 1999. "The Overture of this New-Albion World: King Philip's War and the Transformation of New England," Ph.D. diss., Brandeis University.

Quinn, David. B. 1977. *North America from Earliest Discovery to First Settlements: The Norse Voyages to 1612.* New York: Harper & Row.

Rainey, Froelich G. 1936. "A Compilation of Historical Data Contributing to the Ethnography of Connecticut and Southern New England Indians." *Bulletin of the Archaeological Society of Connecticut* 3(1):89.

Rainey, Mary Lynne. 2005. "The Archaeological Signature of Historic Native American Households on Nantucket Island, Massachusetts." Paper presented at the Eastern States Archaeological Federation, Williamsburg, Va., November 9–12.

Rawson, Grindal, and Samuel Danforth. [1698] 1809. *Account of an Indian Visitation, a.d. 1698.* Copied for Dr. Stiles, by Rev. Mr. Halwey, missionary at Marshpee, from the printed account published in 1698. Massachusetts Historical Society, Boston, Mass. Collections, 1st ser., Vol. 10:129–134.

"Report of a Committee on the State of the Indians in Mashpee and parts Adjacent, 1767." 1767. Massachusetts Historical Society, Boston, Mass. Collections, 2nd ser., Vol. 3:12–17.

Robinson, Paul A. 1990. "The Struggle Within: The Indian Debate in Seventeenth-Century Narragansett Country," Ph.D. diss., Department of Anthropology, State University of New York, Binghamton.

———. 1994. "Narragansett History from 1000 b.p. to the Present." In *Enduring Traditions: The Native Peoples of Southern New England,* ed. Laurie Weinstein, 79–89. Westpoint, Conn.: Bergin & Garvey.

———. 1996. "Lost Opportunities: Miantonomi and the English in Seventeenth-Century Narragansett Country." In *Northeastern Indian Lives 1623–1816,* ed. Robert S. Grumet, 13–28. Amherst: University of Massachusetts Press.

Robinson, Paul, Marc Kelley, and Patricia E. Rubertone. 1985. "Preliminary Biocultural Interpretations from a Seventeenth-Century Narragansett Indian Cemetery in Rhode Island." In *Cultures in Contact: The European Impact on Native Cultural Institutions in Eastern North America, a.d.* 1000–1800, ed. James Fitzhugh, 107–30. Washington, D.C.: Smithsonian Institution Press.

References

Rogers, Alisdair. 1995. *The Urban Context: Ethnicity, Social Networks, and Situational Networks.* Oxford: Berg.

Róheim, G. 1945. *The Eternal Ones of the Dream: A Psychoanalytic of Australian Myth and Ritual.* New York: International Universities Press.

Ronda, James P. 1974. "Red and White at the Bench: Indians and the Law in Plymouth Colony, 1629–1691." *Historical Collections of the Essex Institute* 110:200–15.

———. 1981. "Generations of Faith: The Christian Indians of Martha's Vineyard." *William and Mary Quarterly* 38:369–94.

Ronda, James P., and Jeanne Ronda. 1974. "The Death of John Sassamon: An Exploration in Writing New England Indian History." *American Indian Quarterly* 1(2):91–102.

Rosaldo, Renato. 1980. *Ilongot Headhunting: A Study in Society and History.* Stanford University Press.

———. 1993. *Culture and Truth: The Remaking of Social Analysis.* Boston: Beacon Press.

Rosier, James. 1930. "A True Relation of the Voyage of Captaine George Waymouth." In *Early English and French Voyages chiefly from Hakluyt 1534–1608*, ed. Henry S. Burrage, 353–94. New York: Charles Scribner's Sons.

Rowlandson, Mary. [1682] 1913. "Narrative of the Captivity of Mrs. Mary Rowlandson." Reprinted in *Narratives of the Indian Wars 1675–1699*, ed. Charles H. Lincoln, 107–67. New York: Charles Scribner's Sons.

Rubertone, Patricia. 2001. *Grave Undertakings: An Archaeology of Roger Williams and the Narragansett Indians.* Washington, D.C.: Smithsonian Institution Press.

Russell, Howard S. 1980. *Indian New England Before the Mayflower.* Hanover, N.H.: University Press of New England.

Rutman, Darrett B. 1967. *Husbandmen of Plymouth: Farms and Villages in the Old Colony, 1620–1692.* Boston: Beacon Press.

Sahlins, Marshall. 1983. "Other Times, Other Customs: The Anthropology of History." *American Anthropologist* 85(3):517–44.

———. 1985. *Islands of History.* Chicago: University of Chicago Press.

———. 1993. "Goodby to Tristes Tropes: Ethnography in the Context of Modern World History." *The Journal of Modern History* 65(1):1–25.

References

―――. 1999. "Two or Three Things That I Know about Culture." *The Journal of the Royal Anthropological Institute* 5(3):399–421.

Sainsbury, John A. 1971. "Miantonomo's Death and New England Politics, 1630–1645." *Rhode Island History* 30:111–23.

―――. 1975. "Indian Labor in Early Rhode Island." *New England Quarterly* 48:378–93.

Salisbury, Neal. 1974. "Red Puritans: The Praying Indians of Massachusetts Bay and John Eliot." *William and Mary Quarterly* 3rd ser. 31:27–54.

―――. 1981. "Squanto: Last of the Patuxets." In *Struggle and Survival in Colonial America*, ed. David G. Sweet and Gary B. Nash, 241–43. Berkeley: University of California Press.

―――. 1982. *Manitou and Providence: Indians, Europeans, and the Making of New England, 1500–1643.* New York: Oxford University Press.

―――. 1987. "Social Relationships on a Moving Frontier: Natives and Settlers in Southern New England, 1638–1675." *Man in the Northeast* 33:89–98.

―――, ed. 1997. *The Sovereignty and Goodness of God, Together With the Faithfulness of His Promises Displayed: Being a Narrative of the Captivity and Restoration of Mrs. Mary Rowlandson and Related Documents.* Boston: Bedford.

Salwen, Bert. 1978. "The Indians of Southern New England: Early Period." In *Northeast*, ed. Bruce Trigger, 160–76. *The Handbook of North American Indians* Vol. 15. Washington, D.C.: Government Printing Office.

Sanday, Peggy Reeves, and Ruth Gallagher Goodenough, eds. 1990. *Beyond the Second Sex: New Directions in the Anthropology of Gender.* Philadelphia: University of Pennsylvania Press.

Sapir, Edward. 1921. *Language, An Introduction to the Study of Speech.* New York: Harcourt.

―――. [1924] 1949. "Culture, Genuine and Spurious." In *Selected Writings of Edward Sapir in Language Culture and Personality*, ed. David G. Mandelbaum, 308–31. Berkeley: University of California Press.

Savulis, Ellen. 1990. *Continuity and Change in Historic Native American Settlement and Subsistence Traditions: The Simons Site, Mashpee, Massachusetts.* Public Archaeology Laboratory. Pawtucket, R.I.: Terrestrial Cultural Resource Reports.

References

Scollon, Ron, and Suzanne Wong Scollon. 1995. *Intercultural Communication: A Discourse Approach*. Oxford, UK: Blackwell.

Scozzari, Lois. 1995. "The Significance of Wampum to Seventeenth-Century New England Indians." *Connecticut Review* 17:59–69.

Segel, Jerome, and R. Andrew Pierce. 2003. *The Wampanoag Genealogical History of Martha's Vineyard, Massachusetts. Volume I. Island History, People, and Places from Sustained Contact Through the Early Federal Era*. Baltimore: Genealogical Publishing Company.

Sewall, Samuel. 1886. Letter Book. Massachusetts Historical Society, Boston, Mass. Collections, 6th ser., Vol. 1–2.

———. 1973. *The Diary of Samuel Sewall, 1674–1729*. 2 vols. Ed. M. Halsey Thomas. New York: Farrar, Straus, and Giroux.

Shepard, Thomas. [1648] 1834. *The Clear Sun-shine of the Gospel Breaking forth upon the Indians in New England*. Massachusetts Historical Society, Boston, Mass. Collections, 3rd ser., Vol. 4.

Shapiro, Warren. 1998. "Ideology, 'History of Religions,' and Hunter-Gatherer Studies." *The Journal of the Royal Anthropological Institute* 4(3):489–510.

Shimony, Ann Marie. 1994. *Conservatism among the Iroquois at Six Nations Reserve*. Syracuse: Syracuse University Press.

Shurtleff, Nathaniel. 1853–54. *Records of the Governor and Company of the Massachusetts Bay in New England, 1628–1686*. 5 vols. Boston: William White.

Shurtleff, Nathaniel B., and David Pulsifer, eds. 1855. *Records of the Colony of New Plymouth*. 12 vols. Boston: William White.

Sider, Gerald. 1994. "Identity as History: Ethnohistory, Ethnogenesis, and Ethnocide in the Southeastern United States." *Identities: Global Studies in Culture and Power* 1(1):109–22.

Silverblatt, Irene. 2000. "New Christians and New World Fears in Seventeenth-Century Peru." *Society for the Comparative History of Society and History* 42(3):524–46.

Silverman, David. 2001. "The Impact of Indentured Servitude on the Society and Culture of Southern New England Servitude." *New England Quarterly* 74:622–66.

———. 2005. *Faith and Boundaries: Colonists, Christianity, and Community Among the Wampanoag Indians of Martha's Vineyard, 1600–1871*. Cambridge: Cambridge University Press.

References

Silverstein, Michael. 1998. "Contemporary Transformations of Local Linguistic Communities." *Annual Review of Anthropology* 27:401–26.

Simmons, William S. 1970. *Cautantowwit's House*. Providence, Brown University Press.

———. 1975. "Southern New England Shamanism: An Ethnographic Reconstruction." *Algonquian Conference Papers* 7:217–56. Ottawa: Carleton University.

———. 1979. "Conversion from Indian to Puritan." *New England Quarterly* 52(2):197–217.

———. 1981. "Cultural Bias in the New England Puritans' Perception of Indians." *William and Mary Quarterly* 38(1):56–72.

———. 1982. "The Earliest Prints and Paintings of New England Indians." *Rhode Island History* 41(3):73–85.

———. 1983. "Red Yankees: Narragansett Conversion in the Great Awakening." *American Ethnologist* 10:253–71.

———. 1986. *Spirit of the New England Tribes: Indian History and Folklore, 1620–1984*. Hanover: University Press of New England.

———. 1990. "The Mystic Voice: Pequot Folklore from the Seventeenth Century to the Present." In *The Pequots in Southern New England: The Fall and Rise of an American Indian Nation*, ed. Laurence M. Hauptman, and James D. Wherry, 141–76. Norman: University of Oklahoma Press.

———. 1992. "Of Large Things Remembered: Southern New England Indians Legends of Colonial Encounters." In *The Art and Mystery of Historical Archaeology: Essays in Honor of James Deetz*, ed. Anne Elizabeth Yentsch and Mary C. Beaudry, 317–30. Boca Raton, Fla.: CRC Press.

———. 2002. "From Manifest Destiny to the Melting Pot: The Life and Times of Carlotte Mitchell, Wampanoag." In *Anthropology, History, and American Indians: Essays in Honor of William Curtis Sturtevant*, ed. William L. Merrill and Ives Goddard, 131–38. *Smithsonian Contributions to Knowledge* 44.

Simmons, William, and Cheryl L. Simmons. 1982. *Old Light on Separate Ways: The Narragansett Diary of Joseph Fish 1765–1776*. Hanover: University Press of New England.

Simmons, William S., and George F. Aubin. 1975. "Narragansett Kinship." *Man in the Northeast* 9:21–31.

References

Simon, Brona. 2002. "Discussion on 'Continuity in Native Coastal New England.'" In *Native Coastal New England*, ed. Herbster Holly Herbster and Elizabeth Chilton, 89–92. *Northeast Anthropology* 64.

Simon, Isaac. 1767. Letter to the Commissioners of the Society for the Propagation of the Gospel daybooks, 1715–1735. Boston: New England Historical Genealogical Society.

Slotkin, Richard. 1973. *Regeneration Through Violence: The Mythology of the American Frontier, 1600–1860.* New York: Harper Perennial.

Slotkin, Richard, and James K. Folsom, eds. 1978. *So Dreadfull a Judgement: Puritan Responses to King Philip's War, 1676–1677.* Middletown, Conn.: Wesleyan University Press.

Smith, John. [1624] 1912. "The Generalle Historie of Virginia, New-England, and the Summer Isles. The Sixth Booke: The Generall History of New England." In *Forerunners and Competitors of the Pilgrims and Puritans* Vol 2, ed. Charles Herbert Levermore, 650–753. Brooklyn: The New England Society of Brooklyn.

Smits, David D. 1987. "We Are Not to Grow Wild: Seventeenth-Century New England's Repudiation of Anglo-Indian Intermarriage." *American Indian Culture and Research Journal* 11(4):1–31.

Snow, Dean. 1976. "The Solon Petroglyphs and Eastern Abnaki Shamanism." In *Papers of the Seventh Algonquian Conference*, ed. William Cowan, 281–88. Ottawa: Carleton University.

———. 1980. *The Archaeology of New England.* New York: Academic Press.

Snow, Dean, and Kim M. Lanphear. 1988. "European Contact and Indian Depopulation in the Northeast: The Timing of the First Epidemics." *Ethnohistory* 35:15–33.

Society for the Propagation of the Gospel in North America. Papers. Philip's Library of the Peabody, Essex Museum, Salem, Mass.

Speck, Frank. 1904. "A Modern Mohegan-Pequot Text." *American Anthropologist* new series 6:469–76.

———. 1928a. "Native Tribes and Dialects of Connecticut: A Mohegan-Pequot Diary." In *43rd Annual Report of the Bureau of American Ethnology for the Years 1925–1926*, 199–287. Washington, D.C.: Government Printing Office.

References

————. 1928b. "Territorial Subdivisions of the Wampanoag, Massachusett, and Nauset Indians." In *Indian Notes and Monographs* 44. New York: Heye Foundation.

Spicer, Edward. 1961. *Perspectives in American Indian Culture Change.* Chicago: University of Chicago Press.

Spiess, Arthur E., and Bruce D. Spiess. 1987. "New England Pandemic of 1616–22: Cause and Archaeological Implications." *Man in the Northeast* 34:71–83.

St. Jean, Wendy B. 1999. "Inventing Guardianship: The Mohegan Indians and Their 'Protectors.'" *New England Quarterly* 72:362–87.

Starbuck, Alexander. 1924. *The History of Nantucket, County, Island, and Town, Including Genealogies of the First Settlers.* Boston: C. E. Goodspeed.

Starbuck, Mary, and Nathaniel Starbuck. 1662–1757. Account Book. Peter Foulger Museum, Nantucket, Mass.

Starna, William A. 1992. "The Biological Encounter: Disease and the Ideological Domain." *American Indian Quarterly* 16:512–19.

————. 1996. "'We'll All be Together Again': The Federal Acknowledgement of the Wampanoag Tribe of Gay Head." *Northeast Anthropology* 51:3–12.

Stewart-Smith, David. 1998. "Pennacook-Pawtucket Relations: The Cycles of Family Alliance on the Merrimack River in the Seventeenth Century." *Papers of the Algonquian Conference* 25:445–68.

Stiles, Ezra. 1762a. *A Narragansett Indian Vocabulary Dated 6 September 1769.* Beinecke Library, Yale University, New Haven, Conn.

————. 1762b. "A Vocabulary of the Pequot Indians Obtained in 1762 at Groton, Connecticut." Manuscript. Beinecke Library, Yale University, New Haven, Conn.

————. 1787. Vocabulary of Naugatuck. Manuscript of Words Obtained from Sarah Maweek. Beinecke Library, Yale University, New Haven, Conn.

————. 1916. *Extracts from the Itineraries and Other Miscellanies of Ezra Stiles, D.D., L.L.D, 1755–1794,* ed. Franklin Bowditch Dexter. New Haven: Yale University Press.

Strathern, Marilyn. 1985. "Kinship and Economy: Constitutive Orders of a Provisional Kind." *American Ethnologist* 12(2):191–209.

References

————. 1988. *The Gender of the Gift: Problems with Women and Problems with Society in Melanesia*. Berkeley: University of California Press.

Strong, John A.1989. "Shinnecock and Montauk Whalemen." *Long Island Historical Journal* 2(1):29–40.

————. 1996. "Wyandanch: Sachem of the Montauks." In *Northeastern Indian Lives* 1623–1816, ed. Robert S. Grumet, 48–73. Amherst: University of Massachusetts Press.

————. 1997. *The Algonquian Peoples of Long Island from Earliest Times to 1700*. Interlaken, N.Y.: Empire State Books.

Sweet, John Wood. 1995. "Bodies Politic: Colonialism, Race, and the Emergence of the American North. Rhode Island, 1730–1830," Ph.D. diss., Department of History, Princeton University.

Szasz, Margaret Connell. 1988. *Indian Education in the American Colonies, 1607–1783*. Albuquerque: University of New Mexico Press.

Tantaquidgeon, Gladys. 1928. "Notes on Gay Head." *Indian Notes and Monographs* 7(1):1–26. New York: Museum of the American Indian, Heye Foundation.

————. 1972. *Folk Medicine of the Delaware and Related Algonkian Indians*. Harrisburg, Penn.: The Pennsylvania Historical and Museum Commission.

Tantaquidgeon, Gladys, and Jayne Fawcett. 1987. "Symbolic Motifs on Painted Baskets of the Mohegan-Pequot." In *Rooted Like the Ash Tree*, ed. Richard G. Carlson, 50–51. Naugatuck, Conn.: Eagle Wing Press.

Teunissen, John J., and Evelyn J. Hinz, eds. 1973. *A Key into the Language of America*, by Roger Williams. Detroit: Wayne State University Press.

Thomas, Nicholas. 1991. *Entangled Objects: Exchange, Material Culture, and Colonialism in the Pacific*. Cambridge: Harvard University Press.

Thomas, Peter A. 1976. "Contrastive Subsistence Strategies and Land Use as Factors for Understanding Indian-White Relations in New England." *Ethnohistory* 23(1):1–18.

————. 1979. "In the Maelstrom of Change: The Indian Trade and Cultural Process in the Middle Connecticut River Valley, 1635–1665," Ph.D. diss., Dept. of Anthropology, University of Massachusetts, Amherst.

References

————. 1984. "Bridging the Cultural Gap: Indian/White Relations." In *Early Settlement in the Connecticut Valley Deerfield, Massachusetts,* ed. John W. Ifkovic and Martin Kaufman, 4–21. Westfield, Mass: Historic Deerfield, Inc. and Institute for Massachusetts Studies, Westfield State College.

Tooker, Elisabeth. 1979. *Native North American Spirituality of the Eastern Woodlands: Sacred Myths, Dreams, Visions, Speeches, Healing Formulas, Rituals, and Ceremonials.* New York: Paulist Press.

Treat, Samuel. 1705. *The Hatchets, To Hew Down the Tree of Sin.* Boston: Nathaniel Green.

Trumbull, James Hammond. 1873. "Notes on Forty Algonkin Versions of the Lord's Prayer." *Transactions of the American Philosophical Society (1869–1896)* 3:113–218.

————. 1881. *Indian Names of Places, etc., in and on the Borders of Connecticut.* Hartford. Conn.: Brown & Gross.

————. 1885. The Trumbull Papers. Massachusetts Historical Society, Boston, Mass. Collections, 5th ser., Vol. 9.

————. 1903. "Natick Dictionary." *Bureau of American Ethnology. Bulletin 25.* Washington, D.C.: Government Printing Office.

Turnbaugh, William A. 1993. "Community, Commodities, and the Concept of Property in Seventeenth-Century Narragansett Society." In *Archaeology of Eastern North America: Papers in Honor of Stephen Williams,* ed. James D. Stoltman, 285–86. *Archaeological Report* No. 25. Jackson, Miss: Mississippi Department of Archives and History.

Underhill, Ruth. 1965. *Red Man's Religion: Beliefs and Practices of the Indians North of Mexico.* Chicago: University of Chicago Press.

Van Lonkhuyzen, Harold W. 1989. "A Reappraisal of the Praying Indians: Acculturation, Conversion, and Identity at Natick, Massachusetts, 1646–1730." *New England Quarterly* 62:396–428.

"Various Accounts of the Indians: Saconet Indians." 1809. Massachusetts Historical Society, Boston, Mass. Collections, 2nd ser., Vol. 10:114.

Vaughan, Alden T. 1995a. *New England Frontier: Puritans and Indians, 1620–1675.* Norman: University of Oklahoma Press.

————. 1995b. *The Roots of American Racism: Essays on the Colonial Experience.* New York: Oxford University Press.

References

Vickers, Daniel 1981. "Maritime Labor in Colonial Massachusetts: A Case Study of Essex County Cod Fishery and the Whaling Industry of Nantucket, 1630–1775, Ph.D. diss., Princeton University.

———. 1983. "The First Whalemen of Nantucket." *William and Mary Quarterly* 40(4):560–83.

Walker, Deward E., ed. 1989. *Witchcraft and Sorcery of the American Native Peoples.* Moscow, Idaho: University of Idaho Press.

Ward, Edward. [1699] 1905. "A Trip to New England with a Character of the Country and People, both English and Indians." In *Sailor's Narratives of Voyages Along the New England Coast, 1524–1624,* ed. George Parker Winship.

Weiner, Annette. 1992. *Inalienable Possessions: The Paradox of Keeping-While-Giving.* Berkeley: University of California Press.

———. 1996. *Women of Value, Men of Renown: New Perspectives in Trobriand Exchange.* Austin: University of Texas Press.

Weinstein-Farson, Laurie. 1991. "Land Politics and Power: The Mohegan Indians in the Seventeenth and Eighteenth Century." *Man in the Northeast* 42:9–16.

Weinstein, Laurie Lee. 1983a. "Indian vs. Colonist: Competition for Land in Seventeenth-Century Plymouth Colony," Ph.D. diss., Southern Methodist University.

———. 1983b. "Survival Strategies: The Seventeenth-Century Wampanoag and the European Legal System." *Man in the Northeast* 26:81–86.

———. 1985. "The Dynamics of Seventeenth-Century Wampanoag Land Relations: The Ethnohistorical Evidence for Locational Change." *Bulletin of the Massachusetts Historical Society* 46(1):19–35.

———. 1986. "'We're Still Living on Our Traditional Homeland': The Wampanoag Legacy of New England." In *Strategies for Survival: American Indians in the Eastern United States,* ed. Frank W. Porter III. *Contributions to Ethnic Studies* 15:132–33. Westport, Conn.: Bergin & Garvey.

———. 1994. *Enduring Traditions: The Native Peoples of New England.* Westport, Conn.: Bergin & Garvey.

White, Richard. 1991. *The Middle Ground: Indians, Empires, and Republics in the Great Lakes Region, 1650–1815.* Cambridge: Cambridge University Press.

References

Whitfield, Henry, John Eliot, and Thomas Mayhew. 1651. "The Light appearing more and more towards the perfect Day. Or, a farther Discovery of the present state of the Indians in New-England, Concerning the Progresse of the Gospel amongst them." Massachusetts Historical Society, Boston, Mass. Collections, 3rd ser., Vol. 4(1834):100–48.

Williams, Mary Beth, and Jeffrey Bendremer. 1997. "The Archaeology of Maize, Pots, and Seashells: Gender Dynamics in Late Woodland and Contact Period New England." In *Women in Prehistory: North America and Mesoamerica*, ed. Cheryl Claassen and Rosemary A. Joyce, 136–52. Philadelphia: University of Pennsylvania Press.

Williams, Roger. [1643] 1973. *A Key into the Language of America*, ed. by John J. Teunissena and Evelyn J. Hinz. Detroit: Wayne State University Press.

———. 1988. *The Correspondence of Roger Williams*. 2 Vols., ed. Glenn W. LaFantasie. Hanover, N.H.: University Press of New England.

Williamson, Margaret Holmes. 2003. *Powhatan Lords of Life and Death: Command and Consent in Seventeenth-Century Virginia*. Lincoln: University of Nebraska Press.

Willoughby, Charles. 1935. *Antiquities of the New England Indians, with Notes on the Ancient Cultures of Adjacent Territories*. Cambridge, Mass.: Peabody Museum.

Winiarski, Douglas L. 1998. "'Pale Blewish Lights' and a Dead Man's Groan: Tales of the Supernatural from Eighteenth-Century Plymouth, Massachusetts." *William and Mary Quarterly* 3rd ser., 55(4):497–530.

———. 2005. "Native American Popular Religion in New England's Old Colony 1670–1770. *Mashantucket Pequot Museum and Research Center Occasional Paper No. 1.* In *Eighteenth Century Native Communities in Southern New England in the Colonial Context*, ed. Jack Campisi, 84–113. Mashantucket, Conn.: Mashantucket Pequot Museum and Research Center.

Winship, George Parker. 1905. *Sailor's Narratives of Voyages Along the New England Coast, 1524–1624*. Boston: Houghton, Mifflin, and Company.

279

References

Winslow, Edward. 1624. *Good News from New England.* In *Chronicles of the Pilgrim Fathers,* ed. John Masefield, 267–357. New York: E. P. Dutton & co.

——. 1649. The Glorious Progress of the Gospel amongst the Indians in New-England. Massachusetts Historical Society, Boston, Mass. Collections, 3rd ser. Vol. 4(1834):69–98.

——. 1910. "Relation." In *Chronicles of the Pilgrim Fathers,* ed. John Masefield, 267–356. New York: E. P. Dutton & co.

Winthrop, Adam, Edward Hutchinson, Henry Flynt, Edward Wigglesworth, and Nathaniel Appleton. 1729. *Report of the Commissioners of Indian Affairs and the Corporation of Harvard College on the Indians of Natick. Publications of the Colonial Society of Massachusetts* 16:575–77.

Winthrop, John. 1996. *The Journal of John Winthrop, 1630–1649,* ed. Richard S. Dunn, James Savage, and Laetitia Yeandle. Cambridge: Balknap Press.

Witherspoon, Gary. 1975. *Navajo Kinship and Marriage.* Chicago: University of Chicago Press.

Witthoft, John. 1949. "Green Corn Ceremonialism in the Eastern Woodland." *Occasional Contributions from the Museum of Anthropology of the University of Michigan* 13:31–77.

Wojciechowski, Franz L. 1985. *The Paugussett Tribes: An Ethnohistorical Study of the Tribal Interrrelationships of the Indians in the Lower Housatonic River Area.* Nijmegen, Netherlands: Catholic University of Nijmegen.

Wolf, Eric. 1982. *Europe and the People Without History.* Berkeley: University of California Press.

Wood, William. [1634] 1977. *New England's Prospect,* ed. Alden Vaughan. Amherst: University of Massachusetts Press.

Woolard, Kathryn A. 1992. "Language Convergence and Language Death as Social Processes." In *Investigating Obsolescence: Studies in Language Contraction and Death,* ed. Nancy C. Dorian, 355–68. *Studies in the Social and Cultural Foundations of Language* 7. Cambridge: Cambridge University Press.

Wroth, Lawrence C., ed. 1970. *The Voyages of Giovanni da Verrazzano, 1524–1528.* New Haven: Yale University Press.

Index

Index

Index

Colonialism, 10–11, 68, 82, 112, 218, 231
Color symbolism, 29–30
Communities, Native, 76, 176, 199–201, 204, 220; Christian, 134, 144, 171, 193, 204; churches in, 159; defined, 7–9, 16; links between, 16, 152, 200–201, 209–11, 224; material setting of, 12; Native language use in, 204; settlement of, 148–56
Congregational church. *See* Churches, Congregationalist
Connecticut: Native languages of, 226; Native people of, 45, 190, 191, 193, 196, 208, 211
Continuity, 14
Conversion, 40, 64–65, 173–75, 182; churches, 159; effects of, 169, 171, 230; of Natives, 67, 69, 72, 170, 193; theories of, 168. *See also* Christianity
Coomes family, 130
Cooper, Thomas, 42
Corlet, Master, 173
Cosmology, Native, 30–32, 35, 38, 40, 77; preservation of, 40
Cottle, Edward, 125
Cottle, Hester, 123, 125
Cotton, John, 66, 174
Cotton, John, Jr., 44, 66–67, 70, 72, 74, 76, 135, 142, 172–77; journal of, 77, 174
Cotton, Josiah, 4, 5, 27, 46, 70, 72, 77–78, 142, 173, 175–77, 214, 224; word list, 77–78
Cotton family, 176, 178
Councilors, 38, 69, 94

Court records, 212
Coweset (Cowweset), 201, 208, *209*
Crime and Native identity, 228
Cultural categories, 14, 27, 30, 223
Cultural change, 5, 13, 16, 39, 57, 82, 217, 219, 233–34
Culturalist approaches, critiques of, 12
Cummaquiddick trading post, 59
Cuper, Nathaneill (Nathaniel), 186–87
Customs, ancient, 3

Daggett, Alice, 66, 123–25
Daggett, Hester, 124–25
Daggett, Israel, 122
Daggett, John, 66, 120–24, 127
Daggett, Joseph, 122–27, 130; descendants of, 125
Daggett, Joseph, Native wife of, 121, 127, 130
Daggett, Thomas, 66, 111, 121
Daggett family, 72, 122–23, 130
Dancing, 5–6, 38, 39, 43, 47–48, 77, 78
Danforth, John, 37
Danforth, Samuel, 172, 174
Dartmouth, Natives of, 228
Debt, 161–62
Deeds, Native, 50–51, 75, 108, 142, 186–87
Deer Island, 151
Deetz, James, 9
Descent and marriage, 102, 107, 108
Dialects, Native, 58, 72, 78, 205, 224, 226. *See also* Language

Index

Grammar, 23–24. *See also*
   Language
Grammar schools, 173
Graphic representations, 34
Great Awakening, 69, 170, 180,
   193
Guardians, 5, 118, 128–30, 214

Hallowell, Irving, 34–35
Hamell, George, 28
Hannit, Japhet, 65
Harden, Shubal, 125
Harvard College, 172–73, 182,
   188–89
Hassanimisco (Hassanamesit),
   153–54, 171, 189–90, 211
Hawaii, Native, comparison with,
   117
Hawley, Gideon, 176
Healers, Native, 167, 218–19,
   221–22. *See also* Powwaws;
   Shamanic activities
Healing, 4, 13, 30–31, 41–45, 76,
   166, 218, 222
Health and well-being, theories
   of, 15, 28–29
Herring Pond, 176
Hiacoomes, 64
Hiacoomes, Joel, 172–73
Hierarchy, 15
Historical sources, bias in, 12
Historicity, 17, 223
Hood, Ned, 177
Hossueit, Zachary (Zachariah), 5,
   48, 69, 73, 77, 141, 156–57,
   159–60, 188, 231
Household items, 135, 140, 141,
   157

Households, Native, 83
Houses, Native, 138, 152, 154

Idioms of ownership, 50
Idolatry, ancient, 3
Illness, theories of, 41–42
Indian Converts, 84
Indian Dialogues, 67
Indian Grammar Begun, 178
Indian Primer, 67
Inheritance, 115
Interpreters, 172
Itineracy, 199, 201, 214, 215

Jefferson, Thomas, 226
Job, Benjamin, 187
Joel, 92, 111, 130
Johnson, Joseph, 191
Jonahauwossuit, 166
Josnin, Betty, 110
Josnin, Joseph, 110

Keateanum, 157
Key into the Language of
   America, 58–59, 201, 204
King Philip's War, 7, 12, 84, 96,
   151, 171, 188–89, 206, 210, 219
Kin groups, multigenerational,
   89–90
Kings, role of, 20
Kin relations and inheritance,
   157–159
Kinship, 76, 85, 88, 112, 126;
   function of, 120; ideology, 102;
   and leadership, 107; marriage
   and, 220; obligations, 164;
   terms, 86, 87; ties of, 157, 201
Kishkuhtukquainnit, 112

Index

Index

Mohegan, 46–47, 59, 64, 99, 170, 193, 222; black dance, 47; housing, 155; language of, 22, 203; reservation, 96, 155
Momatchegin, 65
Momenaqueam, 65
Monchquanum, 127
Montocks, 226
Montowampate (James), 201
Monument Ponds, 176–77
Moravian missionaries. *See* Missionaries
Morton, Thomas, 42
Mount Hope, 176
Mourning, 38–39, 41
Multilingualism, 22, 58, 67, 80–81, 196, 201–205, 224, 227
Munsee, 88

Nanamocomuck, 201
Nanepashemet, 201, 207
Nanoso, 65
Nantucket Natives, 10, 39, 74, 78, 80, 92, 94, 99, 106, 109, 111, 138, 141, 147–48, 162, 166, 226, 228; epidemic among, 80
Naquatim, Ephriam, 110
Narragansett, 8, 12, 21, 58, 60, 63–64, 84, 96, 99, 105, 170, 191, 192, 201–202, 204, 209, 211, 226, 228; language, 22, 24–25, 50, 59–60, 202–204, 208; traders among, 42
Nashamoies, 93
Nashoba, 201, 204
Natick, 79, 84, 94, 109, 115–17, 140, 145, 149, 151–52, 166, 171, 190, 201, 205, 206–208; language of, 25, 225; town of,

149–51, 153; town records of, 151
Nations, 6
Naugatuck vocabulary, 226
Nauset, 7
Ned, Francis, 187
Ned, Josiah (Attaunit), 187
Neesnumun, John, 178
Negotiation, 12
Network analysis, 200
New England Company. *See* Society for the Propagation of the Gospel
New Testament, Mass., 67
Niantics, 4, 25, 58, 63–64, 83, 105, 138–39, 207–208; language, 203; traders among, 42
Nickanoose (Nekonnoossoo), 78–79, 89, 95, 106, 108–12
Nickommo, 38
Niles, Samuel, 191
Ninegret, 9
Ninegret, Betty, 99
Ninegret, Charles, 100
Ninegret, Charles, Sr., 96, 99
Ninegret, George, 100
Ninegret, Mary, 100
Ninegret, Old Queen, 107
Ninegret, Tom, 98–99
Ninegret, wives of, 107
Ninegret I, 84, 107
Ninegret II, 100, 104, 107
Ninegret family, 103, 107
Nipmuck (Neepnet), 6, 39, 168–69, 203–205, 215; language, 203
Nohtooksaet, 157
Nonatuck, 206

288

Index

Nope, 72. *See also* Martha's
  Vineyard
Norwarunnt, 189
Norwottuck, 206
Nukkekummees, 176
Nunpaog, 110, 112

O'Brien, Jean, 5
Occom, Samson, 46, 142, 191,
  193–94, *194, 195*
Occouch family, 130
Occupations, Native, 131
Ohomo family, 130
Ohquanhut, Dorcus, 116
Ohquanhut, Peter, 73, 116
Okomakamesit, 201
Ommaush, Naomi, 49, 88, 136,
  140, 159, 160; will of, 156–58
Ommaush (Able), Nehemiah,
  156–57
Ompahinnit, 157
Omppan, Solomon, 187
Orienting meanings. *See* Shadow
  meanings
Ornaments, 137
Osomehew, 113
Ossueit (Hossueit) family, 130

Pakeponessoo, 109
Pannunnut. *See* Lay, William
Pannupuqua, 64
Papemack, Zacharia, 213
Papenau, 187
Papumahteochohoo, 109–10
Passaconnaway, 201
Passuet family, 130
Patrilineality, 100–101
Paupmunnuck, 214
Pawtucket, 201, 205–207

Peagan family, 154
Pennacook, 206–208
Peonage, 161–63
Pequot, 21, 36, 59, 64, 97, 99,
  128, 192, 208–209, 211–12;
  language, 22, 203–204. *See also*
  Eastern Pequots; Mashantucket
  Pequots; Mashantucket
  reservation
Pequot War, 7, 219
Petitions, 7, 62, 69, 70–71, *71,*
  131, 183, *185,* 185–86, 193
Petroglyphs, 34, 37
Pewter, 158–59
Philip (Metacom), 7, 63, 97, 106,
  134, 172, 189. *See also* King
  Philip's War
Phillips, Beniah, 110
Phillips, Elizabeth, 109–10
Pictographs, 37
Pishgatikuks, 193
Place names, Native, 203–204
Plane, Ann, 107, 110n1
Plurilingualism. *See*
  Multilingualism
Plymouth, Mass., 53, 169, 174;
  court of, 122; establishment of,
  233; Indians of, 21, 38, 52, 70,
  98, 176, 187–88, 214, 228;
  ministry at, 4, 5, 46, 66, 142,
  175, 176, 178; settlement of,
  39, 64
Pocasset, 206
Pocumtucks, 206, 208
Pognit, Elizabeth, 115
Pognit, Mary, 145
Pokanoket, 98, 103, 106, 168,
  176, 206. *See also* Wampanoag
Polygyny, 83–84, 85, 106, 218

Index

Index

111, 118, 127; sachemships, 7, 120; speech styles of, 61, 94–95

Sacred power, 27, 32

Sacrifice of goods, 32, 38

Saggeatanumou, 92, 109, 112

Sahlins, Marshall, 6–7, 14, 18

Sakonnet Indians, 7, 107–108, 111, 113, 120

Sangekantacket, 110, 121, 123–24, 127

Sapir, Edward, 16–17, 19

Sassechuammin, 110n1

Sassiman, John, 172

Satasqua. *See* Waban, Elizabeth

Sauncksquûaog (Sunksqua). *See* Queen sachems

Schaghticoke Indians, 193, 226

Schoolcraft, Henry, 37

Schools, Native, 64–66, 154, 173, 191

Seasonal celebrations, 38, 77

Seiknout (Seeknout), 109, 110n1

Seiknout, Joshua, 109

Sepet, John, 75

Sepet, Old Sary, 75, 190

Sepet family, 75

Sepinnu, James, 65

Sermons, 174, 177–80, *197*

Servitude, Native, 211–12, 214

Settlements, English: effects of, 20–21; at Gay Head, 154; structure of, 148, 149, 153

Sewell, Samuel, 65, 122

Shadow meanings, 26, 27

Shamanic activities, 33, 37–38, 41, 76, 166. *See also* Powwaws

Sharon, N.Y., 193

Shekomeko, N.Y., 193

Shell, 36, 193. *See also* Wampum

Shinicocks, 226

Sibling relations, 84; terminology, 76

Silverstein, Michael, 18, 56, 72

Simmons, William, 27–28, 39–40

Simon, Isaac, 47

Simons site, 141–42

Sissetom, 66

Sissetom, Jonoisquash, 127

Sissetom, Thomas, 124, 127

Sissetom, Keziah, 124, 127

Slocum's Island, 156

Smith, Benjamin, 110

Snakes, symbolic associations of, 33, 36

Social reproduction, 82, 91

Social stratification, 103

Societal change, 20

Society for the Propagation of the Gospel, 4, 7, 63–64, 66–67, 157, 169, 171, 192, 213

Sociolinguistics, 18

Sompanwat, 107

Sorcery, 13, 38. *See also* Bewitching; Witchcraft

Souls, theories of, 32, 34–35

Sowag family, 130

Sowams, 176

Speech, 55–56; codes, 73; events, 56–57, 68; genres, 57, 61–62, 69, 74, 94

Speen, Hannah, 145

Speen, John, 145

Speen, Moses, 145

Speen family, 94

Spirit helpers, 20

Spiritual power, 4, 15, 220. *See also* Manitou

Spoons, 49, 160

Index

Index

293